Cognition and Social Worlds

KEELE COGNITION SEMINARS

Cognition and Social Worlds

Edited by

Angus Gellatly, Don Rogers, and John A. Sloboda
Department of Psychology
University of Keele

KEELE COGNITION SEMINARS: 2

CLARENDON PRESS · OXFORD
1989

Oxford University Press, Walton Street, Oxford OX2 6DP
Oxford   New York   Toronto
Delhi   Bombay   Calcutta   Madras   Karachi
Petaling Jaya   Singapore   Hong Kong   Tokyo
Nairobi   Dar es Salaam   Cape Town
Melbourne   Auckland
and associated companies in
Berlin   Ibadan

Oxford is a trade mark of Oxford University Press

Published in the United States
by Oxford University Press, New York

British Library Cataloguing in Publication Data
Cognition in social worlds. — (Keele
cognition seminars; 2).
1. Man. Cognition
I. Gellatly, Angus   II. Rogers, Don
III. Sloboda, John A.   IV. Series
153.4
ISBN 0-19-852173-1

Library of Congress Cataloging in Publication Data
Cognition in social worlds/edited by Angus Gellatly, Don Rogers, and
John Sloboda.
p. cm. — (Keele cognition seminars; 2)
Includes bibliographies and indexes.
1. Cognition — Social aspects.   2. Cognition in children — Social aspects.
3. Socialization.   4. Cognition and culture.
I. Gellatly, Angus.   II. Rogers, Don.   III. Sloboda, John A.   IV. Series.
BF311.C5488 1989   302 — dc19   88-25029
ISBN 0-19-852173-1

Set by Dobbie Typesetting Limited, Plymouth Devon
Printed in Great Britain by
Biddles Ltd, Guildford & King's Lynn

Preface

This volume is the second in a series on current issues in cognition. It follows *Cognitive processes in mathematics* edited by John A. Sloboda and Don Rogers (1987). As before, in choosing topics for the series we have looked for issues which (a) are of fundamental importance; (b) are attracting interesting research; and (c) involve both empirical and theoretical work. This second volume contrasts with the first, however, in the breadth of the selected topic. Whereas cognitive processes in mathematics was a narrowly defined topic, of interest principally to cognitive psychologists and teachers of mathematics, the relation of cognition to social worlds is a very broad topic that can be approached from within a number of disciplines, a fact reflected in the composition of the contributors'to this volume. Because of this heterogeneity of content and approaches the reader may wish to begin by referring to our introductory chapter which provides an overview of, and a framework for, what follows.

The contributions published here are derived from papers presented at a conference held at the University of Keele in the Spring of 1987. We are grateful to the Nuffield Foundation and the Economic and Social Research Council for providing financial support for the conference. Our thanks are also due to Dorothy Masters, Doreen Waters, and Margaret Woodward for their indefatigable preparation of the manuscript and to Oxford University Press for the smooth transition into print. Finally, we wish to thank the individual contributors for their participation in the original conference, their swift submission of manuscripts, and their tolerant responses to editorial interventions.

Keele   A. G.
1988   D. R.
                                                                                           J. A. S.

Contents

Contributors

Barry Barnes, Science Studies Unit, University of Edinburgh, 34 Buccleuch Place, Edinburgh EH8 9JT, UK.

Robert H. Borys, Department of Psychology, Southern Methodist University, Dallas, TX 75275, USA.

Richard W. Byrne, Psychological Laboratory, University of St Andrews, St Andrews, Fife KY16 9JU, UK.

Liza Catán, School of Social Sciences, University of Sussex, Arts Building, Falmer, Brighton BN1 9QN, UK.

Harry Collins, Science Studies Centre, University of Bath, Bath BA2 7AY, UK.

Alan Costall, Department of Psychology, University of Southampton, Southampton SO9 5NH, UK.

Roy G. D'Andrade, Department of Anthropology, University of California, La Jolla, CA 92093, USA.

Gerard Duveen, School of Social Sciences, University of Sussex, Arts Building, Falmer, Brighton BN1 9QN, UK.

Angus Gellatly, Department of Psychology, University of Keele, Keele, Staffordshire ST5 5BG, UK.

Jim Good, Department of Psychology, University of Durham, Science Laboratories, South Road, Durham DH1 3LE, UK.

Liam Greenslade, 11 Fire Station Square, Salford M5 4NZ, UK.

Meagan Jones, Department of Psychology, Southern Methodist University, Dallas, TX 75275, USA.

Stan A. Kuczaj II, Department of Psychology, Southern Methodist University, Dallas, TX 75275, USA.

Paul Light, School of Education, The Open University, Walton Hall, Milton Keynes MK7 6AA, UK.

Barbara Lloyd, School of Social Sciences, University of Sussex, Arts Building, Falmer, Brighton BN1 9QN, UK.

Katerina Logotheti, Department of Psychology, University of Edinburgh, 7 George Square, Edinburgh EH8 9JZ, UK.

Anne-Nelly Perret-Clermont, Séminaire de Psychologie, Université de Neuchâtel, Quai Robert-Comptesse 2, CH 2000 Neuchâtel, Switzerland.

Don Rogers, Department of Psychology, University of Keele, Keele, Staffordshire ST5 5BG, UK.

Barbara Rogoff, Department of Psychology, University of Utah, Salt Lake City, Utah 84112, USA.

Arthur Still, Department of Psychology, University of Durham, Science Laboratories, South Road, Durham DH1 3LE, UK.

Colwyn Trevarthen, Department of Psychology, University of Edinburgh, 7 George Square, Edinburgh EH8 9JZ, UK.

Andrew Whiten, Psychological Laboratory, University of St Andrews, St Andrews, Fife KY16 9JU, UK.

John A. Sloboda (co-editor), Department of Psychology, University of Keele, Keele, Staffordshire ST5 5BG, UK.

1

The individual and the social in cognitive psychology

ANGUS GELLATLY and DON ROGERS

The relationship of the individual to society can be only too readily conceived as one of mutual exclusion, of figure–ground reversibility. Focusing upon the individual, we may even speak of his or her social *background*. Conversely, we can with Aristotle emphasize the whole rather than the part, and assert that 'Society is something in nature that precedes the individual'. It goes without saying that psychologists are well aware of the competing perspectives and able to recognize their respective merits and defects. But it also goes without saying that academic psychology, defined from its inception in terms of this rigid dichotomy, has been dominated by the individualistic perspective. The image of the stand-alone neural computer in its attractive dermal housing has been especially central to the whole endeavour of cognitive psychology, yet the language of contemporary technology here expresses an idea that has been with us for a long time. Its potency and ready availability in the culture have been variously explained. Some of the contributors to the present volume (Good and Still) attribute to Descartes our fascination with the individual who thinks and knows in splendid isolation; another (Greenslade) finds the cause in Capitalist modes of production and the abstractions they engender. (These two approaches themselves constitute a nice example of the very same dichotomy.)

Exceptions to the general tendency towards individualism are well known. Vygotsky in Russia and Mead in America both attempted to root the individual firmly in a social context but whilst their prescience has been frequently acknowledged their actual impact on mainstream Western psychology was slight, at least until recently. Piaget, too, recognized the importance of social context for cognitive development but, as is well known, in his later and more influential work this insight was almost wholly eclipsed (Light and Perret-Clermont).

In recent years, however, considerable efforts have been spent in trying to convert the long established lip-service paid to Vygotsky, Mead, and others into something more concrete (e.g. Cole and Scribner 1978; Hinde, Perret-Clermont, and Stevenson-Hinde 1985; Richards and Light 1986; Wertsch 1985*a,b*).

What this calls for is not simply a reversal of the prevailing bias — images of the isolate giving way to images of the collective — which would amount to no more than giving up psychology in favour of sociology, but a reconceptualization of the dichotomy individual/society. We have to consider not already given individuals but individuals-coming-into-being-through-relationships. This means that one does not simply concentrate on relationships between autonomous individuals but on the ways in which individuals come to be constituted through particular relationships. For example, Wertsch and Sammarco (1985) cite Luria's remark that in order to understand the highly complex forms of human consciousness it is necessary to go beyond the human organism. They see this going beyond the individual in order to understand the individual as an example of irony. Yet there is irony here only if one already starts from the assumption of self-contained individuality, of rigid boundaries separating the self from the other. Although such an assumption has become second nature to we who have been raised on it, it is not mandatory. As Sampson (1988) argues, the notion of individuality is not an all-or-none affair. It is possible to identify at least two dimensions along which the concept may vary: first, the sharpness and permeability of the boundaries of the self; second, the degree to which agency is located within the self or attributed also to a field of exogenous forces. In practice, variation along the two dimensions tends to be correlated, with sharp and impermeable boundaries being associated with a strongly internal attribution of agency, permeable and diffuse boundaries with attribution to a field of forces (e.g. Western as contrasted with Confucian psychology). But the important point lies in recognition of the different forms of individuality.

Naturally enough, reconceptualizing the relationship of individual and society is itself far from easy, though perhaps easier than putting any new conceptualization to work. As in the above example from Wertsch and Sammarco, automatic reliance on established images is a hard habit to break. Ingleby (1986) discusses a number of examples of this kind of reversion to be found in psychological theorizing. On a more positive note, however, Ingleby also reminds us that the attempt to rethink the relationship between individual and society is not confined to psychology but is part of an endeavour spanning the whole of the social sciences and humanities. The work does not have to be done alone. Insights and developments can be imported and exported across disciplinary boundaries.

An undertaking on such a scale raises issues beyond count, only some of which are of direct relevance to psychologists and of which an even smaller proportion can be directly addressed in a single volume. In the remainder of this short introductory chapter we try to identify some of those issues, how they are approached by the various contributors to this book, and some of the interrelations between them.

Conceptualizing the organism

In the opening chapter, Costall points out that while psychologists have always tended to cut off their subject matter from the social and historical, cognitive psychology has gone one better and cut itself off from the organic as well. He goes on to explain how Gibson's ecological approach (e.g. Gibson 1950) was intended to bridge all of these gaps, and not least the last of them. By defining the environment and the organism in terms of mutual interdependence, Gibson set an example of how to escape the trap of the isolated individual, and did so at a level that necessarily preceded that of social individuality. For, as Gibson stressed, organisms must first be able to survive in the natural environment, on the basis of veridical perceptions, before in the course of evolution social organizations and social identities can develop, and with them potentially erroneous socially mediated perceptions. Costall traces the course of Gibson's ideas over more than forty years, noting the strengths and weaknesses at different points along the way.

Rogoff, in her chapter, also starts from a consideration of the mutuality of organism and environment, in terms of nature and nurture. Working from within a Vygotskian framework, she seeks to escape the notion of biology and culture interacting as independent influences upon the developing infant, conceptualizing them instead as aspects of a single system. Development within the system can be studied at various levels; phylogenetic, ontogenetic, microgenetic, and sociocultural. Simultaneous recognition of all the levels is necessary in order to counteract the tendency, despite initial good intentions, to highlight either biology or culture to the detriment of the other.

The evolutionary question

Phylogenetic development of intellect — cognitive evolution — has usually been understood as a response to physical rather than social features of the environment. Perhaps this is not so surprising. After all, the adaptations of organisms to their physical surroundings are striking in their variation and complexity. Even where the purpose is social, as in the evolution of, for example, species markings and their recognition, the actual signals are themselves manifested as part of the physical environment. Behaviourists, indeed, have tried and still do try to explain even the most complex behaviours in terms of physically specifiable stimuli and reinforcers. Furthermore, for a culture in which the physical sciences are often taken to represent the pinnacle of intellectual achievement, the notion that the mind evolved specifically for the conquest of physical nature is a most congenial one.

It is, none the less, an idea that has been challenged. Whiten and Byrne in their chapter review evidence bearing on the hypothesis that the original function of intellect was the maintenance and facilitation of social intercourse. Co-operating and competing with other members of the species, it is argued, calls for much more complex cognitive operations than does the finding of food and shelter. It requires that the cognitive states of others be perceived and modelled. Primates exerting their own selective pressures on one another may have provided the ratchet for cognitive evolution. It follows that in ontogenetic development cognitive competence is likely to first manifest itself in social rather than non-social capabilities.

Adaptation to a social environment

If ontogenetic development consisted simply in the deployment of general purpose cognitive systems over various 'problem domains', there would be no reason to expect newborn infants to excel at social interaction. Learning to cope with and control the behaviours of others should offer neither more nor less of a challenge than, say, learning about billiard balls. Trevarthen and Logotheti claim that this is far from the case. They argue that the newborn human infant is adapted to attend to people not objects, that he or she comes equipped with a mind already organized in terms of self and other, and that because of this prestructuring emotional sensitivity and the ability to enter into intersubjective communication are present from the start. In other words, infants are specifically adapted to enter a social world. Interest in the physical world is a later arrival on the scene. Trevarthen and Logotheti describe the systematic unfolding throughout childhood of motives that structure the child's social interactions and thereby facilitate integration into a world of emotional relationships and social meanings. The physical world becomes known *through* these, not independently of them. All in all, this view of the period from birth to toddlerdom is greatly at variance with the notion of the child as junior epistemologist or physicist. The emphasis on persons in relationships as opposed to reasoning individuals is, however, wholly consistent with the social intellect hypothesis.

Mechanisms of cultural transmission

Adapted as the young human may be for entry into a social milieu, the meanings, values, habits, and techniques of the culture and the family still have to be passed on in specific acts of learning. Trevarthen and Logotheti outline some of the ways in which the behaviour of both child and adult is suited to this task. Rogoff carries this analysis further by revealing some broad principles of joint involvement in learning in general, while Lloyd and Duveen provide a close look at the roles of child and parent in the passing on of the system for signifying social representations of gender.

Rogoff's account of the joint involvement of child and adult takes as its starting point Vygotsky's influential notion of the 'zone of proximal development'. This idea, that there is a zone of competence extending from the tasks a child can accomplish unaided to those that can be managed only with some adult guidance, is one in which the conception of learning as a social activity is inherent. The unfolding motives of the young child ensure that he or she is enabled to partake in a process of what Rogoff calls 'guided participation' within the zone. Adult behaviour, too, seems to be adapted towards maximizing the child's learning of the taken-for-granted skills and practices of the culture, as well as of more personally distinctive habits. Adults link the novel to the familiar, ensure that new tasks are of an appropriate level of difficulty, and only gradually transfer responsibility for task completion to the child. In so doing they smooth the path of learning.

Transmission of the gender system is possibly undertaken less consciously by adults than is the transmission of many cultural skills. Lloyd and Duveen are able to show, however, that adult behaviour is precisely tailored to the task of inducting the child into the system. Initially, the gender identity of a child is held by the socially adept others who surround him or her, yet by the age of first speech this identity appears to have been successfully internalized. Gender differentiation is marked from birth in the talk of adults and older children. It also appears in more subtle guise in their regulation of play. Gender differences in sensorimotor routines are both instigated and amplified by parents in keeping with cultural stereotypes. As linguistic development proceeds these differences then re-emerge at the level of conceptual activity in a manner which, Lloyd and Duveen acknowledge, might be accounted for within either a Piagetian or a Vygotskian framework.

Explaining cognitive performances

Cognitive psychology might with some justification be defined as the study of what goes on inside the head of an organism engaged in problem solving. This definition captures the out-and-out individualism already remarked upon, but it no more than hints at another bias of the field, namely that in favour of endogenous explanations of cognitive performances. Success on a test of reasoning tends to be explained in terms of some cognitive structure, rule, or principle that has become part of the individual's cognitive make-up. Three of the papers in this volume address themselves to the issues to which this tradition within the discipline has given rise. In the first of these, Light and Perret-Clermont provide an overview of the history of the classic conservation tests and of changes in the way that the data of such tests have come to be interpreted. The central point of their exposition is that whereas conservation tests were originally devised as diagnostic tools for the assessment of individual cognitive functioning, their primary role in recent years has been as vehicles for the illustration of various social influences upon test performance. The importance of consultation with peers, the effects of an unfamiliar form of discourse, the nature of the experiment as a social interaction, and the role of shared meaning in effective communication have all been demonstrated in the context of conservation experiments. On the basis of these changes, Light and Perret-Clermont are led to conclude that the heart of cognitive development is to be found not in the elaboration of structures but in agreements in meaning.

Similar terrain is surveyed by Gellatly and by D'Andrade, though for rather different purposes. Gellatly first establishes that there has been a widespread habit in cognitive psychology of seeking to diagnose supposed cognitive competences in terms of which individual reasoning can be explained. It is then argued that justification for this procedure rests upon a misunderstanding of the nature of medical diagnosis. Finally, it is shown that this 'myth of diagnosis', although its shortcomings have frequently been remarked upon, continues to flourish in various areas of psychology. D'Andrade, in his paper, is also concerned with the explanation of reasoning. Like Gellatly, he favours Johnson-Laird's (1983) theory of mental models, according to which logical problems are solved not by the use of internal rules but through internal modelling of the problem. D'Andrade, however, provides an added twist to the story. He presents data which suggest that as well as constructing models for themselves, members of a culture learn a repertoire of 'culturally well formed' models, or schemata. Problem difficulty is then a function of correspondence with such well formed schemata.

Cognition and expression

Just as performance on various tests of reasoning (conservation, syllogisms, etc.) has frequently been interpreted in terms of abstract internal rules or competences, so too with other forms of cognitive expression. The individualism and mentalism of cognitive psychology favour the view that cognitions take shape internally and are translated into a suitable medium only for purposes of expression, frequently of interpersonal communication. An extreme statement of this idea has been given by Fodor (e.g. 1976) who writes of thoughts being initially formulated in the language of 'mentalese', only later to be translated into, for example, spoken English. However, the assumption that any medium of expression offers a cognitively neutral means for externalizing internal representations is certainly open to question. And, clearly, if media are not neutral in this sense then such factors as the availability, or lack, of a particular medium offers one avenue by which culture may influence cognition. In their chapters both Catán and Kuczaj, Borys, and Jones examine some of the ways in which the medium and the message may be interdependent.

Catán reports three studies of the development of representations of rhythm by young children. Her method was based on that used in studies of literacy by Luria, and her aim was to extend previous research on rhythm representation in adults and older children. By contrast, Kuczaj, Borys, and Jones report two experiments investigating the vexed issue of the relationship between language and thought, with particular reference to the mapping between linguistic and non-linguistic categories. They examine the ways in which experience with novel objects and novel words influence children's ability to categorize the former in terms of the latter.

Learning categories

Two other contributions, in their different ways, also have to do with the nature of categories or concepts. Barnes takes as his topic the relationship between ostensive learning and the nature of knowledge. He begins by reasserting the importance of ostensive learning and by setting forth the view that it is a means by which *precedents* are set for the use of categorical terms. His next step is to distinguish between 'normal objects', which contain their natures within themselves, and 'social objects', the natures of which are contained within the contexts around them. This might seem to establish an abrupt discontinuity between the social and the non-social. Barnes argues, however, that this is not so. On the contrary, he claims that the meanings of both sorts of object are learnt by the same technique of ostension, and hence by use of the same cognitive processes. Collins also begins his chapter with a discussion of ostension, but his purpose is that of emphasizing the weaknesses in our understanding of ostensive learning, as well as of other possible mechanisms of cultural transmission. He goes on to argue, nevertheless, that culturally important skills have to be learnt via some such poorly understood mechanisms and not through explicit teaching, which he refers to as algorithmic learning. In the remainder of his chapter Collins goes on to examine the implications of this view, especially with regard to possibilities for the future development of intelligent machines. His conclusion is conditioned by the belief that since society, rather than the individual, is the repository of knowledge, a truly intelligent machine will first have to be a truly socialized machine.

Social cognition

The discussions of ostension by Barnes and Collins both draw attention to the importance for learning of what is not, or cannot be, said. A similar emphasis on the non-verbal is given by Good and Still in a chapter that in many ways completes a circle by re-presenting a number of topics that figured in early chapters of the book. Like Costall, they take Gibson's ecological psychology both as their starting point and as an alternative to cognitivism. Gibson's theory, they claim, has generally been treated as simply a theory of perception, whereas it is more properly understood as a theory of cognition. The important link can be found in the fact that perception of others is a matter of perceiving social affordances. There is direct perception of the motives and intentions of others and this is, immediately, social cognition. If, as Whiten and Byrne propose, it was the needs of increasingly complex social interactions that drove cognitive evolution, then direct perception of cognitive states is likely to have been an early and important stage in the process. The account of infant adaptation offered by Trevarthen and Logotheti suggests that this is true ontogenetically as well as phylogenetically. In their chapter, Good and Still go on to report studies of the information available in human movement for social cognizing.

Willing conceptual change: a problem of reflexivity

Common to nearly all of the preceding contributions is the express desire either to abandon cognitivism altogether or else to modify it radically. Chapter after chapter points up the pitfalls of an overly individualistic psychology, the need to grasp cognitive skills in their social, or cultural, settings. If exhortation alone can effect such intellectual adjustments, then the outcome of the present struggle should not be in any great doubt. But can it?

In the final chapter of the volume, Greenslade argues from a Marxian perspective that such adjustments cannot be brought about by purely intellectual effort. For him the bifurcation into individual and social is a theoretical objectification of the social relations inherent in capitalism, an expression of entrenched social practices. Until the practices themselves are changed, his argument goes, intellectual effort, however well intended, will not suffice. Every criticism of the dichotomy into individual and society will show itself ultimately to be based upon an assumption of the very same dichotomy. Greenslade provides examples that make this very point. He invites members of the academic community rather to engage in political struggle if they wish to bring about genuine intellectual transformation.

The analysis Greenslade provides is thought-provoking to say the least. Vygotsky and Piaget, amongst others, already acknowledged the potential influence of different power relationships on the course of cognitive development, and the thesis that the power structure of society determines the very categories in terms of which intellectual debate is conducted deserves serious consideration in a book dedicated to the proposition that cognitions are social products. All the same, different slants on the issue are available. For instance, Ingleby (1986) describes a post-structuralist contrast between, on the one hand, productive power relations and, on the other hand, repressive power relations of the kind seemingly assumed in Greenslade's analysis. Sampson's (1988) discussion of alternative conceptions of the individual (see above) also seems to allow for the possibility that such conceptions need not be rigidly determined by the prevailing material base of society. Finally, even if one does follow Greenslade in accepting the overriding importance of the material base in determining consciousness, the existence of at least some two-way traffic need not be precluded. Ideas may be only pebbles as against the boulders of entrenched social relations, but in appropriate circumstances the movement of a few pebbles can initiate an avalanche, as perhaps the impact of Marx's own ideas illustrates.

As with all the chapters that make up this book, however, readers are best advised to look for themselves at what Greenslade has to say and to make up their own minds. What has become clear to us in the course of editing this book, and of organizing the conference from which it is derived, is that the mutual interpenetration of what have been traditionally differentiated as the cognitive and the social is under multiple scrutiny. When we put out a call for papers on 'Cognition and social worlds' we did not fully appreciate the variety of approaches to the topic now being taken. Learning about them has been as enjoyable and instructive for us as we hope it will prove for the reader.

References

Cole, M. and Scribner, S. (1978). Introduction to Vygotsky, L. S. *Mind in society: the development of higher psychological processes*. Harvard University Press, Cambridge, MA.

Fodor, J. (1976). *The language of thought*. Harvester, Hassocks, Sussex.

Gibson, J. J. (1950). *The perception of the visual world*. Houghton-Mifflin, Boston.

Hinde, R., Perret-Clermont, A-N., and Stevenson-Hinde, J. (eds) (1985). *Social relationships and cognitive development*. Oxford University Press.

Ingleby, D. (1986) Development in social context. In *Children of social worlds* (eds. M. P. M. Richards and P. H. Light). Polity Press, Cambridge.

Johnson-Laird, P. N. (1983). *Mental models*, Cambridge University Press, Cambridge.

Richards, M. P. M. and Light, P. H. (1986). *Children of social worlds*. Polity Press, Cambridge.

Sampson, E. E. (1988). The debate on individualism: indigenous psychologies of the individual and their role in personal and social functioning. *American psychologist* **43**, 15–22.

Wertsch, J. V. (1985*a*). *Vygotsky and the social formation of mind*. Harvard University Press, Cambridge, MA.

Wertsch, J. V. (ed.) (1985*b*). *Culture, communication and cognition: Vygotskian perspectives*. Cambridge University Press.

Wertsch, J. V. and Sammarco, J. G. (1985). Social precursors to individual cognitive functioning: The problem of units of analysis. In *Social relationships and cognitive development*. (ed. R. A. Hinde, A.-N. Perret-Clermont, and J. Stevenson-Hinde). Oxford University Press.

2

A closer look at 'direct perception'
ALAN COSTALL

It is . . . a mistake to separate the cultural environment from the natural environment, as if there were a world of mental products distinct from the world of material products. There is only one world, however diverse, and all animals live in it, although we have altered it to suit ourselves (Gibson 1979, p. 130).

Introduction

Cognitivism has been the dominant paradigm within psychology for over a quarter of a century. By cognitivism I do not mean a field of research, the study *of* cognition, but a distinct approach to that study which insists that perception and action can only be explained by appeal to internal representations and the rules or processes by which they are constructed and then transformed so as to 'generate' our behaviour. Certain features of cognitivism are surely worthwhile. For example, its concern with the structure of behaviour has helped to displace the long-standing tradition of associationism within psychology. It has also helped to reassure us that psychology might be more than something to mess around at until the biochemists decide to move in. But I cannot say that I am impressed by its trick of turning the interesting and important problems of human cognition into instant, fundamental solutions. Certainly there is much debate about details: the kind of rules which are supposed to underlie our use of language, or the nature of the inner representations which explain our seeing. After all, this is what the whole cognitivist programme is all about. But the very *existence* of rules and representations—and maps, scripts, and cultural schemas—is simply taken for granted and used to explain everything else, from the ramblings of a rat in a maze to the human practices of actually making representations, and formulating and following rules. Cognition, treated in this way, no longer constitutes a problem so much as a short-cut from one area of ignorance to yet another. The consequences are serious. The appeal to such categories as representations and rules as *primary* pre-empts any truly developmental or evolutionary analysis of human cognition. And the privatization of such rules and representations surely frustrates any adequate historical understanding as well (*see also* Gellatly, this volume).

Edward Sampson (1981) has recently discussed the ideological motives which underlie this curious turn in cognitive psychology. But another important factor, I suspect, is psychology's anxiety about its own identity. It would seem that the foremost requirement of any explanation within psychology is that it should be unmistakably *psychological*. And this is equally true of most of the alternatives to cognitivism, for they attempt to define a self-contained field of enquiry by seeking, as Volosinov once put it, 'to locate a world beyond the social and the historical . . . in the depths of the organic' (Volosinov 1927/1976, p. 14). Cognitivism has, however, been more thorough in this business of isolationism, for in its own search for a purified psychology in the depths of subjectivity, it has managed to mark out for itself a realm beyond not only the social and the historical, but the organic as well.

For me, the importance of James Gibson's ecological approach to psychology lies in its promise of reconnecting psychology to both the organic and the cultural realms. Gibson was an active experimental psychologist over a very long period, from the 1920s until his death in 1979. While most experimental psychologists seem to treat experiments as substitutes for thought (presumably in order to avoid being mistaken for philosophers), Gibson's ultimate aim was to develop a radical alternative to cognitivism, free of the many paradoxes which continue to beset psychology.

In this paper I want to explore a central idea in Gibson's theory, his concept of 'direct perception'. This might well seem a curious choice of topic for this seminar. For it is not at all obvious that Gibson had anything to say about human cognition, let alone its relations to the social and cultural context. After all, he emphatically denied a role for any kind of intellectual process, be it inference, memory, hypothesis testing, or whatever, in direct perception. Furthermore, his overall project looks suspiciously like an old-fashioned attempt to establish an individual psychology of the isolated subject. Yet, in fact, Gibson, in seeking to define what we might have in common with even insects or molluscs, was trying to establish a theoretical framework *from* which we might begin to comprehend the origins of truly human modes of cognition in relation to their social and cultural context.

My discussion of Gibson's concept of direct perception will take the form of an historical analysis. In this way, I will try to show that the social context of cognition was indeed a central concern for Gibson, and one which figured in some of his earliest formulations of his theory (*see also* Reed 1987). But such an analysis also serves to reveal how Gibson's distinction between direct and indirect perception came to hinge upon a number of rather distinct issues. Eventually, Gibson's concept of direct perception became so restrictive that it actually runs counter to a fundamental purpose of his project: the reconciliation of the categories of the natural and the socio-cultural.

Gibson's concept of direct perception

Gibson's theory begins with an account of the environment in which perception occurs. According to Gibson, the environment must be described in terms of its meanings for the organism in question; these meanings and values (*affordances*, to use his term), he insisted, are real properties of the environment, if, nevertheless, relative to the organism. His theory then considers the way that these properties and events in the environment structure light, sound, and other energy forms, for, Gibson claimed, such ambient energy (the optic array, in the case of light) includes structures which constitute potential information for a sentient animal, that is, information which is *lawfully* and *specifically* related to relevant features of that animal's environment. Having thus provided a new description of the environment, and of the structures available to perceptual systems, his theory then finally turns to the problem of perception, and to what Gibson took to be its most basic form. To quote Gibson, 'direct perception is the activity of getting information from the ambient array of light' (Gibson 1979, p. 147). That is to say, *direct* perception is the kind of perception which is possible when the perceiver is free to explore his or her surroundings, and detect, or 'pick up', the wealth of information available in the ambient light, sound, and so on. It is as simple as that — or, at least, that is what I used to think. I am now convinced that Gibson's notion of direct perception is a good deal more interesting and complicated than it first appears.

One thing, at least, is clear, however. For Gibson, the possibility of direct perception really mattered. It mattered logically, for otherwise the origin and validity of indirect modes of awareness would remain a mystery. It mattered epistemologically, for otherwise we could not explain the possibility of our knowledge of our world, including that obtained by our specialized sciences. And, most important, as I will now explain, it mattered morally and politically.

As Gibson makes clear in his autobiography, he was a frustrated social theorist. He felt that social theory, including Marxism to which he was attracted, lacked a satisfactory foundation (Gibson 1967a, p. 135). He mentions specifically his concerns over the international political scene in the 1930s; in fact, he was involved in setting up the Society for the Psychological Study of Social Issues at that time. The long-standing target of his criticism was the constructivist or representationalist theory of perception which claims that our experience of our world is inevitably problematic and distorted by our own preconceptions. As his early writings make especially clear, he felt this traditional approach to perception had very dangerous social implications.

This concern is evident in a paper Gibson (1939) published about the dreadful position of Jewish people in Germany. He argued that the Germans no longer were relating to the Jews in any immediate way, as actual individuals, but, instead, indirectly through the effects of social stereotypes:

A stereotype or prejudice [is] a socially prevalent attitude with emotional roots which is so inflexible as to distort perception and produce behavior that is inappropriate to the objective stimulus. 'We see things', as the saying goes, 'not as they are but as we are'. Our world, more especially our world of social objects, is understood in terms of preconceptions, pre-existing attitudes, habitual norms, standards, and frames of reference. When the preconception is sufficiently rigid, an object will be perceived not at all in accordance with the actual sensory stimulation but in congruence with the preconception (Gibson 1939, p. 165).

In fact, Gibson's treatment of this very serious issue is rather conventional in its appeal to the social psychologists' theory of stereotypes. What is significant about it is his expression of deep contempt for what he saw as the cynicism of many social scientists at that time about the rise of anti-Semitism. For, in the guise of scientific objectivity, they shrugged off the problem as merely further confirmation of 'our inevitable irrationality' (Gibson 1939, p. 166).

Gibson returned to the questions of stereotyping and perception in the early 1950s, in contributions to edited volumes on general and social psychology (Gibson 1950b, 1951, 1953). In one of these papers, he considers the work of Lippman on stereotypes, Bartlett on cultural schemas, and Sherif on group pressure to conform, and the perceptual research by Bruner, Postman, and the transactionalist theorists, on the perceiver's contribution to what is seen:

Considering all the accumulated evidence of this sort, social psychologists began to have a much more ambitious conception of their subject. Social perception was not merely the top layer, as it were, of a man's awareness, but extended downward to its base. Perhaps *all* perception was social perception. Likewise all behavior was social behavior. Social psychology was not something to be studied after learning about individual psychology, but something to be considered as a basis for the discipline. . . . What a man perceives, they say, depends on his personality and his culture. Men of different cultures perceive quite different worlds. There are, in short, folkways of perception (Gibson 1951, pp. 92–4).

Once again, he found the social psychologists, and most notably the so-called 'New Look' theorists, placing an exclusive emphasis on our irrationality and subjectivity, and the inevitably distorting effect of language and other social influences. In response to their pessimism, if not cynicism, Gibson sought to define an additional mode of perception, literal perception, which might be free of such distorting influence. As he pointed out, the theory of socially determined perception was fine as an account of stereotypes and misunderstandings among people of different backgrounds, but it failed to explain veridical perception, or connect meaning with our adaptive behaviour (Gibson 1950*b*, p. 159):

An enthusiasm for social psychology and a sense of the urgency of its problems is something that I share. But I cannot agree with the social perceptionists that the kind of problems they study are the prototype of all problems in perception. . . . There are two possible lines of effort, I suggest, in the study of perception: the attempt to understand misperception and the attempt to understand perception. Only the first is being pursued with any degree of energy. . . . [But] is it not reasonable to suppose that a man can perceive in two different senses of the term [i.e. literal vs. schematic perception]? The literal world is the background for the schematic world. It furnishes a kind of basis for posture and locomotion. The schematic world is a shifting set of prominent meanings from which many of the literal qualities have dropped away. If there are two kinds of perception, two kinds of perceptual theory are needed. The two theories ought not to be contradictory, but supplementary (Gibson 1951, pp. 94–104).

Gibson developed his distinction between literal and schematic perception most fully in his first book, *The perception of the visual world*, published in 1950. He stressed that all the experimental evidence marshalled to show that perception is 'inevitably a constructive process which creates the world to suit the perceiver' (Gibson 1950*a*, p. 210) was in fact obtained from situations deliberately contrived to ensure that errors would occur. But, interestingly, his point was not to deny the validity of such evidence, rather its generality. Indeed, he actually states that, since in everyday life we rely on 'glances and faint or ill-remembered impressions', the results of such experiments are truer to life than those obtained under more optimal conditions (Gibson 1950*a*, p. 210). Nevertheless, he insisted, such results do not provide the whole story:

It is perfectly true that perception can be fluid, subjective, creative, and inexact, but it can also be literal. . . . The student of human nature and society needs to remember this when he is in danger of assuming that men are passive victims of their stereotypes and perceptual customs. The detection of witches by the citizens of Salem . . . is a case of gross misperception, but it does not always happen.

But, as he went on to explain, literal perception does not occur without effort, one must take care:

[The literal visual world] is not simply the world of everyday behavior, since that is a schematic world of cues and signs. . . . Only in an unfamiliar environment or a problem situation do we become fully aware of the literal visual world. One has to pause and look in order to see it (Gibson 1950*a*, pp. 211–2).

On the face of it, Gibson's insistence upon the perceiver's *active* involvement seems a fundamental concession to the constructivist's case. But there is a crucial difference. For the constructivist, the perceiver's 'activity' is supposed to be covert and internal: the attentional scanning of, or puzzled cogitation upon, a fixed and imposed retinal image. In contrast, Gibson has in mind the actual exploration of one's surroundings; the perceiver is active in a very literal and obvious sense (*see*, for example, Gibson 1958, p. 51). As I see it, one of Gibson's many important contributions has been to challenge the long-standing assumption that the active role of the subject in the process of knowing implies its lack of objectivity.

Gibson's distinction in the 1950s between literal and schematic perception is a direct precursor of his later distinction between direct and indirect perception. His concept of direct perception does differ in some important ways, for example, in placing a greater stress on the investigatory role of the perceiver, and in its claim that meaning can itself be directly perceived. But, in his earlier treatment of literal perception, it is already clear that Gibson's emphatically individualist treatment of literal perception was not intended to be self-contained, but complementary to any account of culturally-mediated modes of perception.

However, the version of the constructivist theory of perception promoted so enthusiastically by the social psychologists in the fifties was only one variant of the basic theoretical scheme that Gibson was attempting to counter by means of his concepts of literal and, later, direct perception. After all, the basic idea, that perception is largely a creation of the perceiver, has a long history in both psychological and philosophical treatments of perception. It has also remained central to much of the theorizing within clinical psychology and psychoanalysis. In these versions of constructivist theory, however, the treatment is frankly individualistic. As Gibson noted in one of the papers on stereotyping I referred to earlier:

Clinical psychologists tend to accept the generalization that perception is a creative process which constructs the world to suit the perceiver. . . . In this respect they follow the social psychologists *except that they emphasize the bias of personality instead of the bias of culture* (Gibson 1951, p. 98).

In countering these individualistic versions of constructivist theory, Gibson once again appealed to his distinction between literal and schematic perception, but now, of course, he no longer made appeal to an underlying contrast between individual and socialized modes of perception. His distinction between literal and schematic perception was now based, instead, on the character of the immediate situation facing the perceiver, upon the availability or otherwise of sufficient information. By the 1960s, when he came to replace his earlier term, literal perception, by that of direct perception, it was very much this way of posing the distinction which predominated. Reference to the effects of cultural stereotypes or schemas fell very much into the background, for, by this time, the so-called New Look approach of the social psychologists was no longer so fashionable. Instead, he came

to define indirect perception as a process of inference or guessing on the basis
of incomplete perceptual cues:

Psychologists are accustomed to use stimulus situations with impoverished, ambiguous,
or conflicting information. They have been devised in the hope of revealing the
constructive process taken to characterize *all* perception. In these special situations
there must indeed occur a special process. It could appropriately be called *guessing*.
But I would distinguish perceiving from guessing, and suggest that we investigate
the first and try to understand the second by means of corollaries about deficient
information (Gibson 1963, p. 11).

Gibson's discussion of perception can only properly be understood as a
reaction to whatever happened to be the current, dominant versions of the
constructivist theory of perception. In his earliest formulation, the constructivist theory was primarily the preserve of the social perceptionists, and,
accordingly, Gibson's distinction between literal and schematic perception
entailed a distinction between individual and socialized modes of awareness.
But, as the more traditional versions of constructivist theory became once again
more prominent, Gibson reformulated his basic distinction in terms of the
availability or absence of adequate information to the perceiver: literal or direct
perception is based on available information, and schematic or indirect
perception is essentially inferential and based on impoverished cues; and,
of course, in this formulation, the social dimension becomes quite irrelevant.
It is at this point, I think, that we can begin to appreciate why Gibson's
concept of direct perception eventually became so complicated. For, of
course, his opponents, the constructivists, did not conveniently and
unanimously shift their ground from one variant of their theory to yet
another. Even in his earliest writings, Gibson was well aware of the diversity
of the theoretical opposition, as it were. Yet, by the sixties, a further
complication arose, for Gibson realized that even the more individualistic
versions of constructivist theory were, in fact, making appeal to an essentially
social phenomenon. For the current versions of constructivism had
surreptitiously elevated the concept of representation to a central position
in their theory. But, as Gibson stressed repeatedly, the perception of
representations (images, photographs, music, signs, and symbols) is special
in that it involves the mediating role of other human beings:

The classical theories have assumed that *all* perception is mediated, the 'messages
of sense' being signs or symbols of the outer world. It is as if the process of perception
occurring between an environment and a man could only be understood in terms of
the conveying of information between one man and another. True messages are *coded*,
which means . . . that their effect depends upon social agreement or consensus.
. . . The so-called messages of sense are not coded in this or any meaning of the term.
They are *specific* to objects in mathematical and geometrical ways which we need
to understand as such (Gibson 1959, p. 488).

We tend to think of direct stimuli from the terrestrial environment as being like words and pictures instead of realizing that words and pictures are at best man-made substitutes for those direct stimuli. Language and art yield perceptions at second-hand. This second-hand perception no doubt works backward on direct perception, but knowledge *about* the world rests on *acquaintance* with the world, in the last analysis, and this is our first problem (Gibson 1966, p. 28).

The fallacy of the standard theories of perception consists of taking as a model for vision the kind of indirect visual perception that uses pictures as substitutes for things (Gibson 1972, p. 227; *see also* Gibson 1960, 1961, 1962, 1967*b*, 1974, 1982*a*).

Once again, therefore, the contrast between the individual and the social and cultural became prominent in Gibson's theory of perception. Edward Reed has recently explained how Gibson meant to develop a theory of human cognition in terms of how our social practices of representation — speech, writing, picturing, and map-making — give rise to new modes of indirect awareness (Reed 1987). But Reed also implies that Gibson had, finally, settled upon a simple, unitary definition of indirect perception or awareness as dependent upon, and derived from, our collective modes of representation and communication (Reed 1986, p. 242n). Yet even the few quotations I have just cited suggest that Gibson was actually addressing a number of rather distinct issues by his single, basic distinction between direct and indirect perception (*see*, for example, Gibson 1982*c*). For Gibson contrasts not only direct perception versus perception mediated by another human being, but also direct perception and perception based on coded rather than natural information, direct perception and perception mediated by an intervening object, knowledge *by acquaintance* and knowledge *about*, and first-hand and second-hand experience. Now these different contrasts may seem virtually synonymous, but an examination of just a few examples soon demonstrates otherwise.

Take, for example, pictures, a favourite topic of Gibson's later writings; indeed they are a recurrent theme in his last book, *The ecological approach to visual perception* (Gibson 1979). Why did he say that the perception of pictures was indirect? Well, picture perception certainly counts as indirect in terms of most of the above contrasts; yet Gibson certainly did not consider that the information pictures conveyed was coded or conventional, for he insisted that they present the same kind of information as that available in the natural optic array (*see* Costall 1985). And what about telescopes, microscopes, and even spectacles? These constitute mediating objects in the perceptual process, and are human productions, and hence on Gibson's account yield indirect perception; yet there is an important sense, surely, in which they might be said to facilitate *direct* perception, the exploration and detection of available information (cf. Michaels and Carello 1981, p. 55). Then there is the case of perceiving the affordances of the objects in our surroundings; most of these are actually designed and constructed by humans in order not only to function appropriately but also to be conspicuously meaningful to a potential user. Although such objects do not constitute representations in any obvious sense, the perception of their affordances does nevertheless depend upon the intervention of other people. The objects in our surroundings, as well as our relations to them, are *social* (*see* Noble 1981). Finally, consider the case where someone draws our attention to distinctions we might not otherwise perceive. This might merely involve us noticing something in our immediate surroundings, or else involve a long apprenticeship in learning to detect, for example, significant aspects of the sounds made by a defective motor, or something medically important about the wheezing of a diseased patient. This is not a case of second-hand knowledge, representation, or knowledge *about* as opposed to knowledge *by acquaintance* yet, according to Gibson's scheme, it would presumably have to count as indirect perception, since it again involves the intervention of another human being, and often an important historical process as well.

Conclusion

Clearly, Gibson was attempting to deal with a variety of important issues concerning the problem of human cognition, but these became intricately intertwined around an apparently unitary contrast with direct perception. Gibson himself certainly came to realize that his distinction between direct and indirect perception should not be treated as a rigid dichotomy; in his later writings, he talked of a possible scale of indirectness of perception, and even wondered whether some of the cases he had previously classified as indirect counted as cases of perception at all (Gibson 1980, 1982*b*). But he never properly grasped the underlying source of this problem. His distinction between direct and indirect perception eventually came to perform a number of different but important functions—indeed too many, I believe, for a single distinction effectively to fulfil. In the end, Gibson had introduced so many diverse qualifications to his concept of direct perception that it is difficult to see how any example of *human* perception could ever possibly count as direct in Gibson's terms. Yet such an outcome threatens to undermine completely the very purpose of his whole theoretical enterprise.

Gibson rejected the empiricist theory of perception, with its easy resort to 'past experience', but he was avowedly an empiricist in his epistemology. All knowledge, he insisted, is ultimately based upon perception. He regarded direct perception, therefore, as 'the simplest and best kind of knowing' (Gibson 1979, p. 263). According to Gibson, it is our responsibility to look attentively and look for ourselves. Indeed, he often sounds as though he were promoting the Cartesian ideal of the knower as an isolated being confronting a pre-social world. Certainly, he treated this as the most primitive kind of epistemological relation between an organism and its environment, both from an evolutionary and also, more problematically, from a developmental perspective. But what about the human adult, and the problem of the relation between human language and perception? As I hope I have made clear by now, Gibson did not deny the peculiarities of human culture as a trivial complication. Rather he was concerned to reconcile the categories of the natural and the cultural in his theory. So how did he deal with this problem? Well, in fact, in two ways. The first was by acknowledging that language does indeed make a crucial difference in structuring the ways we attend to our surroundings; as he argued, however, language is not necessarily distorting, since it allows us not merely to *name* things, but also to qualify and elaborate our descriptions by *predication*. Yet, curiously, he offered a second solution to the problem of language and perception. For he also claimed that there is a pre-social and pre-linguistic mode of perceiving still available to us, which persists largely distinct and unchanged, independently of language:

The spontaneous activities of looking, listening, and touching, together with the satisfactions of noticing, can proceed with or without language. The curious observer can always observe more properties than he can describe. Observing is thus not necessarily coerced by linguistic labeling (Gibson 1966, p. 282).

It was on the basis of this conviction—that we can see more than we can tell—that Gibson thought he had saved empiricism as a viable epistemological principle, for then direct perception would still be possible, despite the existence of language. Yet, it seems to me, a fundamental problem remains, for he never properly considered what *kind* of world it is that we might thereby perceive. If he had done this, I think he would have seen the need to disentangle his concept of direct perception from some very important senses of mediated perception. For I am not at all convinced by Gibson's recurrent image of culture as merely a kind of potentially distorting screen partly interposed between us and an independent, 'real' world, a 'wilderness', beyond. This is surely wrong. We are *in* culture; it *is* our world. Indeed, it is the only world we could ever directly perceive.

References

Costall, A. P. (1985). How meaning covers the traces. In *Visual order* (eds. N. H. Freeman and M. V. Cox). Cambridge University Press.

Gibson, J. J. (1939). The aryan myth. *Journal of educational sociology* 13, 164–71.

Gibson, J. J. (1950a). *The perception of the visual world.* Houghton-Mifflin, Boston.

Gibson, J. J. (1950b). The implications of learning theory for social psychology. In *Experiments in social process* (ed. J. G. Miller). McGraw-Hill, New York.

Gibson, J. J. (1951). Theories of perception. In *Current trends in psychological theory* (ed. W. Dennis), pp. 85–110. University of Pittsburgh Press, Pittsburgh.

Gibson, J. J. (1953). Social perception and the psychology of perceptual learning. In *Group relations at the cross-roads* (eds. M. Sherif and M. O. Wilson), pp. 120–138. Harper & Brothers, New York.

Gibson, J. J. (1958). An interpretation of Woodworth's theory of perceiving. In *Current psychological issues: essays in honour of Robert S. Woodworth* (eds. G. S. and J. P. Seward), pp. 39–52. Holt, New York.

Gibson, J. J. (1959). Perception as a function of stimulation. In *Psychology: a study of a science. Vol. 1* (ed. S. Koch), pp. 456–501. McGraw-Hill, New York.

Gibson, J. J. (1960). Perception. In *Encyclopedia of science and technology*. McGraw-Hill, New York.

Gibson, J. J. (1961). Ecological optics. *Vision research* **1**, 253–62.

Gibson, J. J. (1962). The survival value of sensory perception. *Biological prototypes and synthetic systems (Vol. 1)*, pp. 230–2. Plenum, New York.

Gibson, J. J. (1963). The useful dimensions of sensitivity. *American psychologist* **18**, 1–15.

Gibson, J. J. (1966). *The senses considered as perceptual systems*. Houghton-Mifflin, Boston.

Gibson, J. J. (1967a). Autobiography. In *A history of psychology in autobiography, Vol. V* (eds. E. G. Boring and G. Linzey), pp. 127–43. Appleton-Century-Crofts, New York.

Gibson, J. J. (1967b). New reasons for realism. *Synthese* **17**, 162–72.

Gibson, J. J. (1972). A theory of direct visual perception. In *The psychology of knowing* (eds. J. R. Royce and W. W. Rozeboom), pp. 215–49. Gordon and Breach, New York.

Gibson, J. J. (1974). On Ronchi's 'New Optics'. *Leonardo* **7**, 382–3.

Gibson, J. J. (1979). *The ecological approach to visual perception*. Houghton-Mifflin, Boston.

Gibson, J. J. (1980). Foreword: a prefatory essay on the perception of surfaces versus the perception of markings on a surface. In *The perception of pictures, Vol. 1* (ed. M. A. Hagen), pp. xi–xviii. Academic Press, New York.

Gibson, J. J. (1982a). A note on current theories of perception. In *Reasons for realism: selected papers of J. J. Gibson* (eds. E. S. Reed and R. K. Jones), pp. 370–73. Erlbaum, Hillsdale, NJ. [Unpublished manuscript, July 1974.]

Gibson, J. J. (1982b). A note on direct perception, various kinds of indirect apprehension, and degrees of indirectness. In *Reasons for realism: selected papers of J. J. Gibson* (eds. E. S. Reed and R. K. Jones), pp. 289–92. Erlbaum, Hillsdale, NJ. [Unpublished manuscript, May, 1977.]

Gibson, J. J. (1982c). Various kinds of cognition. In *Reasons for realism: Selected papers of J. J. Gibson* (eds. E. S. Reed and R. K. Jones), pp. 292–3. Erlbaum, Hillsdale, NJ. [Unpublished manuscript, July, 1979.]

Michaels, C. and Carello, C. (eds.) (1981). *Direct perception*. Prentice-Hall, Englewood Cliffs, N. J.

Noble, W. (1981). Gibsonian theory and the pragmatist perspective. *Journal for the theory of social behaviour* **11**, 65–85.

Reed, E. S. (1986). Seeing through history. *Philosophy of the social sciences* **16**, 239–47.

Reed, E. S. (1987). James Gibson's ecological approach to cognition. In *Cognitive psychology in question* (eds. A. Costall and A. Still), pp. 142–173. Harvester, Brighton.

Sampson, E. E. (1981). Cognitive psychology as ideology. *American psychologist* **36**, 730–43.

Volosinov, V. N. (1927/1976). *Freudianism: a Marxist critique.* Academic Press, London.

3

Machiavellian monkeys: cognitive evolution and the social world of primates

A. WHITEN and R.W. BYRNE

In this chapter we are taking a functional approach to cognition. We are asking the question, 'what is intellect for?' The answer we shall address has everything to do with the social world, and this differs from the traditional answer offered by academic psychology, one which is fundamentally asocial. The asocial assumption is apparent not only in the case of human intelligence tests, but also in the investigation of animal intelligence by comparative psychologists who present problems which involve the manipulation of objects.

By contrast, the 'Machiavellian intellect hypothesis' proposes that the key to the function of intellect lies in the demands of the particularly complex social life which characterizes not only ourselves, but in a number of respects also our close primate relatives and, we therefore assume, our primate ancestors. This idea is not new and indeed has surfaced independently a number of times (Chance and Mead 1953; Jolly 1966; Holloway 1975; Humphrey 1976). What is exciting at present is that the ideas expressed in these isolated papers have at last taken off in a significant body of empirical research (Cheney, Seyfarth, and Smuts 1986; Byrne and Whiten 1988) and it is this we review here.

The Machiavellian intellect hypotheses

Let us start by getting straight what is being claimed. Whiten and Byrne (1988a) note that the 'Machiavellian intellect hypothesis' actually breaks down into a number of sub-hypotheses.

The first is simply that, despite the historical emphasis on intelligence as the solving of object-based problems, intelligence in the natural life of primates will be found to be concerned also with handling social problems. As a psychologist observing wild gorillas for the time time, Humphrey (1976), for example, was puzzled by the apparent redundancy of the animals' acknowledged, laboratory-proven intelligence when it came to extracting the required resources from the physical environment. But for a gorilla to succeed in life requires interacting with, and often competing against, other gorillas, who are just as intelligent. This, Humphrey suggested, presents a series of social problems to be solved. To illustrate, let us take an example from de Waal's (1982) intensive study of chimpanzees:

on a hot day two mothers are sitting in the shadow of a tree while their two infants play in the sand at their feet. Between the two mothers the oldest female, Mama, lies asleep. Suddenly the infants start screaming, hitting and pulling each other's hair. One mother admonishes them with a soft threatening grunt and the other anxiously shifts her position. The infants go on quarrelling. Eventually one mother wakes Mama by poking her in the ribs several times. As Mama gets up, the mother points towards the two quarrelling infants. As soon as Mama takes one threatening step forward, waves her arm and barks loudly, the infants stop quarrelling. Mama then lies down again and continues her siesta.

De Waal tells us that Mama is the highest ranking female and quite formidable. He also notes that conflicts between infants like this often generate tension and ultimately fighting between their mothers. These two facts are crucial to his interpretation, which is that the mothers in this episode were presented with a social problem: to terminate the squabble between the infants without engendering aggression between themselves. One of the mothers solved this problem by activating a dominant third party, Mama, and guiding her towards the solution of the problem.

Whether or not we are sceptical of de Waal's interpretation, after two decades of intensive primate ethology, many, perhaps most, primatologists would find the episode an entirely plausible example of primate social problem solving. To restate our first sub-hypothesis, then, it is simply that careful examination of the social world of primates will allow us to delineate a rich ecology of intelligence.

The second sub-hypothesis goes further: social intelligence is suggested to be more complex, more advanced, than non-social or 'technical' intelligence. This in turn breaks down into two proposals: that the social world (as opposed to the physical or technical world) makes particularly severe demands on an animal's cognitive systems; and that cognitive systems which handle the social environment are more sophisticated than those which handle the technical world. We shall turn to evidence bearing on these hypotheses later.

The third sub-hypothesis is that (natural) selection for social expertise is the key to explaining the evolution of advanced intelligence in the primate order, including the special braininess of our own species. It is this we shall focus on now: what is special about primate society? Our answer comes in three parts (Table 3.1): *demographic characteristics* (large permanent groups, long life, and long-term residency) create *social complexity* (long-term relationships, multi-party interactions, and co-operation) which is handled by a number of sophisticated components of *social cognition* (we pick out knowledge of relationships, the computation of social trade, and doing 'natural psychology'.

Table 3.1. *Principal components of anthropoid demography, social complexity, and social cognition.*

Anthropoid demography	Social complexity	Social cognition
Large permanent groups	Long-term relationships	Knowledge about relationships
Long life	Multi-party interactions	Computing social trade
Long residency	Co-operation	Natural psychology

Anthropoid demography

Large permanent groups

The primates are traditionally divided into the prosimians, which appear first in the fossil record and are today represented by animals like lemurs, bushbabies, and lorises, and the anthropoids, which include all the monkeys and apes. It is perhaps the latter group to which we should target the Machiavellian intellect hypotheses, for although the claim that the prosimians are 'primitive' is controversial (Bearder 1987) it does appear that it is in the anthropoids that we find a clear modal pattern of permanent groups. Fig. 3.1, for example, contrasts the foraging group sizes of prosimians (with whom we shared a common ancestor about 65 million years ago; see papers in Wood *et al.* 1986) with those found in the monkeys of Africa and Asia (with whom we shared a common ancestor about 30 million years ago). If living in such groups imposes the pressures detailed below, it is thus at this later stage of our ancestry that we must infer a shift in the nature of social cognition.

Long lifetime

Primates are unusually long-lived mammals for their body size (although only as long-lived as we should expect given their brain size relative to body size; Passingham 1982). The implication of this in absolute terms is that anthropoids take years to reach maturity and then breed for many years.

Long residency

The above two characteristics come together in a specific way: monkeys and apes tend to stay in these groups for very long periods. In baboons and macaque monkeys, for example, we know that females generally stay in their natal groups all their lives (Moore 1978; Chepko-Sade and Sade 1979). Although in these species males generally move to a new group before starting their reproductive career, they tend to settle in that group for the rest of their

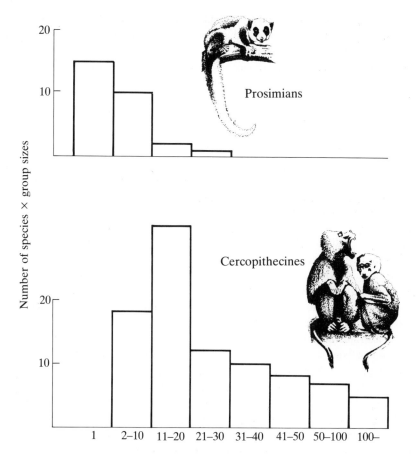

Fig. 3.1. Foraging group sizes of Prosimian and Cercopithecine primates. From data collected in Jolly (1985).

lives or at least for many years (Packer 1979; Lindburg 1969; Sade 1972). Interestingly in our closest relatives, the gorilla and chimpanzee, this pattern tends to be reversed, with the females transferring groups (Harcourt *et al.*, 1976; Nishida 1979), but again any one period of residence is typically of many years' duration and often lasts for a lifetime.

The implications of these characteristics for social complexity will no doubt be clear. We have social groups made up of individuals who, because of their long life and long-term residency, are likely to interact a vast number of times with the same group members. The lifetime is long enough to generate interactions also between several generations of kin. And finally, larger groups permit repeated interactions amongst a huge number of potential partners.

All these factors contribute to social complexity. But 'social complexity' is becoming such an overworked expression that we must now pin it down further to make progress (Whiten and Byrne 1988*b*). In what follows we pick out three features which appear to be special in primates.

Social complexity

Long-term relationships

We can define a relationship between two individuals as constituted by repeated interactions between them (Hinde 1976). The demographic characteristics outlined above clearly create the potential for the development of long-term relationships, and there is now abundant evidence that individual primates fully exploit this potential, with benefits accruing to their ultimate reproductive success.

Amongst non-human primates, an important basis for relationships is grooming. Although mothers groom their infants initially with no reciprocation (Altmann 1980) the developing juvenile increasingly returns this favour and grooming between older individuals becomes simultaneously mutual (Barton 1987) or involves turn-taking, the latter being the common pattern in anthropoids. In those species where we have the necessary long-term knowledge of genealogies, it has been possible to show that individuals of the sex which remain in the natal group tend to develop grooming relationships which are likely to last for as long as the two partners live, and strongly reflect kinship (*see* Wrangham 1980 for references).

But the rules of primate relationships go much beyond a preference for kin. A good example is the 'friendships' which develop between unrelated adult male and adult female baboons—who are not simply 'mates' either (Seyfarth 1978; Altmann 1980). Detailed study by Smuts (1985) has shown that females tend to have two special male associates, and that a complex mesh of benefits to the participants underwrites these relationships, some of which have been found to last as long as six years. To understand these benefits, however, we have to go beyond the consideration of only dyadic interaction.

Multi-party interactions

One of the first and keenest observations that primates were capable of subtle triadic interaction came from the work of Kummer (1967) on hamadryas baboons. These live in a society in which a single large male forms long-term mating relationships with several females. It was within such a 'harem' that Kummer observed what he called 'protected threat': an aggressive tactic in which a female would threaten another female only after manoeuvring into a position between the victim and the adult male. Within this configuration, the victim could not attack back or even threaten the female without simultaneously threatening the male just behind her and risking a dangerous attack by him. The male was thus being used as a social tool — one of the first signs of the Machiavellian nature of primate social competence.

Handling such multi-party interactions will impose greater cognitive demands than will merely dyadic interactions. However, many triadic interactions are yet more demanding, because some of the interactants are involved in offering or withholding their active support to individuals who are in conflict with others.

Co-operation

By co-operating, two individuals can together win a competition with a third, which they would have failed to do if acting by themselves. This has been known to be a feature of primate societies since DeVore and Hall (1965) described such alliances between lower ranking male baboons, allowing them to successfully dominate an individual who outranked each of them in purely dyadic contests.

But we now know that alliances are shifting, in a way which puts extra pressure on the cognitive processes which execute the social behaviour, whether initiating or responding to these shifting relationships. For example, studies of both wild (Nishida 1983) and captive (de Waal 1982) chimpanzees have documented the way in which one male may rise to the highest, alpha rank with the support of a second. The alpha male clearly benefits from this support in maintaining a position allowing him preferential access to resources (notably fertile females and food). But the ally also benefits, because the alpha tolerates a certain amount of mating with females by him. That the ally is offering his support in a Machiavellian fashion, just because there is such a net benefit (he is not a male who could at this point be a serious contender for alpha status himself) is shown by the way in which dramatic cases are observed of a fall in power by the alpha and his replacement by another individual, not because of a gross change in their relative fighting ability, but because of a shift in the allegiance of the third individual, acting as 'kingmaker'. The latter continues with his net benefit of a small ration of matings, rather than none. All this is not to say that there is not *some* shift involved here in the relative power of the changing alpha individuals, independently of actions by the kingmaker; rather, the latter shows enormous social sensitivity to the signs of subtle shifts — not only in the behaviour of the two males but in others' behaviour towards them — and adjusts his behaviour accordingly, tips the scales, and himself remains in a useful social position. It will be clear why, in his detailed account of such power struggles, de Waal (1982) is able to quote in context Machiavelli's (1532) advice to those with high political aspirations:

'He who attains the principality with the aid of the nobility maintains it with more difficulty than he who becomes prince with the assistance of the common people, for he finds himself a prince amidst many who feel themselves to be his equals, and because of this he can neither govern nor manage them as he might wish.'

Many anthropoid relationships have this quality: the ability to adjust social relationships along a knife-edge between conflict and shifting co-operative alliances. In a recent review of the distribution of such alliances in the animal kingdom, Harcourt (1988) finds that in studies of old-world monkeys and apes, 10–30 per cent of contests involve the intervention of a third individual. From the non-primate literature, by contrast, he was able to quote only two isolated examples, and one of these involved support of offspring by their parents. Moreover, data have not yet been offered to contradict Jolly's early finding (1966) that even the most 'monkey-like' (large, diurnal) prosimians do not evidence triadic interactions and alliances. Although, as Harcourt acknowledges, this may yet be because nobody has looked properly at other groups of animals, at present the evidence is in support of the proposition that anthropoids may experience and generate rather special types of social complexity.

What are the implications for social cognition? Below we summarize the evidence that primates often possess prodigious *knowledge* about relationships, that they indulge in difficult computations about *social exchanges*, and that they may often act as *natural psychologists*.

Social cognition

Knowledge about relationships

Social primates appear to have an extensive knowledge about the characteristics of members of their group, about relationships between them, and about what interactions have taken place in the past. They pay avid attention to the 'soap opera' of primate social life.

At perhaps the simplest level, primates discriminate amongst their own relationships with other individuals. For example, macaque monkeys have been shown not only to associate more with close kin, but within kin, to choose those most closely related (Kurland 1977; Datta 1983).

What is more interesting are various lines of evidence that monkeys know a lot about the social world in its own right; that is, about the relationships *between other individuals*:

(1) When infant vervet monkey calls were played back from a tape recorder to the group, mothers paid most attention to the calls of their own infants (Cheney and Seyfarth 1980). This shows simply that mothers could recognize their own infants; much more impressively, it was observed that the *other*

mothers turned and looked towards the mother of the infant; in other words, they knew what specific relationship existed between two other individuals, a mother and her infant.

(2) This has been followed by experimental work with captive social groups, in which monkeys in a discrimination learning task were able to apply a concept of 'mother–infant relationship' to pick out novel pairs of mothers and infants in photographs not presented in the original training sessions (Dasser 1988). Dasser has done the same thing for rank relationships. This shows clearly that these monkeys can operate using an abstract concept about a specific sort of relationship. Seyfarth and Cheney (1988) suggest that this could be an ability of profound functional significance for life in the sort of social world we have been outlining above, for instead of having to learn anew the properties of each of many unique relationships existing in the group, an individual can use pre-existing concepts to help predict the behaviour of others based on only partial information about them.

(3) Bachman and Kummer (1980) have shown experimentally that a male hamadryas baboon will adjust its attempts to disrupt a bond already formed between another male and a female, according to the degree of preference the female has for the male she is already with: if her preference is strong, he expends less energy trying to disrupt the bond. Again there is evidence that one individual distinguishes between relationships existing between two others.

(4) When attacked by one individual, baboons have been found not necessarily to retaliate directly, but to direct aggression preferentially towards an affiliate of the first individual, implying that they know who other individual's friends are (Smuts 1985).

(5) Observations which highlight not only the sophistication of social knowledge but also the fact that it may take years to develop come from work on vervets (Seyfarth and Cheney 1988) where it has been shown that an individual, A, is more likely to express aggression towards another, B, if A has fought not B, but B's close matrilineal kin in the last two hours. The level of social knowledge this implies is found even in vervets younger than three years of age. However, increasing the requisite sophistication leaves such youngsters failing to show what can be demonstrated in individuals older than three years: A is more likely to threaten B if A's close kin have recently been involved in a fight with B's close kin!

Computing social trade

We have already noted above that helping may be reciprocal. In male baboon alliances where one male harrasses a courting male while his partner moves in and mates with the female, the roles tend to be reversed on other occasions, so we have a case of reciprocal altruism (Packer 1977). Now, the males who received help most often were those who gave help most often. Also, males tended to select partners who also preferentially selected them on other occasions: the inference was thus drawn that males promote those reciprocations which work (Packer 1977). We thus have a picture of such a primate constantly computing the net costs and benefits from a series of co-operative interactions, and adjusting its network of relationships accordingly.

This would be hard enough if all reciprocations could be evaluated in the same 'currency' — matings, in the example just described. But primates help each other in various ways: do they compute the value of a relationship by combining the effects in these different currencies — like grooming, and help in fights for example? Evidence that this is happening comes from studies which again exploit the vocalization playback technique. Vervets use a particular call to solicit help from others in aggressive interactions, and this was played back to individuals for whom grooming interactions with others had been recorded in the two hours previous (Seyfarth and Cheney 1984). It was found that if such an individual had been groomed by a non-relative, then it paid more attention to the request for help. Amongst relatives, this distinction was not applied. But for non-relatives, the conclusion was that grooming was traded for help in aggressive encounters on other occasions. This surely adds further complexity to social cognition, for costs and benefits in these different currencies must be tallied over long periods of time.

Natural psychology: mind-reading and deception

Given the picture of primate Machiavellianism sketched so far, we can see that it might be useful for a primate to be able to read the mind of another — to have insights into others' intentions and motivations and thus be a 'natural psychologist' (Humphrey 1980). This idea has been discussed at a theoretical level by a number of behavioural scientists (Menzel and Johnson 1976; Premack and Woodruff 1978; Humphrey 1983; Dawkins and Krebs 1978). However, although many primatologists will confess that the notion is eminently plausible, objective criteria have yet to be agreed upon.

This, however, is an issue we have been forced to consider in our work on what we have called 'tactical deception' in primates (Byrne and Whiten 1985). The project started when we observed several, but relatively infrequent acts of deception during field studies of baboon behaviour. For example, a baboon who was being chased aggressively by another would suddenly stop, rear up, and look intently into the distance as if it had spotted a predator or a baboon from a neighbouring group; yet it was clear under our observation conditions that no such entity was to be seen. The pursuing individual stopped and scanned the horizon for a few minutes and the chase did not resume. Informal discussion with other primatologists led us to the realization that a likely reason that such phenomena had not become established in the literature had to do with a fundamental feature of the phenomenon itself; it would be likely to be rare, because crying wolf too often would be counterproductive (Slater 1983). Because of this we published our own modest corpus of acts of tactical deception (Byrne and Whiten 1985), which we defined as acts from the normal ('honest') repertoire, deployed at low frequency in other contexts such that another individual misinterpreted their significance—as in the above example. We then went on to solicit records of tactical deception from other researchers, and as a result we have assembled a much more comprehensive corpus (Whiten and Byrne 1986).

The range of deceptive tactics in anthropoids (as yet we have only null responses to our requests from prosimian researchers) is diverse, and we have distinguished thirteen different functional classes. It turns out that most of these classes—and indeed most of the individual records—have to do with the *manipulation of attention* (Whiten and Byrne 1988c). As we have already seen, a monkey can, for example, use its own attentional focus deceptively to direct another's attention, with clear benefits to itself.

Now consider another case, where the function of the behaviour is not distraction of the other's attention, but concealment of something from it. The following account was contributed to our corpus by Kummer: it concerns Hamadryas baboons, in which one large 'leader' male typically has long-term exclusive mating and social interactions with several females, but in which the latter can occasionally contrive interactions with other males. Kummer observed a female spend 20 minutes moving into a position where she could groom a subadult male, an action which would not be tolerated if witnessed by her leader male. What is important is that she adjusted her position carefully such that the leader male could see the top part of her, but not the young male, nor the female's hands which were surreptitiously grooming him.

We have proposed that such finesse gives us an objective way in which to talk sensibly about a primate doing natural psychology (Whiten and Byrne 1988d). In the example just described, the female adjusted her behaviour so as to minimize the discrepancy between an actual state of affairs and a goal state, both of which can be specified, not by the female's direct view of the situation, but by the view of the adult male. In other words, the female must be able to mentally represent the male's representation of the world. Using Dennett's (1983) scheme of 'orders of intentionality', we can denote this nesting as a case of second-order social representation, in which individual A is able to represent B's representation.

In apes, our preliminary data indicated that third-order representation may be routine, in that individual A can take account of the ability of individual B's ability to take account of A's attentional focus. They may thus inhibit their gaze with respect to a desirable resource until a competitive situation has waned. The following account we received from Plooij (Whiten and Byrne 1986, 1988d) illustrates this, as well as documenting counter-deception:

One chimpanzee was alone in the feeding area and was going to be fed bananas. A metal box was opened from a distance. Just at the moment when the box was opened, another chimpanzee approached at the border of the clearing. The first chimpanzee quickly closed the metal box and walked away several metres, sat down and looked around as if nothing had happened. The second chimpanzee left the feeding area again, but as soon as he was out of sight, he hid behind a tree and peered at the individual in the feeding area. As soon as that individual approached, and opened the box again, the hiding individual approached, replaced the other and ate the bananas.

Scepticism about such isolated records wanes as more and equally impressive interactions are recorded (de Waal 1986; Savage-Rumbaugh and McDonald 1988). The record just quoted is thus an appropriate one on which to summarize our account so far: we propose that there is now a significant body of evidence that anthropoid primates live in a particularly complex social world, and have powers of social cognition to match.

We conclude, however, by outlining recent attempts to answer the most difficult component of the social intellect hypotheses mentioned at the start of this paper.

Is 'Machiavellian intellect' the key to understanding cognitive evolution in non-human primates, and in humans?

To put the question the other way about, is the social world more potent than the non-social as a selection pressure for cognitive abilities? This is a question which Cheney and Seyfarth (1985) have attempted to answer for a particular subset of cognitive abilities: can primates grasp *relationships* to be detected in the non-social world as well as in the social? The evidence here is limited, but, as far as it goes, it offers the answer 'no', according to Cheney and Seyfarth.

Two findings are particularly worth summarizing. First, a call of a neighbouring vervet was played from an area which it did not in fact inhabit, and the vervets of the study group gave this discrepancy considerable attention. However, they did not react in the same way under the control condition, which involved playing the vocalizations of other species, like hippopotamus, also from areas where they would not normally come. This does not precisely address the social/non-social distinction, but it does indicated that vervets' knowledge is particularly tuned to vervet society.

Secondly, these vervets' sophisticated social knowledge about other group members has already been outlined above. In a number of respects, they are relatively poor at learning other associations, failing, for example, to use the tracks of a python to avoid the bush it is likely to be in, and to avoid a tree containing an antelope carcass—to a human, an obvious indicator of the presence of a leopard.

Turning from data on comparison between matched social and non-social contexts, as soon as we move onto abilities like computing social trade and doing natural psychology, one has in a sense answered the question posed above, for these abilities only exist by virtue of dealing with the social world and its complexities. Anything beyond first-order intentionality (Dennett 1983) is only required in social contexts!

What about the importance of the social world specifically in human cognitive evolution? The traditional view has been that the key to intellectual evolution had to do with the trend towards hunting using tools and weapons—a technical hypothesis. Wynn (1988) has now done a very nice demolition job on this hypothesis, by applying a Piagetian analysis to what must be inferred about the cognitive operations necessary to make the stone tools found at different ages in the archaeological record.

First, he notes that at the time of the first significant brain expansion in Australopithecines dating to 3.5 million years before the present (Myr), there is no evidence of tool use. Then, he shows that at the time of early *Homo*, at 1.8 Myr, with a further expansion in brain size bringing the brain closer to human than chimpanzee size, the capacities required in tool making at that time were early pre-operational, the level achieved by three-year-old children and the living great apes. At this stage there is no indication of tools being fashioned to a standard pattern, a development which appears with *Homo erectus* after 1.5 Myr, with a bigger brain yet. The manufacture of these tools requires attributes of late pre-operational intelligence, like symmetry and interval, which are beyond apes. Nevertheless, brain size continued to expand to modern levels by 300 000 years ago, and yet the basic tool kit changed hardly at all—'there are few things one can point to as inventions in the entire period'—of one million years! Conversely, the principal technological advances have occurred in the last couple of hundred thousand years when there has been very little expansion in brain size.

If the technical intellect hypothesis thus falls by the wayside, perhaps the 'Machiavellian intellect' hypothesis has more mileage in the specific case of human evolution, in addition even to what has been claimed for primate evolution in general. What is required to take this further is investigation along the lines of Cheney and Seyfarth's vervet comparisons described above, for the human case: we need functional and comparative analyses of the manifestation of intelligence by modern humans in both non-social and social worlds. For the latter, of course, the reader can turn to other chapters in this book.

References

Altmann, J. (1980). *Baboon mothers and infants*. Harvard University Press, Cambridge, MA.

Bachman, C. and Kummer, H. (1980). *Behavioural ecology and sociobiology* 6, 315–21.

Barton, R. (1987). Allogrooming as mutualism in diurnal lemurs. *Primates* 28, 539–42.

Bearder, S. K. (1987). Lorises, bushbabies, and Tarsiers: diverse societies in solitary foragers. In *Primate societies* (eds. B. B. Smut, D. L. Cheney, R. M. Seyfarth, R. W. Wrangham, and T. T. Struhsaker). The University of Chicago Press, Chicago.

Byrne, R. W. and Whiten, A. (1985). Tactical deception of familiar individuals in baboons. *Animal behaviour* 33, 669–73.

Byrne, R. W. and Whiten, A. (1988). *Machiavellian intelligence: social expertise and the evolution of intellect in monkeys, apes, and humans.* Oxford University Press.

Chance, M. R. A. and Mead, A. P. (1953). Social behaviour and primate evolution. *Symposia of the Society for Experimental Biology, Evolution* 7, 395–439.

Cheney, D. L. and Seyfarth, R. M. (1980). Vocal recognition in free-ranging vervet monkeys. *Animal behaviour* 28, 362–67.

Cheney, D. L. and Seyfarth, R. M. (1985). The social and non-social world of non-human primates. In *Social relationships and cognitive development* (eds. R. A. Hinde, A.-N. Perret-Clermont and J. Stevenson-Hinde), pp. 23–44. Clarendon Press, Oxford.

Cheney, D. L., Seyfarth, R. M., and Smuts, B. B. (1986). Social relationships and social cognition in nonhuman primates. *Science* 234, 1361–66.

Chepko-Sade, B. D. and Sade, D. S. (1979). Patterns of group splitting within matrilineal kinship groups: a study of social group structure in *Macaca mulatta*. *Behavioural ecology and sociobiology* 5, 67–86.

Dasser, V. (1988). Mapping social concepts in monkeys. In *Machiavellian intelligence: social expertise and the evolution of intellect in monkeys, apes and humans* (eds. R. W. Byrne and A. Whiten). Oxford University Press.

Datta, S. B. (1983). Patterns of agonistic interference. In *Primate social relationships* (ed. R. A. Hinde), pp. 93–103. Blackwell Scientific Publications, Oxford.

Dawkins, R. and Krebs, J. R. (1978). Animal signals: information or manipulation? In *Behavioural ecology: an evolutionary approach* (eds. J. R. Krebs and N. B. Davies), pp. 282–314. Blackwell, Oxford.

Dennett, D. C. (1983). Intentional systems in cognitive ethology: the "Panglossian paradigm" defended. *The behavioral and brain sciences* 6, 343–90.

DeVore, I. and Hall, K. R. L. (1965). Baboon ecology. In *Primates behavior* (ed. I. DeVore). Holt, Rinehart, and Winston, New York.

Harcourt, A. (1988). Alliances in contests and social intelligence. In *Machiavellian intelligence: social expertise and the evolution of intellect in monkeys, apes, and humans* (eds. R. W. Byrne and A. Whiten). Oxford University Press.

Harcourt, A. H., Stewart, K. J., and Fossey, D. (1976). Male emigration and female transfer in wild mountain gorilla. *Nature* 263, 226–7.

Hinde, R. A. (1976). Interactions, relationships and social structure. *Man* 11, 1–17.

Holloway, R. L. (1975). *The role of human social behaviour in the evolution of the brain.* American Museum of Natural History, New York.

Humphrey, N. (1976). The social function of intellect. In *Growing points in ethology* (eds. P. P. G. Bateson and R. A. Hinde), pp. 303–17. Cambridge University Press.

Humphrey, N. K. (1980). Nature's psychologists. In *Consciousness and the physical world* (eds. B. Josephson and V. Ramachandran). Pergamon, London.

Humphrey, N. K. (1983). *Consciousness regained.* Oxford University Press.
Jolly, A. (1966). *Lemur social behaviour and primate intelligence. Science* **153**, 501–6.
Jolly, A. (1985). *The Evolution of primate behaviour.* Macmillan, New York.
Kummer, H. (1967). Tripartite relations in Hamadryas baboons. In *Social communication among primates* (ed. S. A. Altmann). University of Chicago Press, Chicago.
Kurland, J. A. (1977). Kin selection in the Japanese monkey. *Contributions to primatology* **12**, 145. Karger, Basel.
Lindburg, D. G. (1969). Rhesus monkeys: mating season mobility of adult males. *Science* **166**, 1176–8.
Machiavelli, N. (1532/1979). *The Prince.* In *The portable Machiavelli* (eds. P. Bondanella and M. Musa). Penguin Books, Harmondsworth.
Menzel, E. W. and Johnson, M. K. (1976). Communication and cognitive organisation in humans and other animals. *Annals of the New York Academy of Sciences* **280**, 131–42.
Moore, J. (1978). Dominance relations among free-ranging female baboons in Gombe National Park, Tanzania. In *Recent advances in primatology. Vol. I, Behaviour* (eds. D. J. Chivers and J. Herbert). Academic Press, London.
Nishida, T. (1979). The social structure of chimpanzees of the Mahale Mountains. In *The great apes* (eds. D. A. Hamburg and E. R. McCown). Benjamin/Cummings, Menlo Park, CA.
Nishida, T. (1983). Alpha status and agonistic alliance in wild chimpanzees. *Primates* **24**, 318–36.
Packer, C. (1977). Reciprocal altruism in olive baboons. *Nature* **265**, 441–3.
Packer, C. (1979). Inter-troop transfer and inbreeding avoidance in *Papio anubis. Animal behaviour* **27**, 1–36.
Passingham, R. E. (1982). *The human primate.* W. H. Freeman, New York.
Premack, D. and Woodruff, G. (1978). Does the chimpanzee have a theory of mind? *The Behavioral and brain sciences* **1**, 515–26.
Sade, D. S. (1972). A longitudinal study of rhesus monkeys. In *Social communication among primates* (ed. S. A. Altmann). University of Chicago Press, Chicago.
Savage-Rumbaugh, S. and McDonald, K. (1988). Deception and social manipulation in symbol using apes. In *Machiavellian intelligence: social expertise and the evolution of intellect in monkeys, apes, and humans* (eds. R. W. Byrne and A. Whiten). Oxford University Press.
Seyfarth, R. M. (1978). Social relationships among adult male and female baboons. II. Behaviour throughout the reproductive cycle. *Behaviour* **64**, 227–47.
Seyfarth, R. M. and Cheney, D. L. (1984). Grooming, alliances and reciprocal altruism in vervet monkeys. *Nature* **308**, 541–3.
Seyfarth, R. M. and Cheney, D. L. (1988). Do monkeys understand their relations? In *Machiavellian intelligence: social expertise and the evolution of intellect in monkeys, apes, and humans* (eds. R. W. Byrne and A. Whiten). Oxford University Press.
Slater, P. J. B. (1983). The study of communication. In *Animal behaviour, vol. 2: Communication* (eds. T. R. Halliday and P. J. B. Slater), pp. 9–42. Blackwell, Oxford.
Smuts, B. (1985). *Sex and friendship in baboons.* Aldine, Chicago.

de Waal, F. (1982). *Chimpanzees politics*. Jonathan Cape, London.

de Waal, F. (1986). Deception in the natural communication of chimpanzees. In *Deception: perspectives on human and non-human deceit* (eds. R. W. Mitchell and N. S. Thompson). State University of New York Press, Albany.

Whiten, A. and Byrne, R. W. (1986). The St Andrews catalogue of tactical deception in primates. *St Andrews psychological reports no. 10.*

Whiten, A. and Byrne, R. W. (1988a). The Machiavellian intelligence hypotheses. In *Machiavellian intelligence: social expertise and the evolution of intellect in monkeys, apes, and humans* (eds. R. W. Byrne and A. Whiten). Oxford University Press.

Whiten, A. and Byrne, R. W. (1988b). Taking (Machiavellian) intelligence apart. In *Machiavellian intelligence: social expertise and the evolution of intellect in monkeys, apes, and humans* (eds. R. W. Byrne and A. Whiten). Oxford University Press.

Whiten, A. and Byrne, R. W. (1988c). The manipulation of attention in primate tactical deception. In *Machiavellian intelligence: social expertise and the evolution of intellect in monkeys, apes, and humans* (eds. R. W. Byrne and A. Whiten). Oxford University Press.

Whiten, A. and Byrne, R. W. (1988d). Tactical deception in primates. *Behavioural and brain sciences* 11, 233–73.

Wood, B. L., Martin, L., and Andrews, P. (eds.) (1986). *Major topics in primate and human evolution*. Cambridge University Press.

Wrangham, R. W. (1980). An ecological model of female-bonded primate groups. *Behaviour* 75, 262–300.

Wynn, T. (1988). Tools and the evolution of human intelligence. In *Machiavellian intelligence: social expertise and the evolution of intellect in monkeys, apes, and humans* (eds. R. W. Byrne and A. Whiten). Oxford University Press.

4

Child and culture: genesis of co-operative knowing

COLWYN TREVARTHEN and KATERINA LOGOTHETI

Introduction

Recent research describing the emergence of social performances in infancy and early childhood breaks new ground for the social sciences. It demonstrates the primary role of innate emotions and shows up the existence of innate form and time in human expressions for communication. Human individuals are now seen as having motives that make sense and have effect only in relation to an environment of real people who offer and seek affections, meanings, conventions, and co-operative enterprises.

Changes in social capacity from birth indicate the steps by which the young actively engage with their family and then find interest in the wider community around them. Their need for social understanding is manifest in the strong emotions that overcome children with every loss of participation in life with significant others. A child's joy selects universal rewards in the communication which other people afford.

Within the two years of infancy, a baby can be seen to move from practice in direct engagement of interpersonal motives to a sharing mastery of a reality that others find manipulable and learnable. Thus, the child's world is mediated through communication, from the start. The grasp of symbols is a direct product of a seeking for meanings behind others' interests and actions, and of using the world in conventional, sharable ways. This kind of intelligence is different from any social intelligence of animals, even that of apes. While depending upon the recognition of the different social roles of individuals in a group of intimates, cognitive skills that are especially developed in monkeys and apes (Humphrey 1976), human young have additional instincts and cognitive powers to use social knowing for cultural ends (Trevarthen 1979a, 1986a).

Why has this development towards cultural intelligence been misunderstood, as it seems to have been? There seem to be a number of explanations. All our scholarly traditions and implicit philosophical assumptions favour interpretations of ourselves as reasoning individuals, members of the species *sapiens*, and they militate against perception of ourselves as persons in relation (Buber 1937; MacMurray 1961). The nature of culture will only be understood when we have overcome such impediments in our thinking. We must begin by attempting to understand the nature of human 'communitas' (Turner 1974) and of human 'sociality' (Carrithers 1988).

To understand social reality we need to look for explanations outside the cognitive and intentional subjects of traditional psychology; we need to observe what happens *between* people. The psychology of a society exists in engagements, relationships, and conventional beliefs that transcend constraints of time and space in the subjective experience of single minds. Meanings and institutions outlast and outreach the lives of individuals by many times. Conventions and artefacts persist for hundreds of years. An invention, a fashion or 'news' can momentarily absorb the interest of millions scattered all round the world. Social change itself becomes an ideal or institution, in the name of 'progress', 'development', 'decline', or 'revolution'. How do communal and historical concepts such as these arise from the actions of individuals? What connects the senses of people so that they perceive such social realities in similar ways?

In the experimental cognitive tradition of psychology, a single attentive subject perceiving and thinking before choosing to make a response is the basic given. Explanation of psychological functioning has to be in terms of how the subject conducts, associates, and remembers experience as processor of stimulus information. But how could mere existence and stimulation of self-contained minds in society bring forth consciousness of meanings? How could such a subject become the member of a family, a citizen, an actor of social roles, a personality in relation to other persons? There is no clear answer. To escape the paradox, we normally resort to a familiar circle of reasoning that only confirms the impossibility of the task. We observe that humans take on manners and roles, gain prejudices, practise skills, compete for jobs and status, and we call these the effects of social learning. We come up with the explanation that what motivates our learning is pursuit of agreement with others. This is a frustrating, tautological, explanation missing essential facts of human life.

More recently, the 'cognitive revolution' has taught even the most reductionist of psychological scientists to admit that something (usually called 'representation') must go on inside subject's heads. We are now led, with a new kind of hope, to explain social behaviour, not just in terms of learning, but as a consequence of 'social cognition'. But are there special-purpose programs for perceiving and predicting social objects and social changes? One of the aims of the present paper is to question this way of tackling the problem, and the games theory (advantage-taking) descriptions of social encounters that it engenders. The social cognition theory has not, to our mind, really 'grasped the thistle' because it has not explained how we perceive others as people, with minds and feelings like our own.

What we need to understand are the acts and cognitive reactions that effec-tively create and maintain social forms. In short, we shall have to find motives in people for having these kinds of involvement with one another, because social meanings, institutions, symbols, and beliefs are generated and maintained by the ways people choose to interact and co-operate (Trevarthen 1982, 1986a).

Some see promise in an 'ecological' approach that looks for explanations in the structures and processes of surroundings, including the semantic structures of language. It is certainly a step in the right direction to try to see the social and cultural environment as a structured and informative 'life world' (Neisser 1980). But the ecological approach still lacks interest in motives and emotions, which define human engagement and, indeed, lie at the 'heart' of the problem. The ecological subject is a very abstract entity; a point of observation, a moving focus in a flow-field of light and sound; or, more recently, the resultant in a co-ordinated mechanical system, of forces of elasticity, inertia, and contraction, in a body that makes intermittent contact with resistant environmental media (Gibson 1979; Kugler et al. 1982). The ecological subject lives as some kind of substanceless mind–locus at the seat of information pick-up, or at the point of application of the resultant vector, taking profit from reality by selecting where to be and when in the information field, or the force field. What kind of society could ecological beings like this make? Certainly not a co-operative one. Could they conceive a culture? The answer appears to be the old tautological one — 'yes, if they learn language, how to perceive symbols, and to obey conventions of behaviour'. If they imitate and practise acting like others, picking up their sense, they will then be in the same reality and seek the same affordances. Clearly the explanation for social development must not be just in the milieu or in the body.

In the end, all cognitive theories of society have the same shortfall — they do not have an explanation for social co-operation and the collective ambitions that animate traditional social worlds.

If we want to understand human social consciousness, we will have to look directly at the psychological processes of interpersonal and trans-subject communication. What we need to observe is the ongoing interactive, bilaterally or collectively perceived aspect of communication — its intersubjectivity — and underlying this, the emotional basis for interpersonal effort. We have carefully to avoid the restricting connotations of the word 'communication', as it is commonly used. In the psychology of physical information processing by perceiving, learning, and thinking (computing) subject systems, 'communication' has a limited meaning, useless for our purposes. In structural linguistics, sociology, or anthropology, 'communication' also stands for the forms, syntagmata, and semantic terms put outside subjects as products of the activities of communicating — recorded speech, texts, propositions in symbolic form, indeed all symbolic artefacts.

Let us set down three fresh assumptions about the human mind, young or old, in its basic relation to its social world.

Self–other dualism

In the organized mind of every human being there is formed a 'virtual other' (Bråten 1987), who is prepared to take part in a set of 'virtual engagements' with the 'self'. This dual constitution of the human mind, 'virtual other' and 'self', is essential and innate. It becomes active and develops when an actual other meets the self.

Emotions

Regulating the changes of engagement between the self and the other, virtual or actual, are emotions; these are dynamic by nature and organized as a set or field of values with a number of oppositions. Emotions are the communicated aspect of motives, expressed from the surface of the body so they can be picked up (seen, heard, felt, smelled) by others. They arise from the virtual self–other relationship and are, normally, immediately reactive to the expressed emotions of actual others (Trevarthen 1984, 1986*b*).

The sensitivity of emotions in one person to those that are shown to be in another person thus arises from the inherent dual constitution in the mind of 'self' and 'virtual other'. This constitution is ready to be changed, or ready to combine with, the emotional expressions from an actual other. The combining helps give emotions organization, and helps them produce change in an engagement because the emotional system is adapted to interaction with another emotional system. Indeed, the emotional regulation is highly asymmetric; it is much more sensitive to the emotions of others than to the emotions of or about the self, which normally has emotions only through interaction with the other, virtual or actual.

The only way a person can react to his or her own emotions is by placing an emotional description or personality for him- or herself in the position of the virtual other. In other words, the emotional personality of the self is not something one can be aware of, except by creating a 'self-representation' in the position of a virtual other. This kind of self-awareness which is important for personality development and for thinking, has traditionally been considered the cardinal feature of human consciousness (or any consciousness, which is tantamount to saying that animals do not have consciousness). However, we see now that it is a pseudo self-awareness or, at least, an indirect one, important but incapable of existing alone as a primary state. It is derived from the innate 'I–thou' relationship (Buber 1937).

Social consciousness

The hallmark of consciousness (the word 'conscious' has a historical link to the Latin for 'knowing something with others'; Oxford English Dictionary) is the capacity to have an awareness of reality in company or in communication with another, virtual or actual. This part of the meaning of the word has become weaker in our cognitivist tradition. Properly, consciousness is an attribute of a social consensus (and, incidentally, it can exist in animals or humans).

The observation that must change our scientific perspective on social consciousness and self–other relations that are regulated by emotions is the discovery, for science, of the essential duality of the infant mind. Behaviours of newborns show that even they are capable, from the moment of birth, of responding to human expressions of feeling with subtle, appropriate, and effective emotional changes and expressions (Stern 1985; Trevarthen 1983, 1984, 1985, 1986b). This fact demonstrates their possession of the self–other organization which we have just described.

When a mother is in intimate well-regulated engagement with her baby, she has 'stepped into' the baby's virtual other offering emotions that reinforce additional gentle attentions from her (Trevarthen and Marwick 1986). A process of emotional transformation is created, which is jointly controlled. Should her entry be careless or destructive, not 'good enough' (Winnicott 1971), that is, not inter-subjective or generous and grateful enough, then the infant's emotions clearly indicate a state of distress and need. In the extreme, a state of chronic pathology of emotion can be created (or transferred) in this way: an effect that serves as a kind of negative proof of the infant's essential humanness.

Significant findings in the psychology of infants

Using a combination of descriptive methods and experiments, aided by television and improved techniques for keeping a record of freely motivated behaviours of infants in situations that encourage them to explore and test their experience, psychologists have, in the last 20 years, uncovered organized motives that lead infants straight into the social world. A degree of mental structure has been found that was previously thought impossible so soon after birth. An extraordinary precocity for communication has been demonstrated by close observation of what happens when a newborn confronts a responsive person, and subsequent developments have been traced in the interaction between an infant and a familiar other, usually the mother. (Bullowa 1979; Field and Fox 1985; Mehler and Fox 1985; Stern 1985; Trevarthen and Marwick 1986).

The normal course of psychological growth expresses the inherent mechanism by which the child's brain is both self-constructed and adapted to respond and take part in culture. It exposes the changing motives for social responsiveness. Though modified by different styles of upbringing that convey different ethical or practical conventions in society, and adjusted to different personal relationships, these motives and their changes are univeral. That is, they will appear in the development of all young humans. Anthropologists nave described what appear to be widely different customs and beliefs governing the communication of mothers and infants, but no published studies give sufficient information about intimate play at specific ages during the first year to reject the view, gained from research with American, European, and African subjects in their own cultures, that there is a universal pattern of development (*see* Trevarthen 1988). We can therefore summarize the critical age-related features of early human mental growth.

Birth and primary communication

In late fetal stages and early postnatal life the baby shows a primary empathy with voice sounds, human holding, and human movement; an immediate human 'presence' is detected and the baby enters into an intimate 'being in contact'. Even when born 10 weeks premature, newborns show seeking of this contact, moving in order to assist hearing, seeing, and smelling of an affectionate other and seeking to feel skin contact, body warmth, and displacement by gentle movements. Newborns may show a preference for their mother's individual voice at birth; this indicates that they can learn *in utero* the identifying prosodic features of her speech. Hands, eyes, face, arms, trunk, legs, and feet of a quiet-alert newborn move cyclically in intermittent co-ordination and at regulated speed and periodicity. Occasional forms of face movement, vocalization, and hand gesture are oriented to the utterances and expressions of the other. Eye contact is sought, and there can be direct and discrete imitation of eye and mouth movements (Trevarthen 1986*b*). A break in human contact, as well as a feeling of need in absence of support, leads the newborn to express distress (sadness or anger) with powerful effect on others.

These human signs are recognized intuitively by the mother; she finds herself attuning her behaviour in appropriate supportive ways, pacing her brief, evenly spaced expressions of motherese (baby talk) with their characteristic, large changes of pitch (Fernald 1984) to fit with the periodic utterances and gestures of the infant (Trevarthen and Marwick 1986). Within a few weeks she experiences an increased awakening of interest and focusing of attention on the part of the infant, a change which occurs at about 46 weeks gestational age. Protoconversational exchanges are then set up on the shared beat of moving, and both mother and infant adjust intensity of emotion in movements of face, voice, hands, and body posture. The mother's utterances become increasingly regular and conform to patterns of tempo, intonation, and fundamental frequency that transcend social and linguistic conventions: motherese is clearly the same behaviour in Mandarin Chinese and American mothers; the great differences in the adult languages, one tonal, the other not, are left aside when the mothers speak to their infants (Papousek 1987).

The infant quickly identifies the main, most affectionate caregiver, who is given preferential attentiveness in expressions of greater happiness and readiness to make 'utterances'. Unknown persons are regarded with what appears to be suspicion; intently, without pleasure or with expressions of fear and withdrawal (Trevarthen 1984, 1986c). Thus the first instance of human sociability is marked by seeking for affectionate attachment with one (or a few) person(s) — the caregiver(s). Others are distinguished as 'strange' and potentially unpleasant or to be feared. It should be noted that the infant does not give much interest to the impersonal world of things, which is evidently still remote in consciousness. Rejection or withdrawal of affection on the part of the principal caregiver causes acute distress and failures of cognitive growth (Fraiberg 1982).

Attending the world at large

At three months after birth the infant has gained strong muscle support for head and arms, and visual orientation and accommodation are much improved, both in magnitude and in precision. This advance in strength and motor co-ordination is accompanied by a rapid refinement in visual acuity, and also by a marked increase in curiosity and exploration (Trevarthen 1983, 1986b). Physical 'things' increasingly draw the child's attention away from the mother and out into surroundings, which no longer stay in the background of interest. 'Rational' awareness is shown by the baby making systematic efforts to solve problems by strategic deployment of moves that transform experiences of the child's own body or of the outside world (Papousek 1969). For example, the baby works hard to make effects occur again, to bring images into focus, to regulate patterns of sound or light. All events contingent on the baby's moves of orientation or prehension are likely to engage reattention and further examination.

While enjoying emotion-charged play with the affectionate other, the child over three months of age clearly has greater autonomy of reasons and purpose. He or she, still enjoying human contact, may defy or attack a partner in play with an expression of aggressive, 'cheeky' determination. If the child's will is thwarted, this may cause expressions of strong protest. Both 'free' will and the defense of private experience take a stronger position alongside the empathy for other persons as the child gains in consciousness of a wider world and what this offers. There may be considerable cultural or social class differences, as well as differences related to the personalities and histories of different mothers in the way this development is handled (Trevarthen 1988; Trevarthen and Marwick 1986). Nevertheless, an increase of self-regulation and initiative will be evident as a feature of the child at this age.

Early forms of play

From 3 to 6 months, while the infant is starting to consolidate his or her individuality in companionship, the sharing of pleasure in playful combat takes ritual forms (Trevarthen 1983, 1986b; Trevarthen and Hubley 1978). The mother, or other consistent companion to the child, is obliged to transform her behaviour to track the infant's development. Her vocalizations gain in emotional range (in 'voice quality' variation) and are synchronized with large facial expressions and lively gestures; she also moves the baby's limbs or whole body vigorously in time with her utterances and expressions. The infant's interest is captured by the mother singing traditional nursery songs in which the beat and rhythms of interaction and the qualities and melodic forms of voice that signal feelings are brought out clearly.

The songs and chants that mothers perform show many universal musical features that bridge the differences between widely different languages and traditions—they are centred on a *moderato* or *andante* beat and they use universal variations of the beat (*rubato, sforzando, retardando, accelerando*) in such a way as to increase or decrease emotion (Trevarthen 1986b). Comparative study of the songs is helping identify fundamental musical expressions and feelings that all humans respond to.

The infant is excited to play an active part in 'baby songs' and 'baby dances', sharing in their dramatic development. This reflects and enhances the infant's body awareness, as well as favours development of the capacity of the infant to perceive the musical qualities of communicative movement in others. It has been noticed that fathers may play differently than mothers with babies from this age. It seems probable that the child can easily adapt to a number of different styles of play, identifying people with what they offer for sharing. The beat, rhythm, and melody and the regular stanza form of traditional songs sung to infants favour joint control and moving in sympathy—a form of communication which has recreational and therapeutic potential for humans of all ages.

Co-operation, with the mother's support

From birth an infant can link distribution of attention to the world with contact made with the feelings of a partner. A newborn may shift gaze from a mother's face after watching her and becoming animated, and then intensely focus on whatever is seen, as if transferring motivation from her to the thing (Sander 1983). At three months, before they can manipulate objects for themselves, infants show curiosity about others' hands, and they listen to vocalizations others make while acting on things or presenting them. This awareness of aspects of others' agency is proved in imitation tests: 3- to 5-month-olds are able to imitate both the pitch and intonation of vocalizations and certain hand movements (Trevarthen 1986b). Observational learning, watching what others are intending, and what they know and feel is thus revealed to be a primary component of human motivation, not something learned by transfer from acquired sensorimotor practices learned in isolation. It will later assist the child to get experience of manipulative affordances of the world in line with others' interests. This propensity to imitate others' actions on objects and to make an evaluation of objects related to others' feelings (emotional referencing) is also seen in young apes, though it seems to be shown much earlier in humans in spite of their slower sensorimotor development.

In spite of the play companionship that grows strong in the first nine months, objects have, as yet, no conventionally meaningful place in mother–infant communication. The infant primarily shows an independent curiosity about the physical properties of objects and performs on them what Piaget (1962) called 'sensorimotor' play (touching, mouthing, waving, banging).

To be 'good-enough' with her infant, the mother, up to this stage, should be minimally cultural in her attentions, by immediately responding to the infant's natural needs for physical and emotional well-being (security, companionship, responsiveness). Although the mother, as a mature member of her community, certainly assumes culturally specific notions of motherhood, in her actual relating with her infant she cannot make full use of those, precisely because her young partner lacks anything that would directly correspond to them. As we know, the performance of any cultural 'role' depends on reciprocity of assumptions, which happens to be absent in the early mother–infant relationship. No doubt, the same woman can be a more or less 'proper' mother in the eyes of mature members of her community, but it seems that with her child her choice for acting in culturally arbitrary ways is rather limited. She has to respond to her infant's natural feelings, and needs.

At about nine months, however, the world of physical things draws the attention of the child in a new way: objects, either natural or artificial, are now perceived as instruments in the capable hands of others who are performing purposeful actions upon them. The shift of a child's interest towards shared meaning and another person's ideas on specific use of objects was first noted and described in an observational context where the mother was asked to teach the child a simple manipulative task (Hubley and Trevarthen 1979). With a nine-month-old child she was able to do so with an ease documented for the first time at this age and in sharp contrast to earlier performances, in which the infant failed to comply. By demonstration and simple verbal instruction the mother could lead the child to the desired end.

This new orientation of the infant's mind towards people and their use of things, as identified in the psychological literature, combines in the most interesting and sensible way with recent psycholinguistic findings concerning the same age (see below). We have named this orientation Secondary Intersubjectivity or Person–Person–Object Fluency (Trevarthen and Hubley 1978).

Toddlers and nursery school age children

Beginning language

As we have seen, until the age of nine months, communication takes place between the mother and her infant on a directly emotional basis, with voice, gaze, touch, and movement conveying a wide range of feeling that is constantly created and adjusted between them. At about nine months, however, the child sets off for a new type of communication with others. Combining meaning and sound, he or she soon develops a 'family-based' linguistic system capable of conveying a limited but adequate list of semantic units. Halliday calls this 'proto-language' (Halliday 1975; Trevarthen 1987), while Dore, describing something very similar, identifies a number of 'primitive speech acts' in a child's single-word utterances; amongst others including 'labelling', 'requesting', 'calling', 'greeting', and 'protesting' (Dore 1975). Also, Bates *et al.* (1979) distinguish between 'proto-imperatives' and 'proto-declaratives' in the child's first systematic attempts to address and use adults.

We should note here that this first, elementary linguistic system is not directly related to the one regularly used by people surrounding the child: while everybody's mother tongue is characterized, as Halliday (1975) points out, by tri-stratal organization (semantics, lexicogrammar, phonology), 'proto-language' is bi-stratal (semantics and phonology only).

Symbolic play

As we have seen, by their first birthday infants have already understood that the world of things and the world of people can be brought together in the way of conventional uses and elementary symbolic meanings. Let us now outline further developments taking place during the course of the second year.

From studies designed to map developmental trends in the ways infants independently use play material, with the mother minimally present, a shift is reported, around 12 months, from sensorimotor to what is called 'representational' or 'symbolic' play (Lowe 1975; Nicolich 1977; Rosenblatt 1977). This shift was first noted by Piaget (1962), who discussed it as the first instance of the child's ability to represent, i.e. to evoke what is not actually present by means of 'signifiers', in this case by playful or pretend activity. Leslie (1987) sees the same phenomenon as 'an early symptom of the human mind's ability to characterize and manipulate its own attitudes to information' (Leslie 1987, p. 11), achieved by means of primary (literal) representations which are, in their turn, 'meta-represented'.

In the course of the second year, sensorimotor play and the previously conspicuous taste for big, colourful, and sound-making objects is replaced by keen interest for things directly associated with everyday human use, even if the latter are far less impressive in their sensory affordances under observation and manipulation. By 18 months, sensorimotor play reaches its lowest level (about 20 per cent of the child's time with a variety of objects) and stays as low during the months to follow (Rosenblatt 1977). Instead, objects useful in the culture, such as cups and spoons, brushes and telephones, almost compulsively attract the child's attention, who automatically applies on them 'routine representational schemas' (Rosenblatt 1977, p. 36).

Up to the age of 18 months most of a child's pretence is self-directed (brushing one's hair, feeding oneself) but then it gradually becomes doll-related until, by 24 months, it is almost exclusively other-directed (Lowe 1975; Fein 1978). This finding is commonly interpreted as indicating a growing in awareness of the self–other distinction, but such a view should not be emphasized to the extent of assuming that the child has a non-existing self or an all-encompassing other at the beginning of development. At different ages, the child is capable of regulating the balance of self–other distinction in different specific forms of interactive and expressive activity.

Pretend play by the end of the second year is also increased in cognitive complexity, combining now several representational objects and creating whole sequences of action (Lowe 1975; Nicolich 1977). Substitution of one object for another ('double knowledge', Rosenblatt 1977) also makes its appearance by this age, but becomes much more obvious and frequent in the course of the third and fourth year (Lowe 1975; Matthews 1977).

True language

By the middle of the second year, another change takes place in the child's behavioural repertoire. He or she is now prepared to introduce the vocabulary and grammar of adult language to the already operating proto-linguistic system. Of course, this results in major advances in the ability to communicate. In a longitudinal study of mother–infant communication from 12 to 30 months, Stewart-Clarke and Hevey (1981) report linear increase in the child's verbalizations to the mother, until by 30 months, the two partners' contributions to verbal engagements become almost equal. With the use of language, things not currently present easily come into focus as a 'topic' for conversation and, gradually, not only members of the family, but anybody who speaks the same tongue may satisfy the child's growing curiosity about the world, providing information about people and places, real or imaginary, past, present, or yet to come.

First interactions with peers (toddlers)

The existing studies on early interaction with peers provide us with clear enough descriptive and normative reports about this new type of relating with one's human environment during the second year (Eckerman *et al.*, 1975; Goldman and Ross 1978; Mueller and Vandell 1979; Brenner and Mueller 1982; Mueller 1986; Stambak *et al.* 1983). After 12 months, age-mates appear to become increasingly interesting companions for the toddler (Eckerman *et al.* 1975; Mueller and Vandell 1979), in contrast to the very occasional and fleeting contacts of the first year (Buhler 1930).

From descriptions of both playful (Goldman and Ross 1978) and general interactive behaviour (Eckerman *et al.* 1975; Mueller 1979; Stambak *et al.* 1983) one is justified to conclude that the happenings between toddlers have a very rich interactional, but rather poor cultural/symbolic, content. Especially in the American studies, it is emphasized that there is 'a reciprocal interest in physical things' (Mueller 1979, p. 188), with object possession struggle, object exchange, and motor copy scoring highest in toddlers' interactive repertoire. Imitating each other with the use of voice, gesture, and body-movement, repeating at length reciprocal and complementary exchanges, (run-and-chase, hide-and-seek) as well as simply watching each other, happily occupy much of toddlers' time together (Mueller 1986; Stambak *et al.* 1983).

With a peer, children in their second year seem to be enjoying the interaction as such, quite possibly in ways reminiscent of what was taking place with their mother in the period of primary intersubjectivity and in games with her (Trevarthen and Hubley 1978) many months earlier. With very little use of language as such (Stambak *et al.* 1985), toddlers appear most keen to explore the possibilities and dynamics of this new interactional context. In the presence of peers, items with particular cultural significance (toy-telephones, cups, or books) do not seem to be preferably or discriminately used from other 'non-suggestive' ones, like balls or blocks. This finding comes in sharp contrast to what is reported to be the case in interactions with the mother at this same age (Dunn and Dale 1984) and may appear to conflict with the idea of an already keen interest in symbolic meaning and conventional use of objects. But it seems that children know very well what they want, when, and from whom; their imagination in the presence of a trusted adult is different from that they display with another child of the same age as themselves. In summary, during the second year the 'toddlers + toys' communicative system (Mueller 1979) is first introduced and indeed appears to be autonomous in the sense of being able to sustain its own object-centred but interpersonally-driven dynamics, which make it different from, and complementary to, the 'toddler + adult + object' communicative system.

Symbolic role play, with dolls

As we have seen, doll-related pretence becomes dominant by 24 months. Sex-related performances are already present, with a girl being more likely to feed a doll and seat it on a chair, and a boy more likely to put a little man on a vehicle (Lowe 1975). Meal- and bed-time routines are generally performed by both sexes with increasing care for detail while, by 30 months, children practically exhaust all the possibilities that basic play-material offers them. Whole sequences are acted out, absent objects are searched for and, if not found, are substituted by transforming things available. The doll-related performances are gradually organized, especially for girls, around the general idea of a 'caregiver' who may, with a serious and all-knowing face, feed, change, and put the doll to bed or, alternatively, pat it with tenderness or scold it with anger. Such pretend actions mark the beginnings of 'symbolic role play', which precisely implies attribution of cultural/symbolic meaning to human relations, organized around the notion of 'roles' that persons perform in their daily life together.

The first 'role' to be enacted is that of 'mother', and this is observed to occur around the age of 30 months in the presence of a supportive real mother, who may even be playing an active participatory role (Dunn and Dale 1984; Miller and Garvey 1984). The mothering play-theme was found to be the most common one in the mother–daughter pairs at the age of two years observed by Dunn and Dale (1984). As reported in the same study, almost all (97 per cent) play with the mother was, for both sexes, focused upon objects with cultural significance and involved naming them as well as encouraging and instructing the child to make use of them in culturally appropriate ways. In contrast (Dunn and Dale 1984), one-third of the play with a five-year-old sibling was not sustained by object props but evolved around playful use of language and non-verbal interaction (cf. also Keenan 1974). By such comparative findings it is possible to appreciate, once again, the different contributions of qualitatively different ways of relating to a young child's developing interpersonal and cultural sense of self.

Elaborations in play and peer communication (two- and three-year-old children)

Interest in companions of the same age becomes more obvious after the child's second birthday. Unfortunately, detailed information about what peers do together in naturalistic settings with an observational methodology similar to the one used in the early toddler studies, is not directly available for the period between 24 and 36 months. However, suggestive findings about the communicative repertoires of two-year-olds come from a French experimental study on peer imitation (Nadel-Bulfert and Baudonniere 1982; Nadel 1986).

When left alone in a laboratory-playroom with toys available in three identical sets, trios of two-year-old children almost compulsively occupied themselves in imitative activity, mainly focused around those objects (Nadel-Brulfert and Baudonniere 1982; Nadel 1986). What is most interesting is that the very same play-context proved to be offering quite different interactional possibilities to trios of three-year-olds. They would simply ignore the fact that objects were available in multiples, and concentrate, instead, on developing complex joint play-scenarios in which the actual number of toys was not of primary significance. At other times, two of the trio would make friends to the exclusion of the third child emphasizing their alliance by denying him or her access to the remaining objects.

For Nadel (1986), immediate or synchronous imitation, centred around similar or identical objects, is the activity that predominates in peer communication from 2 to 3 years. 'Choosing the choice of the other' (Nadel 1986, p. 125), an option presumably taken on purely emotional and relational grounds (see also Uzgiris 1984), is the fun thing to do. And, as Nadel notes (Nadel 1986, p. 230), adults would better restrain themselves from wondering, in disappointment, what the significance of such elementary and circular behaviour might be; it does appear most meaningful to the children!

By their third birthday children are competent language users (Garvey 1984), have very rich pretence repertoires (Corsaro 1985), and get much out of interacting with peers (Shugar and Bokus 1986; Shugar 1987). It is characteristic that most studies on this and later ages primarily address peer issues and are carried out in peer settings. Friendships (Corsaro 1981; Damon 1977; Gottman and Parkhurst 1980; Rubin 1980), preferential relationships, and discriminate interactions with others (younger versus older, same or different sex, see Lougee et al. 1977; Maccoby and Jacklin 1987), all become quite clear at this stage and have drawn the attention of researchers. Pretence play with peers is increasingly based on complementary enactment of social roles (sociodramatic play, e.g. mother–baby, husband–wife) conveying much of the complexity and subtlety of real life. Also language is beginning to be used in a manner that closely resembles adult performances (Shugar and Bokus 1986). Conversations on non-present 'topics' are now sustained, especially between children with a shared past and an affective relationship, motivated to communicate in a variety of ways (Logotheti, in preparation).

Conclusions

We have discussed evidence that human minds have the following essential characteristics, all of which are somewhat unfamiliar to traditional psychological and sociological theory:

(1) Human consciousness is dominated by meanings that can only be obtained through communication; that is how it is constituted and what it aims to maintain and increase.

(2) Human communication is a mutual engagement of motive states; it is not just an exchange of physical information, but an 'autopoietic' self creative pattern arising between minds in expressive contact with each other. A magnetic field between two metallic forms may be a helpful analogy.

(3) Information about meanings is negotiated by persons matching their motives of interest and intentions to act. Agreements are marked for exchange in symbolic form.

(4) Satisfaction of human motives is achieved through co-operation, exchange of meanings and symbols, and the creation of unique relationships that share learning and a practice of living. Thus, the primary motivation for society is moral and cultural. It is only the individual acting in temporary isolation who can be wholly realistic and practical. Social groups are capable of great practical effect, multiplying their individual capacities, only if the condition of co-operative willingness has been satisfied.

(5) Emotions give the necessary value to relationships and to experiences. Their potential values and oppositions are fully innate and merely gain in efficacy through social experience, and through identifying particular persons as their 'objects'.

(6) Evidence for the motives that generate sharing of culture in society, and for the motives that will regulate relationships, is found in newborn infants. A baby is not vacuous 'biological' material waiting to be socialized, but a being adapted, in the course of evolution, to function intersubjectively, in communication.

(7) Developments through childhood exhibit systematic unfolding of motives that regulate and transform contacts and relations between the child and other persons. Societies and cultures are generated by the emergence of people's enthusiasm for communicating with symbols, for co-operating in complex practices, and for playing defined roles. Young children show this enthusiasm emerging; adults respond in complementary ways to support 'education' of the child in symbolic and cultural communication.

From our point of view, which emphasizes the infant's motivated connectedness with the human world, all the developmental changes described above may be appreciated in one light. The initial orientation and sensitivity to people and especially the mother, then independent interest in physical objects, the progressive decline of sensorimotor activity in parallel with the growing prominence and elaboration of pretend play, the emergence of proto-linguistic and then linguistic skills, the increasing meaningful contact with peers, all these reveal how the 'weaving' of a child's vital links with a community of others takes place naturally, under the control of changing motives of the developing child and in response to experience. For a toddler in his or her second year, the life-style of one's own particular community, in all its complexity of manners, habits and attitudes, becomes an inexhaustible source of interest. Much time and attention is spent in observing others performing their daily routines and also, after 18 months, in actively enquiring about the uses and names of things. Not that every kind of thing can be learnt then, but the critical orientation to learn in this way, the way of culture, is already present.

To our mind, the core of a child's 'representational schemata' is not the product of private, studious exploration of an environment with given properties to be discovered; when present, applied, and elaborated with eagerness and joy, these representations simply show that the child has established a 'living' relatedness with the psychological as well as the cultural environment, an environment that consists of people and of the meaning they attribute to themselves and the world. Of course, some kind of functional relatedness, with its corresponding representations, exists between the child and the physical environment as well, in our society giving rise, at a later stage, to the pursuit of technological and scientific, 'acultural', knowledge. Psychologists should be clear, every time, which sense of 'representation' and 'relatedness' they intend to discuss.

As for a young child's mind, its orientation towards the world may be described as having two complementary sides, one 'receptive' and the other 'expressive', both equally revealing of a genuinely social motivation. The first represents the learning attitude, while its counterpart is met in 'pretend' or 'make-believe play'. In the latter expressive mode, the child does not lose the fascination for the social world nor exhibit a maximum of 'egocentricity', projecting on it an asocial private universe, as has been proposed by Piaget (1962). In a constant alternation between 'receiving' and 'expressing', the child takes possession of what has been learnt and experienced in communication and culture, and then feels the impulse to 'put all of this on stage'. Whether he or she plays alone or in the company of supportive members of the family or with other children, is not such a critical issue any more; the preparedness for learning and expressing is what counts most. Here, the inability of autistic children for 'make-believe' (Baron-Cohen 1987; Wulff 1985) could be a sure indication of the nature of their developmental 'arrest'. Pretence play is simply a child's natural way to take part in life, and life for humans is first and foremost family, friends, society, and culture.

References

Baron-Cohen, S. (1987). Autism and symbolic play. *British journal of developmental psychology* **5**, 139–48.

Bates, E., Camaioni, L., and Volterra, V. (1979). The acquisition of performatives prior to speech. In *Developmental pragmatics* (eds. E. Ochs and B. Schiefflin), pp. 111–29. Academic Press, New York.

Bråten, S. (1987). Dialogic mind: The infant and the adult in protoconversation. In *Nature, cognition and system* (ed. M. Carvallo). D. Reidel, Dordrecht/Boston (in press).

Brenner, J. and Mueller, E. (1982). Shared meaning in boy toddlers' peer relations. *Developmental psychology* **53**, 380–91.

Buber, M. (1937). *I and thou*. T. and T. Clark, Edinburgh.

Buhler, C. (1930). *The first year of life*. John Day, New York.

Bullowa, M. (ed.) (1979). *Before speech: the beginning of human communication*. Cambridge University Press, London.

Carrithers, M. (1988). Sociality, not aggression, is the key human trait. In *Societies at peace* (eds. S. Howell and R. Willis). Tavistock, London (in press).

Corsaro, W. (1981). Friendship in the nursery school: social organization in a peer environment. In *The development of children's friendships* (eds. S. Asher and J. Gottman), pp. 207–41. Cambridge University Press, New York.

Corsaro, W. (1985). *Friendship and peer culture in the early years*. Ablex, Norwood, NJ.

Damon, W. (1977). *The social world of the child*. Jossey-Bass, San Francisco.

Dore, J. (1975). Holophrases, speech acts and language universals. *Journal of child language* **2**, 21–40.

Dunn, J. and Dale, N. (1984). I a daddy: 2-year-olds' collaboration in joint pretend with sibling and with mother. In *Symbolic play—the development of social understanding* (ed. I. Bretherton), pp. 131–58. Academic Press, Orlando. FL.

Eckerman, C. O., Watley, J. L., and Kutz, S. L. (1975). Growth of social play with peers during the second year of life. *Developmental psychology* **11**, 42–9.

Fein, G. (1978). Play revisited. In *Social and personality development* (ed. M. Lamb), pp. 70–90. Holt, Rinehart, and Winston, New York.

Fein, G. (1981). Pretend play in childhood: An integrative review. *Child development* **52**, 1095–1118.

Fernald, A. (1984). The perceptual and affective salience of mothers' speech to infants. In *The origins and growth of communication* (eds. L. Feagans, C. Gavey, R. Golinkoff, *et al.*) pp. 5–29. Ablex, Norwood, NJ.

Field, T. and Fox, N. (eds). (1985). *Social perception in infants*. Ablex, Norwood, NJ.

Fraiberg, S. (ed.) (1982). *Clinical studies in infant mental health: the first year of life*. Tavistock, London.

Garvey, C. (1977). *Play*. Fontana.

Garvey, C. (1984). *Children's talk*. Fontana.

Gibson, J. J. (1979). *An ecological approach to visual perception*. Houghton-Mifflin, San Francisco.

Goldman, B. D. and Ross, H. S. (1978). Social skills in action: An analysis of early peer games. In *Studies in social and cognitive development (vol. 1), The development of social understanding* (eds. J. Glick and K. A. Clarke-Stewart), pp. 177–219. Gardner Press, New York.

Gottman, J. and Parkhurst, J. (1980). A developmental theory of friendship and acquaintanceship processes. In *The Minnesota Symposia on Child Psychology (vol. 1), Cognition, affect and social relations* (ed. W. A. Collins), pp. 197–253. Erlbaum, Hillsdale, NJ.

Halliday, M. (1975). *Learning how to mean.* Arnold, London.

Hubley, P. and Trevarthen, C. (1979). Sharing a task in infancy. In *New directions for child development, vol. 4, Social interaction during infancy,* pp. 57–80. Jossey-Bass, San Francisco.

Humphrey, N. (1976). The social function of intellect. In *Growing points in ethology* (ed. P. Bateson and R. Hinde). Cambridge University Press.

Keenan, O. E. (1974). Conversational competence in children. *Journal of child language* 1, 163–83.

Kugler, P. N., Kelso, J. A. S., and Turvey, M. T. (1982). On the control and coordination of naturally developing systems. In *The development of movement control and coordination* (eds. J. A. S. Kelso and J. F. Clark) Wiley, New York.

Leslie, A. (1987). Pretense and representation: The origins of 'theory of mind'. *Psychological review* 94, 412–26.

Lougee, M., Grueneich, R., and Hartup, W. (1977). Social interaction in same- and mixed-age dyads of preschool children. *Child development* 48, 1353–61.

Lowe, M. (1975). Trends in the development of representational play in infants from one to three years—an observational study. *Journal of child psychology and psychiatry* 16, 33–47.

Maccoby, E. and Jacklin, C. (1987). Gender segregation in childhood. *Advances in child development and behaviour* 20, 239–87.

MacMurray, J. (1961). *Persons in relation.* Faber and Faber, London.

Matthews, W. S. (1977). Modes of transformation in the initiation of fantasy play. *Developmental psychology* 13, 212–16.

Mehler, J. and Fox, R. (eds). *Neonate cognition: beyond the blooming, buzzing confusion.* Erlbaum, Hillsdale, NJ.

Miller, P. and Garvey, C. (1984). Mother–baby role play: its origins in social support. In *Symbolic play—the development of social understanding* (ed. I. Bretherton), pp. 101–30. Academic Press, Orlando, FL.

Mueller, E. (1979). (Toddlers + toys) = (An autonomous social system). In *The child and its family* (eds. M. Lewis and L. Rosenblum), pp. 169–94. Plenum Press, New York.

Mueller, E. (1986). Shared meaning in prelinguistic communication. In *Knowledge and language* (eds. I. Kurca, G. W. Shugar, and J. H. Danks), pp. 465–83. Elsevier, Amsterdam.

Mueller, E. and Vandell, D. (1979). Infant–infant interaction. In *Handbook of infant development* (ed. J. Osofsky), pp. 591–622. Wiley, New York.

Murray, L. and Trevarthen, C. (1986). The infants role in mother–infant communication. *Journal of child language* 13, 115–29.

Nadel, J. (1986). *Imitation et communication entre jeunes enfants.* PUF, Paris.

Nadel-Bulfert, J. and Baudonniere, P. M. (1982). The social function of reciprocal imitation in 2-year-old peers. *International journal of behavioural development* **5**, 95–109.

Neisser, U. (1980). On 'Social Knowing'. *Personality and social psychology bulletin* **6**, 601–5.

Nicholich, L. (1977). Beyond sensorimotor intelligence: assessment of symbolic maturity through analysis of pretend play. *Merrill-Palmer quarterly* **23**, 89–99.

Papousek, H. (1969). Individual variability in learned responses in human infants. In *Brain and early behaviour: development in foetus and infant* (ed. R. J. Robinson), pp. 251–63. Academic Press, New York.

Papousek, M. (1987). Models and messages in the melodies of maternal speech in tonal and non-tonal languages (Paper presented to The Society for Research in Child Development), Biennial Meeting, Baltimore, MD, April, 1987.

Piaget, J. (1962). *Play, dreams and imitation in childhood.* Routledge and Kegan Paul, London.

Rosenblatt, D. (1977). Developmental trends in infant play. In *Biology of play* (eds. B. Tizard and D. Harvey), pp. 33–44. Heinemann, London.

Rubin, Z. (1980). *Children's friendships.* Harvard University Press, Cambridge, MA.

Sander, L. (1983). Polarity, paradox and the organizing process in development. In *Frontiers of infant psychiatry, vol. I* (eds. J. D. Call, E. Galenson, and R. L. Tyson). Basic Books, New York.

Shugar, G. W. (1987). *The nature of early peer discourse* (Plenary lecture delivered at the Fourth International Congress of Child Language Research, Lund, Sweden).

Shugar, G. W. and Bokus, B. (1986). Children's discourse and children's activity in the peer situation. In *Process and outcome in peer relationships* (eds. E. C. Mueller and C. R. Cooper), pp. 189–228. Academic Press, Orlando, FL.

Stambak, M., Ballion, M., Breaute, M., and Rayna, S. (1985). Pretend play and interaction in young children. In *Social relationships and cognitive development* (eds. R. A. Hinde, A.-N. Perret-Clermont, and J. Stevenson-Hinde), pp. 131–48. Clarendon Press, Oxford.

Stambak, M., Barrière, M., Bonica, L., Maisonnet, R., Musalti, T., Rayna, S., and Verba, M. (1983). *Les bébés entre eux.* Presses Universitaire de France, Paris.

Stern, D. (1985). *The interpersonal world of the infant.* Basic Books, New York.

Stewart-Clarke, A. and Hevey, C. (1981). Longitudinal relations in repeated observations of mother–child interaction from 1 to 2½ years. *Developmental psychology* **97**, 127–45.

Trevarthen, C. (1979a). Instincts for human understanding and for cultural cooperation: their development in infancy. In *Human ethology* (eds. M. von Cranach, K. Foppa, W. Lepenies, and D. Ploog), pp. 530–71. Cambridge University Press.

Trevarthen, C. (1979b). The tasks of consciousness: How could the brain do them? In *Brain and mind* Ciba Foundation Symposium, Series 69 (New series), pp. 187–217. Excerpta Medica, Amsterdam.

Trevarthen, C. (1982). The primary motives for cooperative understanding. In *Social cognition: studies of the development of understanding* (eds. G. Butterworth and P. Light), pp. 77–109. Harvester Press, Brighton.

Trevarthen, C. (1983). Interpersonal abilities of infants as generators for transmission of language and culture. In *The behaviour of human infants* (eds. A. Oliverio and M. Zapella), pp. 145–76. Plenum, London and New York.

Trevarthen, C. (1984). Emotions in infancy: Regulators of contacts and relationships with persons. In *Approaches to emotion* (eds. K. Scherer and P. Ekman), pp. 129–57. Erlbaum, Hillsdale, NJ.

Trevarthen, C. (1985). Facial expressions of emotion in mother–infant interaction. *Human neurobiology* **4**, 21–32.

Trevarthen, C. (1986*a*). The structure of motives for human communication in infancy: A ground-plan for human ethology. In *Ethology and psychology* (eds. J. le Camus and J. Cosnier), pp. 91–100. Privat/IEC, Toulouse.

Trevarthen, C. (1986*b*). Development of intersubjective motor control in infants. In *Motor development in children: aspects of coordination and control* (eds. M. G. Wade and H. T. A. Whiting), pp. 209–61. Martinus Nijhof, Dordrecht.

Trevarthen, C. (1986*c*). Form, significance and psychological potential of hand gestures of infants. In *The biological foundation of gestures: motor semiotic aspects* (eds. J.-L. Nespoulous, P. Perron, and A. Roch Lecours), pp. 149–202. Erlbaum, Hillsdale, NJ.

Trevarthen, C. (1987). Sharing makes sense: intersubjectivity and the making of an infant's meaning. In *Language topics: essays in honour of Michael Halliday* (eds. R. Steele and T. Threadgold). John Benjamins, Amsterdam and Philadelphia.

Trevarthen, C. (1988). Universal cooperative motives: How infants begin to know language and skills of culture. In *Ethnographic perspectives on cognitive development* (eds. G. Jahoda and I. Lewis) Croom-Helm, Beckenham, Kent.

Trevarthen, C. and Hubley, P. (1978). Secondary Intersubjectivity: confidence, confiding and acts of meaning in the first year. In *Action, gesture and symbol: the emergence of language* (ed. A. Lock), pp. 183–229. Academic Press, New York.

Trevarthen, C. and Marwick (1986). Signs of motivation for speech in infants, and the nature of a mother's support for development of language. In *Precursors of early speech* (eds. B. Lindblom and R. Zetterstrom), pp. 279–308. Macmillan, Basingstoke, Hampshire.

Turner, V. (1974). *Dramas, fields and metaphors*. Cornell University Press. Ithaca, NY.

Užgiris, I. C. (1984). Imitation in infancy: Its interpersonal aspects. In *Parent–child relations in child development* (ed. M. Perlmutter). The Minnesota symposia on child psychology, Vol 17, pp. 1–39. Erlbaum, Hillsdale, NJ.

Winnicott, D. (1971). *Playing and reality*. Tavistock, London.

Wulff, S. B. (1985). The symbolic in object play of children with autism: a review. *Journal of autism and developmental disorders* **15**, 139–48.

5

The joint socialization of development by young children and adults*

BARBARA ROGOFF

The young child is often thought of as a little scientist exploring the world and discovering the principles of its operation. We often forget that while the scientist is working on the border of human knowledge and is finding out things that nobody yet knows, the child is finding out precisely what everybody already knows (Newman, 1982, p. 26).

This chapter focuses on how young children and adults together manage children's socialization through children's participation in cultural activities with the guidance of adults. Interactions and arrangements between caregivers and infants or toddlers are the basis for the discussion.

Introduction

First to be considered is how such joint involvement can be conceptualized. Then the main part of the chapter describes features of adult–child interactions as well as non-interactive arrangements made between adults and children, in order to examine differing aspects of the joint socialization of children's development. Finally, cultural variations and universals in the goals and means used by young children and adults that may bring about the child's entry into skilled participation in the culture are addressed.

The chapter builds on Vygotsky's concept of the *zone of proximal development*, in which child development is viewed as a social activity with children participating in activities beyond their competence through the assistance of adults or more experienced peers. In social interaction in the zone of proximal development, children are able to participate in activities that are beyond their capabilities when working independently. Through such social guidance, children are presumed to gradually internalize the skills that were practised with adult support so that they can be performed independently (Vygotsky 1978; Wertsch 1979). Thus the zone of proximal development is

*Originally published in *Social influences and behaviour* (eds. M. Lewis and S. Feinman). Plenum, New York. The thoughtful comments of Saul Feinman are acknowledged with thanks.

a dynamic region of sensitivity to learning experiences in which children develop, guided by social interaction.

In Vygotskian theory, children's interaction within the zone of proximal development is part of a larger sociocultural theory that places human skills and achievements in the context of the technologies, practices, and values available through cultural history. These sociocultural technologies and skills include inventions such as literacy, mathematics, mnemonic skills, and approaches to problem-solving and reasoning. In effect, cultural inventions channel the skills of each generation, with individual development mediated by the guidance of people who are more skilled in their use. Children are introduced to the culture through the guidance of its more experienced members (Laboratory of Comparative Human Cognition 1983; Rogoff 1982; Rogoff, Gauvain and Ellis 1984; Vygotsky 1978).

Cole (1981) suggests that the zone of proximal development is where culture and cognition meet. It is in this sensitive zone that variations in social interaction may be expected to yield adaptations of individuals to their specific cultural surroundings. Their adaptations will simultaneously show features that are similar across many cultural contexts, based on cross-cultural commonalities in the processes of communication and of child development, and variations according to the specific goals and means available for appropriate development in each culture.

This chapter extends the concept of zone of proximal development by stressing the *interrelatedness* of children's and adults' roles, in a process of *guided participation*. The thesis is that the rapid development of young children into socialized participants in society is accomplished through a finely tuned combination of children's skills and the guidance of adults (or older children). The elaboration presented in this chapter, while consistent with the Vygotskian approach, differs in its emphasis on the role of children as active participants in their own socialization. They do not simply receive the guidance of adults, they seek, structure, and even demand the assistance of those around them in learning how to solve problems of all kinds. The aim of this chapter is to stress the complementary roles of children and adults in fostering children's development.

Young children appear to come equipped with ways of ensuring proximity and involvement with more experienced members of society, and of becoming involved with their physical and cultural surroundings. The infants' strategies (if one ignores connotations of intentionality) appear similar to those appropriate for anyone learning in an unfamiliar culture: stay near a trusted guide, watch the guide's activities and get involved when possible, and attend to any instruction the guide provides.

Infants' strategies are complemented by features of adult–child interaction that are well adapted to the gradual immersion of children in the skills and beliefs of the society. Adults arrange the occurrence of children's activities and facilitate learning by regulating the difficulty of the tasks and by modelling mature performance during joint participation in activities. While adults may rarely regard themselves as explicitly teaching infants or young children, they routinely adjust their interaction and structure children's environments and activities in ways consistent with providing support for their learning.

In elaborating the concept of the zone of proximal development, Rogoff and Gardner (1984) emphasized that while more experienced people play an important role in socialization, this role is meshed with the efforts of children to learn and develop. Rogoff (1986) proposed that guided participation with school-children involves adults leading children through the process of solving a problem, and the child participating at a comfortable but slightly challenging level:

Adults provide guidance in cognitive development through the arrangement of appropriate materials and tasks for children, as well as through tacit and explicit instruction occurring as adults and children participate together in activities. Adults' greater knowledge and skill allow them to assist children in translating familiar information to apply to a new problem, and to structure the problem so that the child can work on manageable subgoals. The effectiveness of adults in structuring situations for children's learning is matched by children's eagerness and involvement in managing their own learning experiences. Children put themselves in a position to observe what is going on; they involve themselves in the ongoing activity; they influence the activities in which they participate; and they demand some involvement with the adults who serve as their guides for socialization into the culture that they are learning. Together, children and adults choose learning situations and calibrate the child's level of participation so that the child is comfortably challenged (Rogoff 1986, p. 38).

This chapter extends these ideas by focusing on processes of guided participation with younger children. The themes include how adults facilitate the development of infants and toddlers, how children themselves channel their own development and the assistance they receive, and similarities and variations in the processes of social guidance that may occur in varying cultures. First, however, it is necessary to examine the notion of the interrelatedness of the individual child's role and that of the social context — including the adults and older children that provide guidance.

Mutuality of individual effort and social facilitation

This section examines alternative conceptualizations of how mutual involvement of adults and children may contribute to development. It has been common in developmental psychology to focus attention alternatively on the contribution of either partner, in examining how adults teach children, or how children develop independently. This chapter argues for the necessity of considering the mutual involvement of children and the social world in understanding child development. But such mutual involvement could be understood in different ways. In order to explore ways of conceptualizing the mutual roles of adults and children in fostering children's development, it is useful to draw a relationship with the parallel question of nature and nurture, which has long interested psychologists. By analogy, we may regard the role of the child as 'nature' and the role of social partners as 'nurture'.

The history of psychology has long pitted nature against nurture, with questions of how much of development should be credited to one and how much to the other. This traditional view places nature and nurture in opposition. Most developmentalists, as one reads in early chapters of introductory texts, are no longer trying to figure out if development is 'more nature' or 'more nurture'. Instead, they view nature and nurture as interacting to produce development: development does not occur solely through individual effort or preprogramming, nor does it occur entirely under the direction of the environment.

However, the notion of interaction often involves an assumption that the interacting entities are separable (*see* Rogoff 1982). In other words, nature and nurture in such a view can be regarded as independent influences — definable in terms not involving each other — that happen to co-occur.

In contrast to the idea that nature and nurture are separate but interacting influences on development, the present chapter is built on the premiss that nature and nurture (i.e. the child and the social world) are not separable. They are mutually involved to an extent that precludes regarding them as independently definable. In this view, development is made up of both individual efforts or tendencies and the larger sociocultural context in which the individual is embedded and has been since before conception. Thus biology and culture are not viewed as alternative influences but aspects of a system in which individuals develop.

This stance is reflected in Vygotsky's efforts (Wertsch 1985) to study development in terms of four interrelated levels. The level with which developmental psychologists traditionally deal is termed ontogenetic development — changes in thinking and behaviour associated with age. But this is merely a grain of analysis differing from the other three: phylogenetic development is the slowly changing species history that leaves a legacy for the individual in the form of genes. Sociocultural development is the changing cultural history that leaves a legacy for the individual in the form of technologies such as literacy, number systems, and computers, as well as value systems, scripts, and norms for the handling of situations met by the individual. Microgenetic development is the moment-to-moment learning by individuals in particular problem contexts, built upon the individual's genetic and sociocultural background. In this system, the roles of the individual and the social world are seen as interrelated in the levels of analysis reflecting learning, ontogenetic development, phylogenetic development, and sociohistorical development.

A similar concept of embeddedness of nature and nurture is found in Piaget's work. As Furth (1974) explains, contrary to popular belief, Piaget's theory does not stress the importance of nature. Rather, the individual's development in Piagetian theory is based on the species-typical genetic background *and* the species-typical environment, which together form the basis of the individual's effort to construct an understanding of reality.

It should be noted that despite the theoretical adherence of both Vygotsky and Piaget to the idea that nature and nurture are inseparable supports for individual development, both theorists chose to emphasize one or the other aspect for further elaboration in their theories. Thus, Piaget nodded to the role of social arrangements of the environment — and variations in the species environment — while elaborating upon the individual's independent construction of a notion of the world. Vygotsky, on the other hand, allowed an important role for the individual's active efforts in becoming socialized but stressed the sociocultural arrangements that facilitate the individual's socialization. Vygotsky suggested that rather than deriving explanations of psychological activity from the individual's characteristics plus secondary social influences, psychologists should focus on the social unit of the activity and regard individual functioning as derived from that.

The present chapter attempts to keep the roles of both the individual and the social environment in focus, to acknowledge that they build integrally on each other. This perspective is consistent with other work on socialization in the early years (Brazelton 1982; Papousek, Papousek, and Bornstein 1984; Schaffer 1984). Wartofsky (1984) argues for the importance of keeping both angles in view at once — that children are embedded in a social world and that children are active participants in their own development.

The child is *not* a self-contained homunculus, radiating outward in development from some fixed configuration of traits, dispositions, or preformed potencies; and . . . the world, in turn, is not some eternal and objective network of causal factors converging on the neonate to shape an unresisting, passive blob to its external, pregiven structures. To put this positively: the child is an agent in its own *and* the world's construction, but one whose agency develops in the context of an ineluctably social and historical praxis, which includes both the constraints and potentialities of nature and the actions of other agents. Nurture, in short, is both given *and* taken; and so is Nature (Wartofsky 1984, p. 188).

Social facilitation of individual development

Working from observations of adults instructing children aged 6 to 9 years, Rogoff and Gardner (1984) proposed that guided participation involves the following activities:

(1) providing a bridge between familiar skills or information and those needed to solve a new problem,

(2) arranging and structuring problem-solving, and

(3) gradually transferring the responsibility for managing problem-solving to the child.

These activities seem relevant for the guidance of younger children as well. This section elaborates on these three features of adults' and young children's arrangements for socialization and development. It stresses the entwinement of adults' and children's activities, the active role of both participants, and the possibility that teaching and learning can occur tacitly (as well as explicitly) in the arrangements and interaction between adults and young children.

The end of this chapter considers cross-cultural universals and variations, but until then, the terms 'adult' and 'child' refer to the adults and children who have been observed in North American and Western European research—largely middle class and English speaking.

Providing bridges between familiar skills or information and those needed in novel situations

Adults help young children find the connections between what they already know and what is necessary to handle a new situation (D'Andrade 1981; Erickson 1982). For older children this may involve specifying exactly how the new situation resembles the old. For example, in a classification task (Rogoff and Gardner 1984), some mothers made comments such as 'You need to put the things together that go together, just like on Sesame Street when they say "three of these things belong together".'

For very young children, the bridging role of adults involves assisting children in understanding how to act in new situations by provision of emotional cues regarding the nature of the situation, nonverbal models of how to behave, verbal and nonverbal interpretations of behaviour and events, and verbal labels to classify objects and events. All of these adult activities are coupled with young children's efforts (intentional or not) to pick up information about the nature of situations and their caregivers' interpretations.

Emotional and nonverbal communication

From the first year of life, children look to adults to interpret situations that are ambiguous from the child's point of view, in a process termed *social referencing* (Feinman 1982; Gunnar and Stone 1984). Interpretations offered by adults inform infants about the appropriate approach to take to a new situation. For example, if a child is crawling toward its mother and reaches what appears to be a dropoff, the child searches the mother's face for cues regarding the safety of the situation. If the mother's emotional expression indicates fear, the child does not proceed, but if the mother has an encouraging expression, the child carefully crawls across clear glass suspended a foot above what appears to be the floor (Sorce *et al.* 1985).

Young children are so skilled in obtaining information from glances, winces, and mood that one of the greatest challenges of testing preschoolers is to avoid nonverbal actions that may be construed as cues. Children press for and use such cues even when given standardized intelligence tests (Mehan 1976).

Such referencing is facilitated by the ability that appears by 8 to 12 months of age to obtain information from the direction in which caregivers point and gaze (Bruner 1983; Butterworth and Cochran 1980). The development of such skill is supported by the efforts of mothers to regulate joint attention during the first year. If an infant appears not to understand a pointing gesture, mothers facilitate the baby's comprehension by touching the indicated object (Lempers 1979). As early as three months of infants' age, mothers attempt to achieve joint reference by introducing an object between themselves and the baby as a target for joint attention, using a characteristic intonation and shaking the object (Bruner 1983). From ages 6 to 18 months, infants are more than four times as likely to engage in joint attention when interacting with their mothers as when interacting with a peer (Bakeman and Adamson 1984). Bakeman and Adamson attribute this pattern to the mother's socialization of reference, 'embedding it within the interpersonal sphere well before infants can structure this integration by themselves' (p. 1288). Thus the infant's use of social referencing builds on earlier skills and social guidance, providing more advanced means to gather information regarding their mothers' (and others') interpretations of new situations.

Mothers and other adults may at times intentionally attempt to communicate a particular understanding of a new situation through managing their emotional and nonverbal communication. For example, at a doctor's office a mother may try to mask her apprehension when her baby is receiving an injection, in order to minimize the baby's reaction to the situation. Or parental management of cues may enter into instruction in potentially frightening situations, as suggested in the following advice to parents on teaching 3-week-old babies to swim in the bathtub:

Your attitude toward water is important. An infant who sees her mother wince in terror every time she floats in deep water is not going to have a very confident picture of the strange situation. Since panic is the single most deadly factor in water, parents should be acutely aware of their responsibility in teaching their child a healthy respect for water. . . . If you show enjoyment of the water, she will imitate your excitement and pleasure. . . . Lift your baby into the water, and rest her on your bent knees, facing you. Dip your hands into the water, and pat your baby's body to help her adjust to the water temperature. Talk and smile constantly throughout the entire session. Gradually lower your knees until the baby is completely submerged in the water, head resting comfortably on your knees, body on your thighs. Take this part slowly, allowing enough time for your baby to become acquainted with the water (Poe 1982, pp. 12, 20).

Such intentional communication of how to interpret a situation may be rare. But in a less self-conscious fashion, adults handling babies seem almost inevitably to provide interpretation for the baby's actions, their own actions, and events in the environment (Shotter and Newson, 1982). For example, mothers may respond to the baby's attempt to push an approaching spoon away with a running commentary such as 'You getting full? Try another bite, Mama wants you to grow up big and strong'. For babies learning to eat from a spoon, adults frequently provide supplementary cues regarding the appropriate action for the child—they can be observed to open their own mouths wide at the time the baby is to do the same (Valsiner 1984). To ensure a happy response to a potentially startling event, adults make an exaggerated face of surprise and enjoyment, for example, commenting 'isn't that funny'? when concerned that a Jack-in-the-box might startle a baby (Rogoff, Malkin, and Gilbride 1984).

Words as a cultural system for bridging

In addition to such interpretive comments and actions, the provision of a language system teaches children the meanings and distinctions important in their culture. Labels categorize objects and events in ways specific to the language of the child's culture. Roger Brown pointed out this function of language learning in his comments about the Original Word Game:

The Original Word Game is the operation of linguistic reference in first language learning. At least two people are required: one who knows the language (the tutor) and one who is learning (the player). In outline form the movements of the game are very simple. The tutor names things in accordance with the semantic custom of his community. The player forms hypotheses about the categorical nature of the things named. He tests his hypotheses by trying to name new things correctly. The tutor compares the player's utterances with his own anticipations of such utterances and, in this way, checks the accuracy of fit between his own categories and those of the player. He improves the fit by correction. In concrete terms the tutor says 'dog' whenever a dog appears. The player notes the phonemic equivalence of these utterances, forms a hypothesis about the non-linguistic category that elicits this kind of utterance and then tries naming a few dogs himself. . . . In learning referents and names the player of the Original Word Game prepares himself to receive the science, the rules of thumb, the prejudices, the total expectancies of his society (Brown 1958, pp. 194, 228).

Clearly, the Original Word Game requires two active partners. Language development is facilitated by social involvement as well as deriving from the child's natural propensity to learn language. In this view, Chomsky's Language Acquisition Device cooperates with Bruner's Language Acquisition Support System, which 'frames or structures the input of language and interaction to the child's Language Acquisition Device in a manner to "make the system function"' (Bruner 1983, p. 19). Consistent with this emphasis on the social supports for language acquisition are Moerk's (1983) careful analyses of maternal language input to Roger Brown's subject Eve. Eve's mother provided sufficiently rich and frequent input, with semantic and linguistic redundancy, and contingent instructional relationships between mother's and child's utterances, for her framing of Eve's language development to be considered an important contribution to the child's efforts to learn language.

The process of communication, itself a social activity, can be regarded as the bridge between one understanding of a situation and another. For an adult and child to communicate successfully, the adult must search for common reference points, translating the adult's understanding of the situation into a form that is within the child's grasp (Rogoff 1986; Wertsch 1984). Adults insert their interaction into the ongoing activity of an infant, waiting for the infant to be in the appropriate state and providing verbal and nonverbal commentary on the object or event to which the baby is already attending (Kaye 1982; Schaffer 1984).

Adjustment of the adult's perspective in the service of communication is also apparent in the way adults occasionally misclassify an atypical exemplar of a category in order to avoid confusing toddlers about the basic nature of the category. For example, adults may agree that a whale is a fish, or that an electric outlet is 'hot'. Bruner (1983, based on Deutsch and Pechmann) suggests that the fact that a physicist mother is unlikely to share an identical concept of 'electricity' with her 4-year-old does not matter as long as their shared meaning is sufficient to allow their conversation about shocks to continue. This effort to communicate draws the child into a more mature understanding that is linked to what the child already knows. In the process of communicating, adults tie new situations to more familiar ones, drawing connections from the familiar to the novel through the adult's verbal and nonverbal interpretation.

Structuring situations for child involvement

Choice and structuring of situations

Adults frequently make arrangements for children, selecting activities and materials they consider appropriate for children at that age or interest level (Laboratory of Comparative Human Cognition 1983; Valsiner 1984). Such choices may frequently be made without the intention of providing a specific learning experience, but may also be designed explicitly for the socialization or education of the child. Whiting (1980) cogently states the responsibility of parents and other adults for arranging children's learning environments:

The power of parents and other agents of socialization is in their assignment of children to specific settings. Whether it is caring for an infant sibling, working around the house in the company of adult females, working on the farm with adults and siblings, playing outside with neighborhood children, hunting with adult males, or attending school with age mates, the daily assignment of a child to one or another of these settings has important consequences on the development of habits of interpersonal behavior, consequences that may not be recognized by the socializers who make the assignments (p. 111).

By making such choices and adjusting tasks and materials to children's competence and needs, adults tacitly guide children's development. Parents designate some objects as appropriate for children, following the recommendations of toy manufacturers and cultural lore. For example, children of different ages are presented with books adjusted to their interests and skills: cardboard or plastic picture books, paper picture books with a few words, books with pictures and text, books with pure text. Adults determine the activities in which children's participation is allowed or discouraged, such as chores, parental work and recreational activities, television shows, the birth of a sibling, or the death of a grandparent. Adults arrange the social environment to promote or avoid certain relationships, by assigning child care to a sibling, grandparent, or baby sitter, and encouraging or discouraging particular playmates.

It would be misleading to consider the choice of activities to be the sole responsibility of adults. Children are very active in directing adults towards desirable or away from undesirable activities. Children's preferences are clear in their refusal to enter some activities, and their insistence on others. Their attempts to communicate desire for involvement in specific activities begins during the last half of the first year of life. Rogoff, Malkin, and Gilbride (1984) cite an example of a 9-month-old attempting to get an adult to work a Jack-in-the-box: The baby began by pushing the box across the floor toward the adult, and patted the top of the box when the adult asked 'What'? The adult responded to the baby's actions as a request, and asked 'Should we make Jack come out?' The adult tried to get the baby to turn the handle (an action too difficult for this 9-month-old); and the baby responded with a series of frustrated yet determined moves — whining and fumbling with the box — that expressed his desire to have the box opened. Finally the adult began to turn the handle and the baby immediately relaxed. The adult asked sympathetically, 'Is that what you wanted?' and the baby stared at the handle and let out a big sigh of relief.

Structuring situations through division of responsibility

In addition to arranging the structuring learning activities by providing access and regulating the difficulty of tasks, adults structure children's involvement in learning situations by handling more difficult aspects of the task themselves and organizing the child's involvement with the more manageable aspects of the activity. In engaging the child in an appropriate handling of the situation, the adult creates a 'scaffolded' or supported situation in which the child can extend current skills and knowledge to a higher level of competence (Wertsch 1979; Wood, Bruner and Ross 1976). Note that while the term scaffold could imply a rigid structure or one that does not involve the child, most users of the term include notions of continual revisions of scaffolding to respond to children's advancements. Bruner (1983) characterizes scaffolding in language development as the adult acting on a motto of 'where before there was a spectator, let there now be a participant' (p. 60).

An example of adult support is provided by the way adults structure children's developing narration skills by asking appropriate questions to organize children's stories or accounts (McNamee 1980). If the child stops short or leaves out crucial information, the adult prompts, 'What happened next?' or 'Who else was there?' Such questions implicitly provide children with the cues they need to internalize as they develop narration skills. Adults' questions fill in the outline of what narratives involve. Building on Bruner's perspective, McNamee (1980) suggests that 'if story schemas exist for young children, they hover in the air between adults and children as they converse' (p. 6).

Adults interacting with children may structure tasks by determining the problem to be solved, the goal, and how the goal can be segmented into manageable subgoals. For example, the joint clean-up of a toddler's room may require the adult (even with a co-operative toddler) to define the goal of cleaning up the room, to segment the task into subgoals such as picking up dirty clothes and putting toys in their proper places, and to determine the specifics of each subgoal (e.g. can you find all the blocks and put them in the box?). The adult's structuring of the problem may be tailored to the child's level of skill. With a novice, the adult may take responsibility for managing the subgoals as well as making sure the overall goal is met. A more experienced child may take responsibility for the subgoals, and eventually for the whole task. Such changes in the division of responsibility are an important feature of guided participation, in which the child becomes increasingly responsible for managing the situation as skills increase.

Transfer of responsibility for managing situations

Children take on increasing responsibility for managing situations over the course of years as well as through the process of becoming familiar with a particular task. Effective transfer of responsibility for managing a situation requires adults to be sensitive to children's competence in particular tasks so that responsibility is given when the child is able to handle it. Similarly, such decisions require knowledge (again, it may be tacit) of what skills and knowledge are needed in order to be able to independently handle that situation, and facilitated by knowledge of the course of development of skill in handling that particular situation. In addition to adults' adjustment of support according to children's skills, children are active in arranging for participation at an appropriate level.

Adults' adjustment of support

Scaffolding requires revision as the child gains in understanding. One form of scaffolding involves providing sufficient redundancy in messages so that if a child does not understand one aspect of the communication, other forms are available to make the meaning clear. As children develop greater understanding, adults and older children adjust the level of scaffolding necessary to support the young child's learning and performance by reducing the level of redundancy.

For example, mothers assisting preschoolers in a counting task adjusted the level of their assistance to children's correctness (Saxe, Gearhart, and Guberman 1984). When children made accurate counts, mothers shifted their directives to a more superordinate level in the task structure so that children had more responsibility for determining the subgoals regarding how to obtain one-to-one correspondence, and when children counted inaccurately, mothers shifted to a subordinate level in the task structure, taking over management of the subgoals themselves.

In early parent–child communication, adults facilitate infants' language acquisition by supporting verbal messages with enough redundant nonverbal information to ensure understanding (Greenfield 1984). As infants become able to comprehend verbal messages, adults decrease the nonverbal information. Messer (1980) observed that maternal discourse was organized in episodes referring to specific objects, and within the episodes the mothers provided great redundancy regarding which thing was the object of reference. This organization of maternal speech was greatest for younger children, again suggesting that the structure of maternal communication provides a continually modified scaffold for learning.

Researchers in pre-linguistic development have noted that adults carry on conversations with infants in which the adult's role as conversational partner is adjusted to the baby's repertoire:

The mothers work to maintain a conversation despite the inadequacies of their conversational partners. At first they accept burps, yawns, and coughs as well as laughs and coos — but not arm-waving or head movements — as the baby's turn. They fill in for the babies by asking and answering their own questions, and by phrasing questions so that a minimal response can be treated as a reply. Then by seven months the babies become considerably more active partners, and the mothers no longer accept all the baby's vocalizations, only vocalic or consonantal babbles. As the mother raises the ante, the child's development proceeds (Cazden 1979, p. 11).

Caregivers simplify their own language, they repeat and expand upon infants' contributions, and they provide visual supports and redundant information to assist an infant's understanding (Bruner 1981, 1983; Hoff-Ginsberg and Shatz 1982; Messer 1980; Moerk 1983; Snow 1977; Zukow, Reilly, and Greenfield 1982). Mothers report that their conversations with 2-year-olds help the children learn to talk (Miller 1979).

The modification of discourse by adults speaking to infants and young children may provide support for children's conversation and language learning. In the earliest months, the restriction of parental baby talk to a small number of melodic contours may enable infants to abstract vocal prototypes (Papousek, Papousek, and Bornstein 1985).

Caregivers make the context of statements explicit by clarifying their own and the child's intentions and specifying the referents of a statement (Ochs 1979). Such provision of background knowledge is reduced as children gain language facility. The structure of mother–child discourse allows children to participate in conversations that are beyond their competence in discourse and may help children advance their skills (Bernstein 1981). Some evidence regarding the impact of adult language input on children's language development is discussed in a later section on the influence of guided participation.

Children's role in arranging participation

While it is certainly true that adults carry great responsibility in socialization—they are more knowledgeable and have authority—children are also very active in gaining skill through social interaction. Children participate by indicating their readiness for greater responsibility or even by managing the transfer of information. Adults do not simply solve problems and report their solutions, nor do children passively observe adults and extract the relevant information spontaneously. An adult assesses a child's current understanding of the material and adjusts the scaffolding to support the child's developing skill, while the child simultaneously adjusts the pace of instruction and guides the adult in constructing the scaffold.

An example of an infant seeking a more active role is found in Rogoff, Malkin, and Gilbride's (1984) description of an adult and a 12-month-old working a Jack-in-a-box together. Initially, the adult performed all aspects of manipulating the toy (turning the handle to get the bunny out of the box, and pushing the bunny back into the box), while the baby concentrated solemnly on the actions. In the second episode of play with the Jack-in-a-box, the baby attempted to push the bunny back in the box, and the adult encouraged, 'close it up', while helping the baby push the lid down. In the third episode, the baby began to participate in cranking the handle, and in the fourth episode the baby seemed to demand some independence in managing the handle while the adult encouraged this involvement:

The baby grabbed the box on its sides and shoved it back and forth on the tray, and the adult paused in cranking. The baby looked at the crank and slowly reached for it, confirming the adult's interpretation that he had been demanding a turn. Putting the baby's hand on the crank and turning the crank, the adult said, 'Okay now, you do it' (pp. 40–1).

Over the course of this interaction, the baby eventually participated in winding the handle, pushing the bunny back in the box, and closing the box, while the adult supported the baby's involvement by winding the handle to near the end of the cycle and assisting the baby in holding the lid down on the springy bunny.

Negotiations regarding level of participation and the nature of the activity can be managed by babies through eye contact, joint attention, smiles or cries, and posture changes. Babies can indicate interest by looking eagerly toward an object or event, leaning forward and gesturing toward the object or event with arms, and making enthused grunts. In a negative situation, or if the adult seems not to understand the baby's cues, the baby's activity may change from joint attention to listlessness, then gaze aversion, and finally to turning entirely away. Kaye (1977) found that 6-month-old infants' actions, especially gaze aversion, controlled their mothers' efforts to teach them to reach around a barrier.

In addition to their contribution to managing joint interaction, young children influence their participation in adults' ongoing activities that may not have interaction with the child as a focus. Children's attempts to learn from adult activities may go unnoticed by parents, who are likely to view children's attempts to 'help' or be involved in adult activities as just an inevitable aspect of childhood. During the first year, babies seem to be automatically interested in whatever object an adult is handling, and try to grasp it themselves. An adult's manipulation of a toy facilitates contact by 11- to 13-month-olds with the same toy, with markedly similar actions performed on the toy (Eckerman, Whatley, and McGhee 1979). Toddlers follow their parents around the house, trying to be involved in ongoing activities. Rheingold (1982) found that children aged 18 to 30 months spontaneously and energetically helped their parents or a stranger in the majority of the household chores that the adults performed in a laboratory or home setting. Many of the parents reported that they commonly circumvented their child's efforts to participate at home by trying to do chores while the child was napping, to avoid the child's 'interference'.

The propensity to seek proximity to and involvement with adults assists infants and toddlers in acquiring information about the environment and about the activities of the person who is followed (Hay 1980). Their eagerness to be involved may force a busy parent to give them some role in activities, allowing them to stir the batter, put tape on the present, carry the napkins to the table, help turn the screwdriver, and so on.

In such activities, the adult's and child's roles are likely to fit the characteristics of guided participation. For pragmatic reasons, the adult may try to keep the child from getting involved in an aspect of the activity that is too far beyond the child's skill, e.g. to avoid broken eggs, torn wrapping paper, or damage to the child or to objects. Nevertheless, the child is likely not to be satisfied with an aspect of the job that is too simple, and will insist on greater involvement if given an obvious make-work role. Thus even in interaction with a reluctant adult, the adult and child together may contribute to the child's learning through guided participation.

An example of how a child's insistence on involvement may be instrumental is provided by my daughter, who at age 3½ years was interested in sewing. I was getting ready to leave the house, and noticed that a run had started in the foot of my stocking. My daughter volunteered to help sew the run, but I was in a hurry and tried to avoid her involvement by explaining that I did not want the needle to jab my foot. I began to sew, but could hardly see where I was sewing because my daughter's head was in the way, peering at the sewing. Soon she suggested that I could put the needle into the stocking and she would pull it through, thus avoiding sticking my foot. I agreed and we followed this division of labor for a number of stitches. When I absent-mindedly handed my daughter the needle rather than starting a stitch, she gently pressed my hand back toward my foot, and grinned when I glanced at her, realizing the error. The same child at four years of age asked me, as we worked in the kitchen, 'Can I help you with the can opener by holding onto your hand while you do it? . . . That's how I learn'. These incidents illustrate the eagerness with which children approach the possibility of learning through involvement with adult activities, as well as their active role in the 'instruction'. The child arranges for participation in the activity, and the adult tacitly (sometimes unwillingly) provides access and information.

Does guidance participation influence learning and development?

Thus far, I have suggested that the integrated role of children seeking involvement and structuring their participation, and of adults providing information and arranging for children's activities, may in part be responsible on a day-to-day basis for the rapid progress of children in becoming socialized participants in the intellectual and social aspects of their society. But the existence of such interaction and arrangements between adults and children does not prove that they are influential in children's learning and development.

I would argue, however, that guided participation does play a role in children's learning and development. So much of what children are able to do requires being embedded in their culture. They would certainly not learn English without exposure to that language, nor would they develop scripts for restaurants, peek-a-boo, or book reading without involvement in those as observers or participants. Many of the skills that developmental gists study are tied closely to the technology (e.g. books, number anguage, logic, television) of the culture in which children develop and which children learn to master, with the assistance of people who already participate skillfully in culturally important activities.

A variety of studies find an association between children's experiences and their independent skills. In Rogoff, Malkin, and Gilbride's (1984) observations of adults and infants playing with a Jack-in-the-box, the infants' understanding of the game script and skill in manipulating the toy improved over the course of repeated episodes in single sessions. Babies who participated in monthly games of roll-the-ball with their mothers were able to return the ball almost two months earlier than they returned any items in a standard test of infant development (Hodapp, Goldfield, and Boyatzis 1984). The extent to which mothers expand on infants' pointing gestures by labelling objects is associated with the number of object names in the child's vocabulary (Masur 1982), and the pattern of joint adult–child construction of propositions from one-word utterances appears to form the foundation of children's combinations of words (Scallon 1976).

Several studies provide evidence that an important function of social interaction with adults may be the direction of young children's attention. Attention may be an important individual activity that can be channeled by the highlighting of events by social partners. Mothers who more frequently encourage their 4-month-olds' attention to objects, events, and environmental properties have babies with greater speaking vocabularies and Bayley scores at age 12 months, even when the effect of 4-month infant vocalization and the effect of 12-month maternal stimulation are partialled out (Papousek, Papousek, and Bornstein 1984). In an experiment in which the level of maternal focusing of attention was increased (by having an encouraging observer comment on the effectiveness of the mother's naturally occurring efforts to stimulate her infant), infants showed greater exploratory competence as much as two months after the intervention (Belsky, Goode, and Most 1980). Active involvement of a supportive parent or experimenter in children's exploration of novel objects, compared with these adults' more passive presence, led to more active object exploration by 3- to 7-year-olds (Henderson 1984a,b).

It is hardly surprising that children learn what they are taught; it is but a short extension to argue that on a day-to-day basis what children learn and are taught contributes to the development of what they know. In this perspective, development is built upon learning and, at the same time, learning is based on development. Children contribute to their own development through their eagerness and management of learning experiences as well as through their employment of the knowledge they already have at hand. At the earliest ages this 'knowledge' includes their reflexes and aspects of behavior necessary for eating and protection, as well as primordial schemas for social interaction and learning systems such as language (Slobin 1983). Soon, however, their inborn behavioural repertoire is modified with experience to reflect their history of learning experiences in the knowledge they bring to each new situation.

Cultural universals and variations in guided participation

Most research on the zone of proximal development, guided participation, scaffolding, and adult–child interaction has involved middle class parents and children in North America and Britain. How then do the processes observed in such samples relate to the broader spectrum of child-rearing practices around the world? How do observations made in non-industrial societies compare with and extend the theory? In this final section, some speculations are offered regarding cultural universals and variations in the processes of guided participation.

Universality of guided participation

The general outline of guided participation may appear in diverse cultural groups. Caregivers around the world are likely to play an instrumental role in helping children extend their existing knowledge to encompass new situations. Caregivers and children around the world are likely to devote attention to the arrangements of activities for children, and to revise children's roles in activities as their skill and knowledge develop. They are likely to participate in joint activities that serve the function of socializing children to more mature roles in their culture.

Ethnographic accounts of teaching and learning in different cultures suggest that adults structure children's activities and provide well-placed instruction in the context of joint activities, and that children are active participants in their own socialization (Fortes 1938; Greenfield 1984; Rogoff 1986; Ruddle and Chesterfield 1978). Children participate in the cultural activities of their elders, with adjustment of their responsibilities according to their own initiative and skill. Adults may provide guidance in specific skills in the context of their use. For example, toddlers in India learn at an early age to distinguish the use of their right and left hands, as the former is the clean hand used for eating, and the latter is the 'dirty' hand used for cleaning oneself after defecation.

If a child did not learn to eat with the right hand by participation and observation, a mother or older sister would manipulate the right hand and restrain the left until the child understood and did what was required. One of the earliest lessons taught a child of one-and-a-half to two years of age was to distinguish between the right and left hand and their distinctly separate usages. . . . Although we judged that the Indian style of eating required considerable manipulative skill, we observed a girl, not quite two, tear her chapati solely with her right hand and pick up her vegetable with the piece of chapati held in the right hand. (Freed and Freed 1981, p. 60).

It is notable that the caregivers relied on children's participation as well as structuring the situation, and the children achieved an impressive understanding of the difficult concept required to differentiate right and left. Joint participation and learning through social activity may be especially available to young children, who spend so much of their time in intimate contact with the activities and interpretations of more skilled members of their culture.

Cultural variations in what is learned and the means of transmission

Though the process of guided participation may have widespread use in socialization of children around the world, there are striking cultural differences in such adult–child interaction as well. Different cultural groups vary in the skills and values that are fostered, as well as the means used to transmit these culturally appropriate skills and values.

Differences in skills and values promoted

The most important differences across cultures in the social guidance of development involve variation in the skills and values that are promoted. Relevant skills (e.g. reading, weaving, sorcery, healing, eating with the right hand) vary from culture to culture, as do the objects and situations available for the practice of skills and the transmission of values.

Cross-cultural psychologists and sociocultural theorists have argued that basic to the differences in behavior across cultural (or historical) groups are the tools developed for the solution of problems (Cole and Griffin 1980; Rogoff, Gauvain, and Ellis 1984; Vygotsky 1962, 1978). For example, there is speculation that modes of remembering and classifying information vary as a function of the possibility of making lists (Goody 1977), and that the presence of literacy and Western schooling influence the specific cognitive skills that are practiced and learned (Rogoff 1981b; Scribner and Cole 1981). Mathematics skills vary as a function of the technology available — notches on sticks, paper and pencil long division, or hand calculators. Currently, speculations abound regarding the effect computers have on the thinking of children who learn to use them (Papert 1980). Television's effects on children's thinking and social skills has long been a matter of discussion. Such technologies have been termed 'cultural amplifiers', and their function is an integral part of the practice of the skills developed in each culture (Cole and Griffin 1980).

Skills for the use of cultural amplifiers such as literacy are socialized by parents of very young children even before children have contact with the technology itself. Middle-class United States parents teach their children 'literate' forms of narrative in preschool discourse, as they embed their children in a way of life in which reading and writing are an integral part of communication, recreation, and livelihood (Cazden 1979; Taylor 1983). Picture-books made of durable materials are offered to babies, and bedtime stories become a part of the baby's daily routine.

A fascinating comparison of middle-class school-oriented practices for inculcating literacy with those of families from two communities whose children have difficulty in reading is available in Heath (1982). Parents in a white Appalachian milltown taught their preschool children a respect for the written word but did not involve book characters or information in the children's everyday lives; their children did well in the first years of learning to read but had difficulty when required to *use* literate skills to express themselves or interpret text. Preschool children of rural origin in a black milltown learned a respect for skillful and creative use of language but were not taught about books or the style of analytic discourse used in school; they had difficulty in learning to read which kept them from making use of their creative skills with language in the school setting. Early childhood in both of these communities did not include reading and writing in the texture of daily life, and the children experienced difficulties in the use of literacy in school.

Differences in the means by which adults and children communicate

Research indicates that adult–child communication strategies vary across cultures (Leiderman, Tulkin, and Rosenfeld 1977; Field, Sostek, Vietze, and Leiderman 1981). Such cultural variations in communication strategies would deeply influence the ways in which parents and children collaborate in the child's socialization. If such differences are not recognized, it may be easy for Western researchers to overlook the structuring and joint participation that occurs in other cultures, since it may be at variance with child-rearing practices familiar in middle class Western settings.

The most striking cultural differences may involve the explicitness and intensity of verbal and nonverbal communication, the interactional status roles of children versus adults, and the extent of reliance on face-to-face interaction.

The extent of reliance on explicit, declarative statements compared with tacit, procedural, and subtle forms of verbal and nonverbal instruction appears to vary across cultures (Jordan 1977; Rogoff 1982; Scribner and Cole 1973), with an emphasis on explicit verbal statements in cultures that emphasize Western schooling (Rogoff 1981b; Scribner 1974). Differences in use of explicit statements may also relate to cultural values regarding the appropriate use of language, subtlety, and silence, as well as to the adequacy of other forms of communication for most purposes. For example, among the Navajo, who have frequently been characterized as teaching quietly by demonstration and guided participation (e.g. Cazden and John 1971), talk is regarded as a sacred gift not to be used unnecessarily.

Though researchers have focused on talking as the appropriate means of adult–child interaction, this may reflect a cultural bias in over-looking the information provided by gaze, postural changes, and touch. United States infants have been characterized as 'packaged' babies who do not have direct skin contact with their caregiver (Whiting 1981), and often spend more than a third of their time in a room separate from any other people. This may necessitate the use of distal forms of communication such as noise. In contrast, children who are constantly in the company of their caregivers may rely more on nonverbal cues such as direction of gaze or facial expression. And infants who are in almost constant skin-to-skin contact with their mother may manage effective communication through tactile contact in squirming and postural changes. Consistent with this suggestion that vocalization may be less necessary when there is close contact between adults and infants, Freed and Freed (1981) report work by Lewis in 1977 showing that United States infants and small children are less likely to vocalize when held on the lap, and more likely to vocalize when out of the mother's arms and lap.

Another important cultural difference in adult–child communication involves the interactional status of children. In some societies, young children are not expected to serve as conversational peers with adults, initiating interactions and being treated as equals in the conversation (Blount 1972; Harkness and Super 1977). Instead, they may speak when spoken to, replying to informational questions or simply carrying out commands.

Ochs and Schieffelin (1984) suggest that there may be two cultural patterns of speech between children and their caregivers. In cultures that adapt situations to children (as in middle class United States families), caregivers simplify their talk, negotiate meaning with children, co-operate with children in building propositions, and respond to verbal and nonverbal initiations by the child. In cultures that adapt the child to the normal situations of the culture (as in Kaluli New Guinea and Samoan families), caregivers model unsimplified utterances for the child to repeat to a third party, direct the child to notice others, and build interaction on situational circumstances to which the caregiver wishes the child to respond.

In both patterns, the child participates in activities of the society, but the patterns vary in terms of the child's versus the caregiver's responsibility to adapt in the process of learning or teaching the more mature forms of speech and action. It seems likely that the adaptation of caregivers to children may be more necessary in societies that segregate children from adult activities, thus requiring them to practise skills or learn information outside of the mature context of use (Rogoff 1981a). In societies in which children are integrated in adult activities, the child is assured a role in the action (at least as an observer), and socialization may proceed with less explicit child-centred interaction to integrate the child in the activities of society.

Efforts to instruct children may thus vary in terms of the children's responsibility to observe and analyse the task, versus the caregivers' responsibility to decompose the task and motivate the child. Dixon, Levine, Richman, and Brazelton (1984) noted that Gusii (Kenyan) mothers taught their 6- to 36-month-old infants using clear 'advance organizers' in instruction, often modelling the expected performance in its entirety, appearing to expect the task to be completed exactly as specified if the child attended to it, giving the children the responsibility for learning. This contrasted with the efforts of American mothers, who concentrated on arousing the child's interest and shaping the child's behaviour step by step, providing constant encouragement and refocusing, taking the responsibility for teaching.

Related to the cultural differences suggested here in the interactional role of children are differences that have been observed in the use of face-to-face interaction. Face-to-face interaction may be a prototype in United States research on mother–child communication due to the didactic role assumed by middle class American mothers, relying on their own efforts to motivate children to learn, in contrast with mothers who give the responsibility for learning to the children. There appears to be cultural variation in the extent to which mothers rely on this position for communication. Mothers in many cultures commonly hold infants facing away from them (Martini and Kirkpatrick 1981; Sostek, Vietze, Zaslow, Kreiss, van der Waals, and Rubinstein 1981).

Variation in infant positioning from facing the mother to facing the same way as the mother may reflect cultural values regarding the social world in which the child is to be embedded, as well as the means by which children are socialized. Martini and Kirkpatrick (1981) note that Marquesan mothers (in the South Pacific) appeared strained and awkward when asked to interact with their babies in a face-to-face orientation. In everyday activities, babies were usually held facing outward and encouraged to interact with and attend to others (especially slightly older siblings) instead of interacting with the mother. The authors report that this is consistent with a general cultural value of embeddedness in a complex social world. Marquesan infants learn a different lesson in their socialization than do American infants engaged in face-to-face interaction, but their mothers appear to provide similarly rich guidance in developing culturally appropriate skills and values. Marquesan mothers actively arrange infants' social interactions with others; if babies appear to get self-absorbed, mothers interrupt and urge attention to the broader social environment:

[Mothers] consistently provided the infant with an interactively stimulating world, first by interacting, next by encouraging and making effective his attempts to make contact, and finally by directing others to interact with the infant. Caregivers . . . shaped the infants' attention towards others and objects, and shaped their movements towards effective contact and locomotion. By the end of the first year, infants were becoming interactants able to accompany and learn from older children in an environment supervised by adults (Martini and Kirkpatrick 1981, p. 209).

Summary

This paper proposes that middle class Western children as well as children in other cultures learn and develop in situations of joint involvement with more experienced people in culturally important activities. Adults and children collaborate in children's socialization as they negotiate the nature of children's activities and their responsibilities in participation. They work together to adapt children's knowledge to new situations, to structure problem-solving attempts, and to regulate children's assumption of responsibility for managing the process. This guidance of development includes tacit forms of communication and distal arrangements of children's learning environments, as well as explicit verbal interaction. The mutual roles played by adults and children in children's development rely both on the adults' interest in fostering mature skills and on children's own eagerness to participate in adult activities and push their own development.

These joint socialization roles may be universal, although cultures vary in the goals of socialization and the means used to implement them. Cultures vary in the explicitness or subtlety of verbal and nonverbal communication, the orientation of the infant towards parents versus siblings or other caregivers, the adaptation of children to the adult world or vice versa, and the accesibility of caregivers to infants through proximal and distal forms of communication. The variations as well as the similarities across cultures in how adults and infants interact may be instrumental in the rapid socialization of infants to be participating members of their cultures.

References

Bakeman, R. and Adamson, L. B. (1984). Coordinating attention to people and objects in mother–infant and peer–infant interaction. *Child development* **55**, 1278–89.

Belsky, J., Goode, M. K., and Most, R. K. (1980). Maternal stimulation and infant exploratory competence: Cross-sectional, correlational, and experimental analyses. *Child development* **51**, 1163–78.

Bernstein, L. E. (1981). Language as a product of dialogue. *Discourse processes* **4**, 117–47.

Blount, B. G. (1972). Parental speech and language acquisition: Some Luo and Samoan examples. *Anthropological linguistics* **14**, 119–30.

Brazelton, T. B. (1982). Joint regulation of neonate–parent behavior. In *Social interchange in infancy* (ed. E. Z. Tronick), pp. 7–22. University Park Press, Baltimore, MD.

Brown, R. (1958). *Words and things*. Free Press, New York.

Bruner, J. S. (1981). Intention in the structure of action and interaction. In *Advances in infancy research vol. 1* (ed. L. P. Lipsitt), pp. 41–56. Ablex, Norwood, NJ.

Bruner, J. S. (1983). *Child's talk: learning to use language.* Norton, New York.

Butterworth, G. and Cochran, G. (1980). Towards a mechanism of joint visual attention in human infancy. *International journal of behavioral development* 3, 253–72.

Cazden, C. (1979). Peekaboo as an instructional model: Discourse development at home and at school. In *Papers and reports on child language development*, No. 17. Stanford University, Department of Linguistics, Stanford, CA.

Cazden, C. B. and John, V. P. (1971). Learning in American Indian children. In *Anthropological perspectives in education* (eds. M. L. Wax, S. Diamond, and F. O. Gearing), pp. 252–72. Basic Books, New York.

Cole, M. (1981). The zone of proximal development: Where culture and cognition create each other. Center for Human Information Processing Report No. 106, University of California, San Diego.

Cole, M. and Griffin, P. (1980). Cultural amplifiers reconsidered. *The social foundations of language and thought* (ed. D. R. Olson), pp. 343–64. Norton, New York.

D'Andrade, R. G. (1981). The cultural part of cognition. *Cognitive science* 5, 179–95.

Dixon, S. D., Levine, R. A., Richman, A., and Brazelton, T. B. (1984). Mother–child interaction around a teaching task: An African–American comparison. *Child development* 55, 1252–64.

Eckerman, C. O., Whatley, J. L., and McGhee, L. J. (1979). Approaching and contacting the object another manipulates: a social skill of the one-year-old. *Developmental psychology* 15, 585–93.

Erickson, F. (1982). Taught cognitive learning in its immediate environments: a neglected topic in the anthropology of education. *Anthropology and education quarterly* 13, 149–80.

Feinman, S. (1982). Social referencing in infancy. *Merrill-Palmer quarterly* 28, 445–70.

Field, T. M., Sostek, A. M., Vietze, P., and Leiderman, P. H. (1981). (eds.) *Culture and early interactions.* Erlbaum, Hillsdale, NJ.

Fortes, M. (1938). *Social and psychological aspects of education in Taleland.* Oxford University Press.

Freed, R. S. and Freed, S. A. (1981). *Enculturation and education in Shanti Nagar, vol. 57, Part 2,* Anthropological Papers of the American Museum of Natural History, New York.

Furth, H. G. (1974). Two aspects of experience in ontogeny: Development and learning. In *Advances in child development and behavior vol. 9* (ed. H. Reese), pp. 47–67. Academic Press, New York.

Goody, J. (1977). *The domestication of the savage mind.* Cambridge University Press.

Greenfield, P. M. (1984). A theory of the teacher in the learning activities of everyday life. *Everyday cognition: its development in social context* (eds. B. Rogoff and J. Lave), pp. 117–38. Harvard University Press, Cambridge, MA.

Gunnar, M. R. and Stone, C. (1984). The effects of positive maternal affect on infant responses to pleasant, ambiguous, and fear-provoking toys. *Child development* 55, 1231–6.

Harkness, S. and Super, C. M. (1977). Why African children are so hard to test. In *Issues in cross-cultural research* (ed. L. L. Adler), *Annals of the New York Academy of Sciences* 285, 326–31.

Hay, D. F. (1980). Multiple functions of proximity seeking in infancy. *Child development* 51, 636–45.

Heath, S. B. (1982). What no bedtime story means: Narrative skills at home and school. *Language in society* **11**, 49–76.

Henderson, B. B. (1984*a*). Parents and exploration: The effect of context on individual differences in exploratory behavior. *Child development* **55**, 1237–45.

Henderson, B. B. (1984*b*). Social support and exploration. *Child development* **55**, 1246–51.

Hodapp, R. M., Goldfield, E. C., and Boyatzis, C. J. (1984). The use and effectiveness of maternal scaffolding in mother–infant games. *Child development* **55**, 772–81.

Hoff-Ginsberg, E. and Shatz, M. (1982). Linguistic input and the child's acquisition of language. *Psychological bulletin* **92**, 3–26.

Jordan, C. (1977). Maternal teaching, peer teaching, and school adaptation in an urban Hawaiian population. Paper presented at the meetings of the Society for Cross-Cultural Research, Michigan.

Kaye, K. (1977). Infants' effects upon their mothers' teaching strategies. In *The social context of learning and development* (ed. J. D. Glidewell). Gardner Press, New York.

Kaye, K. (1982). Organism, apprentice, and person. In *Social interchange in infancy* (ed. E. Z. Tronick). University Park Press, Baltimore.

Laboratory of Comparative Human Cognition (1983). Culture and cognitive development. In *History, theory, and methods* (ed. W. Kessen). *Handbook of child psychology* (ed. P. H. Mussen) *vol. 1*, pp. 294–356. Wiley, New York.

Leiderman, P. H., Tulkin, S. R., and Rosenfeld, A. (eds.) (1977). *Culture and infancy*. Academic Press, New York.

Lempers, J. D. (1979). Young children's production and comprehension of nonverbal deictic behaviors. *Journal of genetic psychology* **135**, 93–102.

Martini, M. and Kirkpatrick, J. (1981). Early interactions in the Marquesas Islands. In *Culture and early interactions* (eds. T. M. Field, A. M. Sostek, P. Vietze, and P. H. Leiderman), pp. 189–213. Erlbaum, Hillsdale, NJ.

Masur, E. F. (1982). Mothers' responses to infants' object-related gestures: Influences on lexical development. *Journal of child language* **9**, 23–30.

McNamee, G. D. (1980). The social origins of narrative skills. Unpublished dissertation, Northwestern University.

Mehan, H. (1976). Assessing children's school performance. In *Worlds apart* (eds. J. Beck, C. Jenks, N. Keddie, and M. F. D. Young). Collier McMillian, London.

Messer, D. J. (1980). The episodic structure of maternal speech to young children. *Journal of child language* **7**, 29–40.

Miller, P. J. (1979). *Amy, Wendy, and Beth: learning language in South Baltimore*. University of Texas Press, Austin.

Moerk, E. L. (1983). *The mother of Eve—as a first language teacher*. Ablex, Norwood, NJ.

Newman, D. (1982). Perspective-taking versus content in understanding lies. *Quarterly newsletter of the Laboratory of Comparative Human Cognition* **4**, 26–9.

Ochs, E. (1979). Introduction: What child language can contribute to pragmatics. In *Developmental pragmatics* (eds. E. Ochs and B. Schieffelin). Academic Press, New York.

Ochs, E. and Schieffelin, B. B. (1984). Language acquisition and socialization: Three developmental stories and their implications. In *Culture and its acquisition* (eds. R. Schweder and R. LeVine). University of Chicago Press, Chicago.

Papert, S. (1980). *Mindstorms*. Basic Books, New York.

Papousek, M., Papousek, H., and Bornstein, M. H. (1985). The naturalistic vocal environment of young infants. In *Social perception in infants* (eds. T. M. Field and N. Fox). Ablex, Norwood, NJ.

Poe, P. (1982). Beginning in the bathtub. *American baby* **44 (19)**, 12–20.

Rheingold, H. L. (1982). Little children's participation in the work of adults, a nascent prosocial behavior. *Child development* **53**, 114–25.

Rogoff, B. (1981*a*). Adults and peers as agents of socialization: A Highland Guatemalan profile. *Ethos* **9**, 18–36.

Rogoff, B. (1981*b*). Schooling and the development of cognitive skills. In *Handbook of cross-cultural psychology vol. 4* (eds. H. C. Triandis and A. Heron), pp. 233–94, Allyn & Bacon, Boston.

Rogoff, B. (1982). Mode of instruction and memory test performance. *International journal of behavioral development* **5**, 33–48.

Rogoff, B. (1986). Adult assistance of children's learning. In *The contexts of school based literacy* (ed. T. E. Raphael). Random House, New York.

Rogoff, B. and Gardner, W. P. (1984). Guidance in cognitive development: an examination of mother–child instruction. In *Everyday cognition: its development in social context* (eds. B. Rogoff and J. Lave), pp. 95–116. Harvard University Press, Cambridge, MA.

Rogoff, B., Gauvain, M., and Ellis, S. (1984). Development viewed in its cultural context. In *Developmental psychology* (eds. M. H. Bornstein and M. E. Lamb). Erlbaum, Hillsdale, NJ.

Rogoff, B., Malkin, C., and Gilbride, K. (1984). Interaction with babies as guidance in development. In *Children's learning in the "zone of proximal development"* (eds. B. Rogoff and J. V. Wertsch), pp. 31–44. Jossey-Bass, San Francisco.

Ruddle, K. and Chesterfield, R. (1978). Traditional skill training and labor in rural societies. *The journal of developing areas* **12**, 389–98.

Saxe, G. B., Gearhart, M., and Guberman, S. B. (1984). The social organization of early number development. In *Children's learning in the "zone of proximal development"* (eds. B. Rogoff and J. V. Wertsch), pp. 19–30. Jossey-Bass, San Francisco.

Schaffer, H. R. (1984). *The child's entry into a social world*. Academic Press, London.

Scallon, R. (1976). *Conversations with a one-year-old*. University Press of Hawaii, Honolulu.

Scribner, S. (1974). Developmental aspects of categorized recall in a West African society. *Cognitive psychology* **6**, 475–94.

Scribner, S. and Cole, M. (1973). Cognitive consequences of formal and informal education. *Science* **182**, 553–9.

Scribner, S. and Cole, M. (1981). *The psychology of literacy*. Harvard University Press, Cambridge, MA.

Shotter, J. and Newson, J. (1982). An ecological approach to cognitive development: implicate orders, joint action, and intentionality. In *Social cognition studies in the development of understanding* (eds. G. Butterworth and P. Light), pp. 32–52. Harvester, Sussex.

Slobin, D. I. (1973). Cognitive prerequisites for the development of grammar. In *Studies of child language development* (eds. C. A. Ferguson and D. I. Slobin). Holt, Rinehart, and Winston, New York.

Snow, C. (1977). Mother's speech research: From input to interaction. In *Talking to children* (eds. C. Snow and C. Ferguson). Cambridge University Press, New York.

Sorce, J. F., Emde, R. N., Campos, J. J., and Klinnert, M. D. (1985). Maternal emotional signaling: Its effect on the visual cliff behavior of 1-year-olds. *Developmental psychology* **21**, 195–200.

Sostek, A. M., Vietze, P., Zaslow, M., Kreiss, L., van der Waals, F., and Rubinstein, D. (1981). Social context in caregiver–infant interaction: a film study of Fais and the United States. In *Culture and early interactions* (eds. T. M. Field, A. M. Sostek, P. Vietze, and P. H. Leiderman). Erlbaum, Hillsdale, NJ.

Taylor, D. (1983). *Family literacy.* Heinemann Educational Books, Exeter, NH.

Valsiner, J. (1984). Construction of the zone of proximal development in adult–child joint action: The socialization of meals. In *Children's learning in the 'zone of proximal development'* (eds. B. Rogoff and J. V. Wertsch), pp. 65–76. Jossey-Bass, San Francisco.

Vygotsky, L. S. (1962). *Thought and language.* M.I.T. Press, Cambridge, MA.

Vygotsky, L. S. (1978). *Mind in society: The development of higher psychological processes.* Harvard University Press, Cambridge, MA.

Wartofsky, M. (1984). The child's construction of the world and the world's construction of the child. In *The child and other cultural inventions* (eds. F. S. Kessel and A. W. Siegel), pp. 188–215. Praeger, New York.

Wertsch, J. V. (1979). From social interaction to higher psychological processes. *Human development* **22**, 1–22.

Wertsch, J. V. (1984). The zone of proximal development: Some conceptual issues. In *Children's learning in the 'zone of proximal development'* (eds. B. Rogoff and J. V. Wertsch), pp. 7–18. Jossey-Bass, San Francisco.

Wertsch, J. V. (1985). *Vygotsky and the social formation of mind.* Harvard University Press, Cambridge, MA.

Whiting, B. B. (1980). Culture and social behavior: A model for the development of social behavior. *Ethos* **8**, 95–116.

Whiting, J. W. M. (1981). Environmental constraints on infant care practices. In *Handbook of cross-cultural human development* (eds. R. H. Munroe, R. L. Munroe, and B. B. Whiting), pp. 155–79. Garland, New York.

Wood, D., Bruner, J. S., and Ross, G. (1976). The role of tutoring in problem solving. *Journal of child psychology and psychiatry* **17**, 89–100.

Zukow, P. G., Reilly, J., and Greenfield, P. M. (1982). Making the absent present: Facilitating the transition from sensorimotor to linguistic communication. In *Children's language, vol. 3* (ed. K. Nelson). Gardner Press, New York.

6

The reconstruction of social knowledge in the transition from sensorimotor to conceptual activity: the gender system
BARBARA LLOYD and GERARD DUVEEN

Introduction

This presentation is, like Gaul, divided into three parts. First we consider the interpretations of experience and knowledge which shape the presentation of the main material. The principal province is an account of a series of studies over the past decade exploring the development of children's knowledge of gender. Finally we examine the contribution this material might make to the developmental study of social cognition.

We use our recent theoretical statement on social gender identity as a framework for presenting the empirical material (Duveen and Lloyd 1986). We have deliberately eschewed the more traditional search for sex differences and employed instead a semiotic approach, viewing gender as a system of signs. From this perspective the results of a number of studies are interrogated in order to demonstrate how young children gain access to this sign system in which the relationships between signifiers and signifieds are socially agreed and arbitrary.

The gender system is a particularly fruitful model to consider in the context of a discussion of cognition and social worlds. It is amenable to semiotic analysis for at least two reasons: first, all societies employ biological sex differences in an obligatory and ubiquitous semiotic system in which social representations of gender are the signified, and second, in all societies it is necessary for individuals to acquire social gender knowledge and to create for themselves a social gender identity.

The data which we present have been gathered in quasi-naturalistic settings; we brought mothers to our laboratory to play with unfamiliar infants, and we arranged that preschool friends play together in our observation room. We used these tactics, not only because we are trained in the quantitative and empirical traditions of academic psychology, but also because we believed that it would be difficult to collect sufficient naturalistic evidence to comment upon the relevant psychological issue in the acquisition of a social gender identity.

In this introductory section we will pose some psychological questions which have guided the collection and analysis of our data on gender understanding. The second and major section is an account of the development of social identities from birth until four years of age. This is not intended as a review of published studies; rather the evidence from other research will be invoked only when it makes a particularly salient point about an issue on which our own data are silent.

As developmental psychologists who focus on gender we have pre-empted an answer to the question Robert Siegler posed in the title of his book *Children's thinking: what develops*? We assert that what develops is a social gender identity. Infants are born with a biological sex which is used as a signifier in assigning them to a social gender category. This category is part of a partially arbitrary but consensually agreed gender system. This system resides in the members of a particular society as a shared set of beliefs about the nature, behaviour, and value of females and males. Individuals, both adults and older children, realize the gender system in their social gender identities when interacting with each other and in interaction with infants.

The developmental problem which this view poses is how do infants enter into this system? Initially the social gender identities of infants are held by adults and older children; it is they who locate the infant within a social world and whose representations function as scaffolding or indices for infants seeking order in their social worlds. Eventually infants internalize their society's gender system.

The psychological questions we seek to address concern this process. As Piagetians we can describe this development as the emergence of the semiotic function, by which Piaget meant that children become capable of representing objects and events in their absence, and are able to use these representations to regulate their activity. Thus infants move from regulation in terms of the social gender identities of others and those which others ascribe to them to being able to invoke a social gender identity when interacting with others. In familiar Piagetian language this is described as the construction of representational knowledge from indexical or sensorimotor knowing.

Vygotskian psychology offers another framework within which to pose questions about the acquisition of gender understanding and a social gender identity. The world of the infant is, *par excellence*, an interpersonal one as Winnicott (1945) noted long ago. Thus the development of a social gender identity from birth to four years can be examined as an example of interiorization, semiotic relations moving from the interpersonal plane to the intrapersonal plane.

At its most general, the question is whether data collected about a particular aspect of social life can inform our understanding of the development of children's thinking.

The development of a social gender identity

Birth

Birth is the starting point for an account of the development of social gender identities because it is the moment in which biological characteristics are invoked to assign the new individual to a gender category. Although legal definitions of paternity have changed, and it is no longer necessary to specify whether a child is born in wedlock, it is still mandatory, where births are registered, to declare whether an infant is male or female. The procedure is relatively straightforward: assignment is made on the basis of dimorphic, physical criteria. In rare instances, where the external genitalia are ambiguous, further investigations designed to assess genetic sex are undertaken through examination of cells taken from the lining of the mouth. Assignment may be relatively straightforward, but the consequences of this assignment are complex and enduring.

The physical characteristics of infants are crucial in assignment to a gender category, but it is the socially shared beliefs about the nature, behaviour, and value of males and females which guide interaction with the newborn. This gender system operates before birth and, it has been suggested, may influence parental decisions about abortion when the genetic sex of the fetus is known. There is no doubt that the social gender system is operative once the biological sex of the newborn is announced. The biological sex assigned to infants is interpreted by parents in terms of the gender system; it becomes a sign signifying gender characteristics.

Within hours of birth parents of first borns are reported to describe their daughters as significantly more beautiful, small, and cute while fathers describe their sons as firmer, larger featured, more alert, stronger, and better co-ordinated (Rubin *et al.* 1974). As the male and female infants in this study did not differ in birth weight, birth length, or Apgar scores, it is social gender identities functioning as ideal types which organize parents' perceptions of their first-born children.

In the first year

A further example of the use which adults make of their access to social gender identities is to be found in our cross-dressing studies undertaken with six-month-old infants (Smith and Lloyd 1978; Smith, unpublished thesis 1982). In a series of studies we have systematically observed mothers playing for 10 minutes with one of our unfamiliar six-month-old infants, two boys and two girls. The dress of each infant varied so that half the time they were presented as being assigned to the gender congruent with their biological sex, and half the time as the other gender. In these exchanges the mothers knew only the baby's gender differentiated name, i.e. Jane or John, and could observe that the infant was wearing either a ruffled dress and socks or a 'babygro'. They were unaware that there might be a discrepancy between gender and biological sex. The mothers' choice of an initial toy for the baby matched the baby's ascribed social gender identity. Regardless of the biological sex of the infant, when the infant was presented as a boy mothers were likely to offer the hammer or rattle, but when the same infant was presented as a girl the doll was the favourite toy to be offered first. Across the 10-minute observation period the clear gender-based toy choice of mothers was moderated by infants' interest and, as this interest was not yet differentiated, gender did not influence significantly the length of time the gender marked toys were used.

Other aspects of the behaviour of mothers were also influenced by the ascribed social gender identity of the infants. Although there were no measured differences in the motoric behaviour of the two girl and two boy babies who participated in the study, mothers' responses to the babies varied in terms of the presentational social gender identity of the baby. When named and dressed as boys mothers offered all infants more verbal encouragement to gross motor activity. In addition, when the babies were presented as boys rather than as girls mothers responded to their gross motor activity with further stimulation. With a baby dressed as a girl this behaviour often led to efforts to soothe and calm the infant. At six months therefore, infants experience gender-specific play outcomes; although they have no direct access to the sign system which regulates gender, their participation in pleasurable play routines is regulated by adult choices made on the basis of the infant's ascribed social gender identity.

The beginning of the second year

In the second year infants begin to manifest their social gender identities through preferences for different play routines. In a well known study, Goldberg and Lewis (1969) observed 13-month-olds playing for 15 minutes in a room with their mothers and reported gender differences in time spent playing with toys and in related behaviour. Girls spent significantly more time playing with blocks, a peg board, and two toys with faces, a cat and a dog. Girls were observed spending significantly more time sitting and combining toys and boys more time being active and banging. Goldberg and Lewis asserted that girls chose toys which involved more fine motor than gross motor co-ordination. Although mothers were instructed to watch their children's play and to respond to it in any way they desired, mothers' feedback to girls and boys was not compared. These results are interpreted as evidence of gender differentiation originating with the infant. The toys afford different possibilities for activity, and it is the infant's preference for particular play routines or activity which result in differential amounts of time spent playing with the various toys.

In two partial replications in our laboratory Caroline Smith (unpublished thesis 1982) observed 13-month-olds playing for 10 minutes with a similar array of toys. In her first study the mallet was the only toy which provided evidence of statistically significant gender-differentiated use, and in the second no single toy was used differentially.

Smith also measured gross motor play and fine motor manipulative play with toys. Gross motor play including bang, shake, throw, and push, occurred more than five times as much as manipulative which included fit, place, and handle. Quantitatively boys engaged in more of the former and girls in more of the latter, but in the first study only the gender difference in gross motor play was statistically significant. The view that toys afford different possibilities for play is supported by Smith's observation that differences in duration of play with particular toys are confounded with differences in styles of play. She observed that boys spent a significantly greater proportion of the time they were in contact with the mallet banging it.

Smith added a condition in her second study; after the initial 10-minute period mothers were asked to play actively with their 13-month-olds for a further 10 minutes. Although only one significant gender difference in toy use was reported in either condition, there were clearer differences in types of activity. Again boys engaged in significantly more gross motor play and girls in significantly more fine motor manipulative play with toys. But the participation of mothers had a highly significant and gender-specific effect on styles of play. The gross motor play of boys (but not of girls) increased significantly when mothers engaged actively in play. Though the manipulative play of girls (but not of boys) increased in frequency, the effect failed to reach conventional levels of significance ($P < 0.09$). It appears that the 13-month-old's mother amplifies the child's developing social gender identity.

In order to understand the nature of mother–child interaction Smith also examined children's first action after their mothers brought a toy to their attention. Children's social gender identity did not predict whether they would make a response nor whether they would hold the toy to themselves. However, boys were significantly more likely to use the toy in some gross motor activity such as banging or hitting, and there was a trend in the direction of girls using the toy to engage in manipulative activity.

In interaction with their mothers, the behaviour of 13-month-olds is regulated in terms of their social gender identity. The mechanisms which govern this gender regulation are unclear. Somewhat surprisingly, in view of the work with 6-month-olds, Smith found no difference in the frequency with which mothers of boys and mothers of girls joined in their children's gross motor play.

In discussing development in the first year, we suggested that mothers may contribute to the development of gender-differentiated patterns of sensori-motor activity through their active influence on infants' practical activity, by their encouragement of and reward for gender-appropriate toy choice and play style. If this hypothesis is well grounded, it may be that by 13 months this gender regulation is already a well established feature of children's practical activity, with the consequence that active influence by the mother is no longer necessary. Over a shorter time span, six to nine months, Vandell and Wilson (1987) showed that infants who engaged in proportionally longer turn-taking sequences with their mothers at six months engaged in proportionally longer sequences with a sibling at nine months. Interaction with mother may encourage the development of sensorimotor routines just as it facilitates the development of social interaction skills and language (Bruner 1975).

Developmental changes from the second year through the fourth year

From around the beginning of the second year, infants begin to manifest a social gender identity in their styles of play and related choice of objects for motoric activity (*see* above). The second year is a time of major changes, and these have important implications for the expression of a social gender identity. Increasing mobility and the use of language in communication provide new media for the expression of social gender identities. Money and Ehrhardt (1972) have suggested, on the basis of their evidence showing that sex reassignments undertaken between 18 months and three or four years are unlikely to have successful outcomes, that a gender identity is already formed by the time children begin to speak. Where, formerly, it was adults and older children who exercised regulation of infants' activities in terms of gender, these new competences may facilitate the child's internalization of gender regulation. The process of this internalization can be traced through the development of children's social interactions with their peers and their play with toys.

To illustrate some of these changes we present data from two studies which included children from 18 months to four years. (Duveen and Lloyd 1988; Lloyd 1987; Lloyd and Smith 1985; Lloyd *et al.* 1988). All the children in the samples walked confidently and had begun to speak.

Language and social gender identities

Alongside locomotor changes in the second year there are major sensorimotor and cognitive/linguistic developments. Modern studies of language acquisition based upon the speech corpora of a very few children (e.g. Brown 1973) have not focused on gender, but the superior linguistic development of girls in the preschool years is a widely accepted generalization in the field of sex differences (Maccoby and Jacklin 1975; Coates 1986). Results may not always yield statistically significant effects but the direction of findings consistently favours girls. More interesting from the perspective of the infant's construction of a social gender identity is Lieberman's (1967) report that even before the appearance of speech infants adapt the pitch of their voices to the pitch of the person they are addressing; the pitch used with fathers is lower than that addressed to mothers. Although Lieberman's results are limited, they suggest that in the first year infants are already becoming sensitive to features which mark the gender of the person with whom they interact.

Our own linguistic recognition and production data from 18 months onwards suggest that this knowledge of gender quickly finds other means of expression as children gain access to the linguistic code. When children of 18 to 23 months were shown photographs of a man and a woman *or* a girl and a boy they could select the pictures which corresponded to the gender marked nouns MAN, LADY, DADDY, MUMMY, BOY, and GIRL 60 per cent of the time. In the three- to four-year-old groups recognition was virtually perfect, 99 per cent. These same children found the matching of photographs to the pronouns SHE, HE, HER, and HIM much more difficult; the youngest children responded infrequently and then were rarely correct although the oldest children were correct 95 per cent of the time.

Children's ability to produce the same terms was also tested in the context of a recognition task. Once the child selected the photograph which matched the given noun the child was then asked to name the other picture. The children's replies were scored along four dimensions—gender, age, part of speech, and precise complement. Thus, after choosing the picture which matched the term LADY, a child was expected to supply the word, MAN. The scoring procedure was such that the word DADDY would not be scored as totally correct. The increasingly adequate performance across the age range is scarcely surprising. In part this can be explained by the very strict criteria of the task and the failure of many of the youngest children to respond at all. More interesting to consider is the finding that when errors did occur gender confusion accounted for only 2.4 per cent and age confusion, 3.5 per cent. Even the youngest children were able to categorize according to social dimensions of gender and age; it is the other dimensions of the linguistic code, part of speech and particular complement, which they found more difficult.

Play and social gender identity

Observing gender-marked play   The same children whose linguistic development was reported in the previous section were observed and video-recorded while playing for six minutes with mothers and familiar peers in a room which contained a variety of gender-marked toys. Parents of local primary school children rated an array of toys described in published reports as appropriate objects for girls and boys. The female-marked toys selected on the basis of the parental ratings were irons and ironing boards, comb, brush, and mirror sets, large white hats, shopping bags, saucepans and stove top, and baby dolls and cradle. The male-marked toys were a sit-and-ride fire engine, construction trucks, firemen's hats, briefcases, pegbenches with hammers, and guns. Crayons and paper were also available but they were not reported to be or rated as gender-marked. The toys were matched intuitively for possibilities of use in active play, and duplicates were provided to reduce quarrels.

In the first study, analysis was based upon data from 60 pairs of children accustomed to playing together. They were blocked in four age groups: up to 2 years, 2½ years, 3 years, and 3½ years, and each age cohort was divided into five girl/girl pairs, five boy/boy pairs and five girl/boy pairs. In a replication and extension study 120 children of three to four years were recruited from the same community. These children, selected in triads, were also accustomed to playing together. All children were observed playing with their mothers and one child, designated the target child, was also observed playing with a girl and a boy. Children were blocked for age; the replication group included children up to 3½ years old, the extension group children up to 4 years. In each age group there were 10 target girls and 10 target boys.

Duration of toy use in action play   The duration of play with each toy was coded directly from the video record using a computer assisted, video-linked keyboard which functioned as a multi-channel event recorder (Smith *et al.* 1982). Total time spent in action play was coded for each child in each of the 60 pairs in the first study. In the second study only the action play of target children was coded.

The analysis of duration of toy use in the first study is based upon pair data, i.e. the separately coded scores for each child in a pair were combined and used as a dependent variable in a three-way analysis of variance with four age groups, three pair types, and toys summed to yield totals for female and male toys. The main effects were not significant, although an overall preference for male toys almost achieved significance, $P = 0.053$ ($F = 3.95$; df 1, 48). The data (mean for play with male toys, 336.6 seconds and for female toys, 261.3 seconds) just fail to support the assertion that all the children spend more time playing with male toys.

There was a significant Pair type × Toy type interaction ($F = 13.09$; df 2, 48; $P < 0.001$), but the only paired comparisons of means which achieved significance indicate that boy/boy pairs used male toys more than female toys and that boy/boy pairs used male toys more than girl/girl pairs. None of the comparisons relating to female toys reached significance (Table 6.1). These results show that when playing with a boy, boys assert a social gender identity through their greater use of male toys; girls playing together, however, do not show a preference for female-marked toys.

The three-way interaction including age was also significant ($F = 3.33$; df 6,48; $P < 0.01$). Comparisons of all pairs were assessed using Scheffe tests, but none of these were statistically significant. However, in the groups of

Table 6.1. *Duration of toy use in action play by pair type (in seconds)*

Pair type	Female toys	Male toys
Girl/girl		
Mean	380.1	214.0
S.D.	152.5	130.1
Boy/boy		
Mean	155.2	463.6
S.D.	180.6	276.0
Girl/boy		
Mean	248.7	332.1
S.D.	130.9	175.3

children approaching 3 and 3½ years of age, the results were consistent with those already reported. In the two oldest groups boy/boy pairs tended to play more with male toys than with female toys and boy/boy pairs tended to play more with male toys than did girl/girl pairs. Boys' assertion of a differentiated social gender identity through toy use in play with other boys is a developmental phenomenon appearing in the two oldest groups of boy/boy pairs.

In the second study only the action play of target children was coded. Thus the analysis of duration of toy use appears in a different form. The results reported here are for play with first partner only, as these are directly comparable to the first study. The analysis of variance has four factors with two values on each: target child's gender, gender of partner, toy type, and age group. Both target child's gender and toy type were significant, indicating that boys spend more time in action play and that children in general play more with male toys (Table 6.2).

Table 6.2. *Duration of toy use in action play by gender (in seconds)*

Gender	Female toys	Male toys	Combined mean
Girls			
Mean	210.1	281.7	245.9
S.D.	144.1	180.9	
Boys			
Mean	46.5	534.7	290.6
S.D.	32.6	139.8	
Combined mean	128.3	408.2	

The gender of target child by toy type interaction was highly significant, and when the six possible pair comparisons were analysed using the Scheffe test the only one which failed to achieve significance was the comparison of girls' use of female toys and male toys. In other words, boys assert a social gender identity by using male toys more than female toys, using female toys less than girls do and by using male toys more than girls do. There is a more limited differentiation of female and male toys in the gender identity asserted by girls in action play; girls use male toys less than boys do and female toys more than boys do, but their use of female and male toys is not significantly differentiated. Overall, girls do not differentiate their play with toys according to gender markings, while boys show a strong tendency to play with male-marked toys and to avoid female-marked toys.

Paradigmatic and syntagmatic toy choices   Analyses of duration of toy use in action play demonstrated that girls and boys assert different social gender identities through the use of toys in action play. Duration is a crude measure in the sense that the HOLD TOY code functions so that once children sit down on a sit-and-ride or place a hat on their heads the count begins and only ceases when the activity stops. A more sensitive measure was constructed in order to assess the element of choice in toy use. For this analysis every time a child made a toy choice it was classified as either paradigmatic or syntagmatic. [A similar distinction was introduced by Catherine Garvey (1977) in her analysis of the elements of ritual play in young children.] The selection of a toy marked for the child's own gender constituted a paradigmatic choice, while selecting a toy marked for the opposite gender constituted a syntagmatic choice. Thus for a girl choosing a female-marked toy was paradigmatic and a male-marked toy syntagmatic, while for a boy a paradigmatic choice was a male-marked toy, and a syntagmatic choice a female-marked toy.

The toy choices of the 3- to 4-year-old children from the second study were analysed using these categories. The number of paradigmatic and syntagmatic choices made by the target child in each recorded session (with mother, with a girl peer, and with a boy peer) was used as a dependent variable in an analysis of variance with four factors, age, target child's gender, choice type, and partner, with repeated measures on the last two factors. The results showed that, overall, girls made more toy choices than boys (mean for girls 8.7; mean for boys 6.9; $F = 5.6$; df $= 1,36$; $0.05 > P > 0.01$), and that paradigmatic choices (mean $= 9.6$) were more frequent than syntagmatic choices (means $= 6.0$; $F = 18.5$; df $= 1,36$; $P < 0.001$). A Gender by Toy Choice interaction ($F = 22.0$; df $= 1,36$; $P < 0.001$) showed that while girls made roughly equal numbers of paradigmatic and syntagmatic choices, boys made many more paradigmatic than syntagmatic choices (Table 6.3).

Table 6.3. *Type of toy choice by gender*

Gender	Paradigmatic choices	Syntagmatic choices	Combined mean
Girls			
Mean	8.5	8.8	8.7
S.D.	3.3	4.6	
Boys			
Mean	10.6	3.3	7.0
S.D.	3.5	1.9	
Combined mean	9.6	6.0	

Table 6.4. *Boys types of toy choices with each partner*

Partner	Paradigmatic choices	Syntagmatic choices	Scheffe test
Mother			
Mean	10.2	3.2	$P < 0.01$
S.D.	4.3	3.1	
Girls			
Mean	10. 5	4.7	$P < 0.01$
S.D.	4.0	3.8	
Boys			
Mean	11.2	1.9	$P < 0.01$
S.D.	5.0	1.8	

Further analyses by Scheffe test of all the possible pair comparisons among these means showed that the only significant ($P < 0.01$) difference occurred between boys' scores for the two types of choices. The consistency of this response is shown by the detailed analysis of the significant three-way interaction Gender × Toy Choice × Partner (Table 6.4; $F = 3.99$; df $= 2,72$; $0.05 > P > 0.01$).

Although boys' syntagmatic choices were highest when playing with girls and lowest when playing with boys this comparison was not significant. None of the complementary comparisons for girls were significant. Indeed there were no significant variations as a function of partner for girls' or boys' use of either choice type. Comparisons between girls' and boys' use of paradigmatic choices also showed no differences as a function of partner. However, comparison of girls' with boys' scores did show one further significant difference in their use of syntagmatic choices. Girls (mean = 9.7) produced significantly more syntagmatic choices when playing with a boy than did boys (mean = 1.9; $P < 0.01$ for the Scheffe test). Girls do not discriminate between type of choice in any context, whereas boys always showed a marked preference for paradigmatic over syntagmatic choices in every context. Boys are likely to assert a differentiated social gender identity through their choice of gender-appropriate toys whether playing with another boy, a girl, or their mothers. Girls, however, do not assert a differentiated social gender identity in play either with girls or boys. Syntagmatic choice by girls cannot be ascribed to any lack of awareness of the stereotypical value of toys since they sorted photographs of the toys for gender more successfully than boys (Lloyd 1987). Although toy use and toy choice are significant media through which boys express a differentiated social identity, they do not have the same significance for girls.

Pretend play   Pretend play was coded separately from action play using written transcriptions made from the video record of each child's speech and action. A unit of pretend play was identified when children showed clearly that they were fantasizing by introducing elements that were not inherent in the toy as object, e.g. saying 'This is my baby' while hugging the doll. The child's speech identifies the unit as pretend play and places it in Nicolich's (1977) symbolic stage.

Pretend play was more common in the replication and extension groups and could be analysed using parametric statistics. In a four-way analysis of variance with the number of units of pretend play as the dependent variable there were two values on each of the factors, target child's gender, partner's gender, age group, and type of toy. Only two terms were significant at a level between $P = 0.05$ and $P = 0.01$; they were the interaction of age and gender of target child, and toy type and gender of target child (Table 6.5).

Table 6.5.   *Units of pretend play by toy type*

	Female toys	Male toys
Girls		
Mean	5.9	4.5
S.D.	6.8	4.0
Boys		
Mean	2.4	6.0
S.D.	3.0	5.4

Pair comparisons failed to achieve significance in either of the Scheffe test analyses. The only comparisons to approach significance were the comparisons of girls' and boys' use of female toys and boys use of female and male toys. In action play duration and toy choice boys displayed a social gender identity through the choice of male toys. In pretend play it appeared only as a trend. Although weaker, the pattern in these pretend play data repeats that found in duration and toy choice measures in action play. Boys use male toys more than female toys; they also use female toys less than do girls. On none of these measures have we observed any differences in girls' use of female and male toys.

Scripted play   In the previous section children's pretend play creations were examined in a simple quantitative manner. Each unit was also analysed in detail for evidence of children's discursive skills and the incorporation of social representations of gender into pretend play. To assess their grammatical competence, mean length of utterance (MLU) was computed for the 30 oldest children in the first study and for all target children in the second (cf. Brown 1973). In addition, the dialogic characteristics of pretend speech were analysed following Nelson's work (Nelson and Seidman 1984); discontinuous, continuous, and scripted discourse were identified. Analysis of the content of scripts allowed the assessment of gender knowledge.

Analysis of MLU in the first study yielded an expected result in that the MLU of the 15 oldest girls was significantly longer ($P < 0.05$) than that of the 15 oldest boys on a one-tailed t test. In the analysis based on the speech of target children in the second study there were no effects due to the child's own gender, though both girls and boys had longer MLUs when speaking with a girl than when speaking with a boy. It thus appears that the social gender identities of these older children take account of the gender marking of their partners. There is here an echo, at the level of representation, of the difference noted by Lieberman at the level of action.

The three discourse measures, discontinuous, continuous, and scripted dialogue were each correlated significantly with MLU suggesting their inter-related nature as measures of linguistic development. However, scripts were still relatively rare in the fourth year. Only 14 of the 40 target children produced at least one script while playing with a girl and only 12 while playing with a boy. Although the gender marking of their partner was not related simply to the target children's script production, there is a different relationship between MLU and script production in the two gender contexts (Table 6.6). The MLUs of the fourteen children who produced a script when playing with a girl were, on average, half a morpheme longer than those of the twenty-six who failed to produce a script, though this difference was not statistically significant. When playing with boys, however, the twenty-eight children who failed to produce a script had a significantly lower MLU than

Table 6.6.   *Averaged mean lengths of utterance (MLU)*

Children	With girls	With boys
Producing scripts	5.6 (n = 14)	5.5 (n = 12)
Not producing scripts	5.0 (n = 26)	4.6 (n = 28)

the twelve children who produced at least one script ($t = 2.67$; df $= 38$; $P < 0.05$), the difference amounting to approximately one morpheme. Once again the gender context of play influences the expression of social gender identities.

Structural and content analyses were also undertaken on the scripts produced in the two gender contexts. When the structures of the scripts produced by children in the oldest group in the first study and the two groups of the second study are compared, it can be seen that differentiation between actors, roles, locations, properties, and goals only becomes clear in the oldest group. This differentiation allows the coding of content as masculine and feminine. In the content analysis of the scripts of younger children between 70 and 85 per cent could not be marked for gender. This proportion falls to 40 per cent in the scripts of the 20 target children approaching four years of age. The gender marking of their scripts was skewed with 19 involving feminine role enactment and only three of them masculine roles.

The content analysis of scripts showed that over half of those produced by the older group of children (those approaching four years) were concerned with traditionally feminine roles, while very few related to traditionally masculine roles. Many of the scripts were located in domestic settings (ironing, cooking, shopping, etc.) which usually featured women. This difference suggests that feminine roles are more accessible to young children for re-creation in scripted pretend play. There was a sense in which feminine scripts were children's reconstructions of their own experience and observation of family life. When men were represented in scripts they figured in roles which were available to the children through the media of public representations (television, books, etc.) rather than through participant observation. Thus while children were able to give quite intricate performances of domestic routines, their enactments of occupational roles were impoverished.

Gender and developmental social cognition

This review of data provides evidence for two complementary systems through which knowledge of the gender system is expressed — the linguistic and the ludic systems.

At birth, new parents employ gender-marked descriptions in speaking about their infants. By six months mothers address different instructions to infants according to their social gender identities. In the second half of the first year, the sounds infants make are modulated to suit the pitch of the parents' voices. Two-year-old children begin to use the formal linguistic system to express their understanding of gender categorization. Children approaching four years use language to re-create the routines of social life in scripted play.

The ludic or play system also begins with parental regulation. At six months, toy choice is regulated by mothers' gender marking, but duration measures reflect the absence of any gender marking by infants. At thirteen months, infants express different social gender identities in their styles of play, and these differences are amplified in play with mothers. Our presentation of the 18-month- to four-year-old play data was deliberately structured in terms of an increasing developmental and conceptual complexity. Between eighteen months and four years, duration measures express different social gender identities of girls and boys with more differentiated gender marking by boys in duration, toy choice in action play, and in pretend play.

Pretend play only becomes frequent in the oldest groups when children employ the linguistic system to introduce new elements in their interaction with toys. At this point feminine concerns become salient and domestic, traditionally female routines are enacted by both girls and boys.

Our account of children's internalization of the gender system in their first four years can be encompassed by either a Vygotskian or a Piagetian account. There is evidence of gender regulation moving from the interpersonal to the intrapersonal plane, but the evidence can also be marshalled to demonstrate the reconstruction of sensorimotor knowing into representational understanding. All of our results are based upon cross-sectional group comparisons. These data do not address the possibility of conflict between these two perspectives. To do so we require a more detailed appreciation of the processes of internalization. Perhaps the time has come for students of social cognition to follow their colleagues in child language in undertaking detailed longitudinal studies of individual children. Piaget's three books on infancy are testimony to the fruitfulness of this approach for wider developmental issues.

Acknowledgements

The research reported was funded by SSRC and ESRC Research grants (No. HR 5871 and No. C00232113) to B.L. We are grateful to Dr C. Smith for her contribution to the research and for her helpful comments on this paper.

References

Brown, R. (1973). *A first language: the early stages*. Harvard University Press, Cambridge, MA.

Bruner, J. S. (1975). From communication to language—a psychological perspective. *Cognition* **3**, 255-87 .

Coates, J. (1986). *Women, men and language*. Longman, London.

Duveen, G. and Lloyd, B. (1986). The significance of social identities. *British journal of social psychology* **25**, 219-30.

Duveen, G. and Lloyd, B. (1988). Gender as an influence on the development of scripted pretend play. *British journal of developmental psychology* **6**, 89-95.

Garvey, C. (1977). *Play*. Fontana, London.

Goldberg, S. and Lewis, M. (1969). Play behavior in the year-old infant: early sex differences. *Child development* **40**, 21-31.

Lieberman, P. (1967). *Intonation, perception and language*. MIT Press, Cambridge, MA.

Lloyd, B. (1987). Social representation of gender. In *Making sense: The child's construction of the world* (ed. J. Bruner and H. Haste). Methuen, London.

Lloyd, B. and Smith, C. (1985). The social representation of gender and young children's play. *British journal of developmental psychology* **3**, 65-73.

Lloyd, B., Duveen, G., and Smith, C. (1988). Social representations of gender and young children's play: a replication. *British journal of developmental psychology* **6**, 83-88.

Maccoby, E. E. and Jacklin, C. N. (1974). *The psychology of sex differences*. Stanford University Press, Stanford, CA.

Money, J. and Ehrhardt, A. A. (1972). *Man and woman, boy and girl*. Johns Hopkins University Press, Baltimore.

Nelson, K. and Seidman, S. (1984). Playing with scripts. In *Representing the symbolic world in play: reality and fantasy* (ed. I. Bretherton). Academic Press, New York.

Nicolich, L. M. (1977). Beyond sensorimotor intelligence: assessment of symbolic maturity through analysis of pretend play. *Merrill-Palmer quarterly* **23**, 89-99.

Rheingold, H. and Cook, K. (1975). The contents of boys' and girls' rooms as an index of parents' behavior. *Child development* **46**, 459-63.

Rubin, J. Z., Provenzano, F. J., and Luria, Z. (1974). The eye of the beholder: parents' views on the sex of new borns. *American journal of orthopsychiatry* **44**, 512-19.

Siegler, R. (ed.) (1978). *Children's thinking: what develops*? Erlbaum, Hillsdale, NJ.

Smith, C. (1982). Mothers' attitudes and behaviour with babies and the development of sex-typed play. Unpublished D. Phil. Thesis, University of Sussex.

Smith, C. and Lloyd, B. B. (1978). Maternal behavior and perceived sex of infant: revisited. *Child development* **49**, 1263-5.

Smith, C., Lloyd, B. and Crook, C. (1982). Instrumentation and software report: computer-assisted coding of videotape material. *Current psychological reports* **2**, 289-92.

Vadell, D. L. and Wilson, K. S. (1987). Infants' interactions with mother, sibling and peer: contrasts and relations between interaction systems. *Child development* **58**, 176-86.

Winnicott, D. W. (1945/1958). Primitive emotional development. In *Through paediatrics to psycho-analysis*. Hogarth Press, London.

7

Social context effects in learning and testing
PAUL LIGHT and ANNE-NELLY PERRET-CLERMONT

Introduction

Within academic developmental psychology the dominant view of cognitive development has always had a more or less maturationalist flavour. In the 1940s and 50s cognitive development was frequently characterized as unfolding through stages regulated by internal biological mechanisms (e.g. Gesell 1943). In the 1960s and 70s, under the influence of Piaget, this conception was elaborated into a view of intelligence as a progressive construction involving feedback. The basic ingredients of development (the body with its physiological and psychological regulatory processes) are given at birth. Development proceeds step by step, and involves the integration of the child's experiences into cognitive functioning. However, such integration is constrained by the fact that the child's capacity for experience is itself determined by his or her present intellectual structures or schemas.

This conception of cognitive development bears all the hallmarks of 'cognitivist' approaches in psychology generally. It is focused very heavily upon the *individual* and upon the characteristics of the individual's endogenous mental organization at different stages of development. Development consists essentially in the stage by stage construction of new logical or 'operational' competences. Procedures developed by Piaget and his associates were refined and formalized in order to provide precise diagnostic tests for these various competences. Conservation (the understanding that number, volume, weight, etc. remain invariant across various transformations) emerged for Piaget as perhaps the most critical element in the genesis of operational thought (e.g. Piaget 1968, p. 121), and the conservation test became one of the 'trade marks' of the Piagetian approach in developmental psychology and education. In the present chapter we shall use the conservation test as a case study in an examination of emerging alternatives to the long dominant maturationalist/Piagetian view.

Any essentially maturational view of cognitive development necessarily relegates social factors (language and social experience in the family, the peer group, the school, etc.) to a secondary role. Such factors may facilitate or inhibit but they have no genuinely constitutive function. By contrast, in the alternative 'sociogenic' tradition reaching back to the work of G. H. Mead and Vygotsky, cognitive development is treated as essentially a social–cultural product. A combination of social and symbolic factors associated with the family, the school, peer groups, mass media, social ritual, and work and play activities are constitutive of cognitive processes. Language is seen as having a crucial part to play. Since the mid 1970s the developmental literature has reflected a marked revival of interest in this approach, with both theoretical and empirical interest centring more and more clearly on the conception of cognitive development as a social/symbolic process. Interestingly, many students of the social conditions of learning and development have found in the conservation test a useful microcosm for the study of socio-cognitive processes. Thus if conservation has continued to hold a central place in the concerns of psychologists, it is partly because it serves as a useful bridge or point of connection between contemporary socio-cognitive work and the large corpus of Piagetian work built up over recent decades.

In the sections which follow we shall focus first on a line of predominantly Swiss research concerned with the developmental potential of child–child interaction in the context of conservation. Then we shall review some predominantly British work in which the conservation test has been examined as a social interaction between tester and child, governed by 'conversational' rules. In the latter part of the chapter we shall explore the recent signs of convergence between these two lines of research and will argue a case for seeing cognitive development (and in particular conservation) in terms of a socially grounded process of co-construction of meanings.

Peer interaction and conservation

In some of his early work (especially *The moral judgment of the child* 1932) Piaget had suggested a privileged role for child–child interaction in 'decentring' the child's thought. At very much the same time Mead (in *Mind, self and society* 1934) and Vygotsky (in *Thought and language* 1934/1962) emphasized the establishment of shared meanings in interaction and the role of play and 'inner speech' in the development of thought. It took some forty years for these ideas to spawn any strong tradition of empirical work on cognitive development. Paradoxically, perhaps, the conservation test, itself a product of Piaget's later much more individualistic psychology, provided one of the main vehicles for this development.

In the mid 1970s in Geneva Doise, Mugny, and Perret-Clermont embarked on a series of experimental studies designed to address the issue of the role of peer interaction in cognitive development (Doise, Mugny, and Perret-Clermont 1975; Perret-Clermont 1976). This work (together with parallel work elsewhere in Europe, e.g. Carugati, De Paolis, and Mugny 1979; Rijsman, Zoetebier, Ginther, and Doise 1980) involved a three-step procedure.

First, individual children, typically 4- to 7-year-olds, were pre-tested. Then some were assigned to pairs or small groups for an interaction session, while others (controls) worked alone. Finally, all children were individually post-tested.

In the case of conservation of liquids (Perret-Clermont 1980), for example, the experimental procedure might take the following course. At the pre-test stage a conservation of liquid test is administered to each child individually. Two identical glasses are filled to the same level and the child is asked whether they each contain the same amount. When he or she has agreed that they do, the contents of one are poured into, say, a taller, thinner glass. The child is then asked whether the two glasses still contain the same amount of liquid. Justifications are sought. Other more or less closely related conservation procedures may also be included in the pre-test. About a week later, each child who failed to conserve at pre-test is allocated to an interaction or control condition. The interaction session might for example involve being paired with another child (conserver or non-conserver) in order to 'play a game' involving sharing out juice equally. The adult experimenter gives one child a glass which is taller and thinner than the other child's and tells the non-conserving child to pour out equal shares. A third glass, identical to one of the others, is available for their use. The 'game' ends when the children agree that they both have the same amount to drink. The post-test session a week later mirrors the pre-test.

The results of such studies (e.g. Perret-Clermont 1980; Perret-Clermont and Schubauer-Leoni 1981) show that, under certain circumstances, children who participated in the interaction session show significantly more pre- to post-test progress than control subjects who do not have the opportunity to interact with a peer. Pairing with a partner who presented the *correct* response did not appear to be a necessary condition for progress. Other studies using different conservation tasks or other types of task involving spatial transformations or co-ordinations have obtained similar results (e.g. Ames and Murray 1982; Doise and Mugny 1981; Glachan and Light 1982).

The interpretation of these findings was principally in terms of *socio-cognitive conflict*. In the peer interaction situation, according to this explanation, the child is confronted with alternative and conflicting solutions which, while not necessarily offering the correct response, suggest some relevant dimensions which the child might otherwise have neglected. Moreover, the social context in which these conflicting solutions are proferred is of such a character that each child has to take account of his or her partner's view in order to pursue the social interaction in which they are jointly involved.

Progress occurs through a conflict of centrations which can only be resolved by the achievement of a new 'decentred' cognitive schema which can account for the various points of view. Thus socio-cognitive conflict can occur whenever partners to an interaction offer differing solutions, whether or not any of these solutions is correct.

Socio-cognitive conflict is an inherently social mechanism, in that progress is envisaged as resulting from interindividual conflict (conflict between the viewpoints of different persons) rather than from intraindividual cognitive conflict or dissonance. However, while this interpretation offers a clear role for social interaction, such interaction remains essentially an 'external' factor, stimulating the child's cognitive development but not determining its content or direction. Put in very simple terms, maybe the child, in this interpretation, does not progress towards operational thinking entirely on his or her own, but only needs a little help from a friend.

There were indications right from the outset that children's responses in these three-step experiments were influenced by wider socio-cultural factors (Mackie 1980; Perret-Clermont 1980, Perret-Clermont and Mugny 1985), but rather than pursue these at this stage we shall introduce in the next section a separate strand of work, also developed through the late 1970s and early 80s, which approached the role of social interaction in a rather different way.

The conservation test as an interactional setting

Doise, Mugny, and Perret-Clermont, in the works to which we have been referring, have been grappling with the problem of how children *learn* to conserve. A rather different concern has been central to the work of Donaldson (1978), and others in Britain and the United States, who have been concerned primarily with how children's understanding of conservation can be validly *assessed*. For this reason, their experimental work has typically involved single-session testing rather than the three-step procedures described in the previous section.

McGarrigle and Donaldson's (1975) 'Conservation accidents' paper remains probably the best known in this literature, and exemplifies very clearly the central concern with how the child represents or understands *what is going on* in the conservation test. Four- and five-year-olds were given a variety of conservation tests in the usual way and, as expected, few showed any understanding of conservation. However, they were also tested using a variation of the procedure in which instead of the transformation of materials (the curling up of string in a length conservation task or the bunching up of counters in a number conservation task) being achieved by a deliberate and focused act of the adult experimenter, it resulted from an apparently haphazard or mischievous action of a Teddy bear. 'Naughty teddy' was in actual fact manipulated by the experimenter, but McGarrigle and Donaldson hoped by using it to avoid a misleading suggestion which they felt was implicit in the usual procedure. They suggested that the usual conservation testing procedure created an ambiguity, since whereas the experimenter referred verbally (in his questions), to, let us say, number, he referred nonverbally (through his actions in transforming the materials) to a different factor such as spacing or length of rows. Certainly the use of the naughty teddy bear to achieve the transformations resulted in substantially higher levels of correct response.

Other ways have also been found of rendering the transformation of materials 'incidental' to the proceedings. Light, Buckingham, and Robbins (1979) used a badly chipped beaker as a reason for pouring the contents from one container to another. This produced correct conservation judgements from 70 per cent of a sample of 5- and 6-year-olds, compared to 5 per cent success in a control sample tested in the usual way. Similar results have been obtained by Hargreaves, Molloy, and Pratt (1982), Miller (1982) and others.

The central argument underlying these studies was that the young child's non-conserving responses may reflect not so much a misunderstanding of the effects of the transformation (i.e. a lack of grasp of conservation) as a misunderstanding of the experimenter's *intentions*. The confusion is not so much conservational as conversational. From the perspective of an analysis of the conservation task as a piece of discourse, the way that the transformation of materials is handled is by no means the only important factor. Rose and Blank (1974) pointed out that typically in a conservation task the pre- and post-transformation questions are exactly the same. It seemed possible that repetition of the question by the experimenter might lead the child to suppose his or her first answer to have been wrong, and therefore to change the response. Or alternatively, the repetition of the question after the transformation might lead the child to suppose that the transformation must, after all, have been relevant to the question. Rose and Blank showed that, although normally all children answer the pre-transformation question (the question about initial equality of amounts) correctly, simply leaving it out led to a significant increase in the level of correct responding to the crucial post-transformation question. Rose and Blank (1974) used number conservation, and although attempts to replicate this study have not always succeeded, it has been replicated successfully by Samuel and Bryant (1984) not only for number but for several other conservation tasks.

In another analysis of the 'conversational assumptions' which might influence the child's responses to the conservation task, Perner and colleagues (Perner, Leekam, and Wimmer 1984) have drawn attention to the shared knowledge which exists between experimenter and child. The child knows that the amounts were equal before transformation—and the initial questioning ensures that he or she and the experimenter *both* know about this. This being so, Perner argues, the child cannot readily treat the post-transformation question as a straightforward request for information, since everything that the child knows, the experimenter also obviously knows. Of course the experimenter is really interested not in the equality or otherwise of amount, but rather in *what the child knows*. Perhaps the child's difficulty lies in dealing, not with conservation *per se*, but with this type of 'examination' question which, as Elbers (1986) has argued, involves a significant departure from the patterns of communication to which the child will be accustomed at this age. Perner *et al.* (1984) offered some evidence that, as would be predicted from this argument, the child's difficulty can be alleviated by introducing a second experimenter, apparently naive to the pre-transformation state of affairs, to ask the post-transformation question. Such a 'naive experimenter' can ask about the equality or inequality of amounts as a straightforward request for information, since after the transformation the equality or otherwise is far from obvious perceptually.

Light, Gorsuch, and Newman (1987) have recently confirmed this observation in a study with 5- and 6-year-olds, tested in pairs. The task began with a heap of dried peas on a table. The children had to help the experimenter to divide this heap into two equal piles. The experimenter put the peas from one pile into one glass container and those from the other pile into another, differently shaped container, and then asked whether there was the same 'amount of peas' in each. Less than 20 per cent of children responded correctly. However, another sample of children followed exactly the same procedure except for an interruption which occurred just after the peas had been placed in the glass containers. Another adult, already familiar to the child, popped her head round the door and said that the experimenter was wanted on the telephone. The incoming adult then took over the experimenter's role and asked the crucial conservation question. Even though the wording of the question was exactly the same, over 50 per cent of children succeeded in this condition.

This experiment also provided an opportunity to test the efficacy of another factor which had more or less surreptitiously crept in to a number of previous studies (e.g. Light *et al.* 1979). This concerns the introduction of a *game* between the participants, in which the requirements of fair competition make equality of amounts an important issue. The Light *et al.* (1987) study just described had an alternative format, in which before the heaps of peas were divided up the pairs of children were told that they were going to play a game which involved moving the peas into a target bowl (by sucking them with straws), and that the one who finished first would be the winner. During the initial division into two piles the importance of fairness was reiterated, but otherwise the procedure and the questions were as described earlier. In this game format over 50 per cent succeeded in the single experimenter condition and over 70 per cent when the second experimenter was introduced to ask the post-transformation question. Statistical analysis of the results of this experiment showed significant main effects both for standard versus game context and for the one- versus two-experimenter conditions, with no significant interaction between these effects.

In this section we have considered a family of related empirical studies of conservation testing, which have demonstrated that various more or less subtle 'discourse cues' available in the testing situation can have a major impact on the child's reading of the situation, and on his or her response to it. There is certainly room for doubt as to whether correct judgements given in response to these various modified tasks necessarily indicate a full grasp of the principles of conservation (cf. Gellatly this volume). Donaldson (e.g. 1978) has tended to take the view that the modified procedures show that many 4-, 5-, and 6-year-olds really do understand about conservation, and that their failure in standard Piagetian tests reflects the inherently misleading and confusing nature of these tests. Others (e.g. Light et al. 1979) have been more sceptical, arguing that children's correct responses in the modified contexts of task presentation cannot be regarded as independent of the support which those contexts offer. Some broader issues relevant to this debate will be discussed in the final section of the chapter, but first we shall turn our attention back to the peer interaction/socio-cognitive conflict research introduced in the previous section. Our purpose is to outline recent developments in this research, and in particular to explore the ways in which it has converged with the (originally rather separate) research tradition which has been the subject of the present section.

Social interaction and the co-construction of meanings

We sketched out earlier the basic three-step experimental paradigm used in cognitive development. The 'continental' (mostly Genevan) work, up to 1980, concentrated upon identifying the conditions under which cognitive changes occurred (see Mugny, Perret-Clermont, and Doise 1981, for a review). In particular, studies were directed at establishing the cognitive prerequisites necessary for progress, the efficacy of different combinations of cognitive level in the pair or group, the importance of assigning particular roles to individuals in the group, and so on.

To counter the criticism that children were merely learning the right response to conservation problems by superficial imitation or cueing, considerable attention was given to demonstrating that at post-test the children who had made gains were able to satisfy all the various Piagetian criteria for conservation. These include justification of responses, generalization to related tests, and durability of gains. So the question of whether success on the standard conservation post-tests was indicative of an understanding of conservation was addressed in detail. By contrast, the complementary question as to whether *failure* on standard conservation pre- and post-tests was indicative of an *absence* of an understanding of conservation attracted little attention.

This issue of the significance of failure on the standard task, which is so obviously raised by the work discussed in the previous section, did come to the surface in one aspect of the Genevan peer interaction work, namely that concerned with socio-cultural differences. Perret-Clermont (1980) observed that working-class children tended to perform significantly less well than middle-class children in conservation pre-tests, but that in the experimental groups this class difference largely or entirely disappeared by post-test. Differential benefit from interaction has also been shown in more recent work in Neuchatel. For example, Nicolet (personal communication) has found recovery from initial disadvantage as a result of the peer interaction session in children from rural (farming) backgrounds compared with those whose parents have more urban occupations.

An explanation of such findings in Piagetian terms might be that the initial disadvantage of working-class children reflected a social milieu less conducive to the development of cognitive structures, and that the interaction sessions provided the requisite stimulation to allow rapid development. But this is hardly convincing. How could an interaction session of perhaps 10 minutes duration compensate for a 'deficient social milieu', and bring about such a profound cognitive advance almost instantly? An alternative approach to interpretation of such findings is to suppose that perhaps the initial pre-test differences may reflect not so much a class difference in the children's understanding of conservation, but rather a class difference in their understanding of the test situation itself.

Grossen (1988) has recently confirmed the finding that at around five years of age, in both conservation of number and (in a separate sample) conservation of liquid quantity, twice as many middle-class as working-class children respond correctly. Role-playing techniques reveal that conservers and non-conservers understand the task differently and their verbal justifications of questions and answers differ not only on cognitive grounds.

Also in Neuchatel, Bell (personal communication) has obtained rather similar results with respect to occidental and non-occidental children in context of an international school. Success rates were substantially higher amongst the former, but there were various indications that this arose from differences in the extent to which the children were able to achieve a shared understanding with the experimenter about the topic and nature of the discourse. For example, the non-occidental children more often asked questions about why the experimenter was pouring the juice, and they more frequently justified their responses in terms which were seemingly irrelevant (or at least would seem so to the classically trained Piagetian experimenter expecting 'logical' interpretation).

Another pointer to the fact that the conservation test is not functioning as a neutral 'litmus test' of logical reasoning comes from the observation that differences in the presentation of the test have differential effects for different social class groups. Thus Perret-Clermont and Schubauer-Leoni (1981) showed that for a middle-class sample it did not make any difference whether a liquid conservation task was presented in terms of juice having to be shared between two identical dolls or between the experimenter and the child. For the working-class sample not only did the children do worse overall, but they also found the dolls condition significantly more difficult. Grossen (1988) found similar results in a conservation of liquid task in which the type of beaker received by the non-conserving child was manipulated in such a way that in one condition the non-conserving child always had the illusion of having *more* juice than his or her partner (advantage condition) and in the other always *less* juice (disadvantaged condition). The results show that the conditions of beakers attribution did not have the same effects for every social class and that the working-class subjects were the only ones to react to the difference of conditions, giving more conserving judgments in the disadvantage condition.

The issue of *sharing*, and the associated norms of equality and of fairness, may themselves be very important factors contributing to the efficacy of peer interaction in stimulating correct conservation responses. We saw evidence in the previous section on contextual modifications of the conservation test that setting the test within the context of a competitive game, with explicit reference to the norm of fairness, led to significantly better results. As indicated in the second section of this chapter, the typical procedure for a peer interaction experiment involves explicit reference to establishing equal shares. Even where this is not explicitly the objective of the peer interaction session, the issue of fairness will almost inevitably arise (at least implicitly) whenever children are working together on the distribution of quantities. Thus it may be that the efficacy of the peer interaction procedure arises not (or not only) from the socio-cognitive conflict mechanism outlined earlier, but from the introduction of a norm of equality which serves to support correct responses which are then carried over to the individual post-test.

This interpretative shift has indeed been evident in much of the recent European work. The concept of 'social marking' has been introduced to describe the way in which the ease or difficulty of a cognitive task can be affected by the extent to which it can be mapped on to social norms or rules with which the child is familiar (e.g. Doise and Mugny 1981; Doise 1985; Girotto 1987; Roux and Gilly 1984). In the case of conservation the importance of the norm of equality is becoming increasingly apparent. Doise, Rijsman, Van Meel, Bressers, and Pinxten (1981) showed that pairs of 'nonconserving' children given a series of liquids conservation tests were significantly more likely to succeed if they were told at the outset that since they deserved equal rewards they should have equal amounts of juice. This superiority carried over to individual post-test.

Nicolet and Iannaconne (in press) found that the norm of fairness did not act 'in vacuo' nor did the setting of the conservation task in the context of a game suffice to produce high levels of conservation, but that the impact of the recall of the norm depended on the type of interpersonal relationship (co-operative or competitive) experienced previously in the game. Zhou (1987) has independently obtained very much the same results.

Doise et al. (1981) also included an individual condition in their study. Here the child worked alone with the experimenter, but an emphasis on equality of rewards was introduced in terms of equality with another child 'who will come in a minute'. This condition proved to be just as effective as its two-child counterpart. This finding perhaps serves to highlight the difference between the position we have now arrived at and that described (in terms of socio-cognitive conflict) at the end of our second section. Socio-cognitive conflict is, as we suggested earlier, a mechanism which reflects the importance of the 'social other' as embodying an alternative perspective to the child's own. Social marking, by contrast, is a mechanism which does not require the physical presence of others, but it is social in the wider and perhaps more fundamental sense that the child's social experience elicited by symbolic means (e.g. the evocation of a norm) provides the framework within which the problem is understood.

Work with the 'three step' experimental paradigm is actively continuing, at Neuchatel and elsewhere. For example Perret-Clermont and Brossard (1985) have been examining where (or at whom) the subjects look at critical points in the procedure. But (as is evident from this example) the interpretative framework within which these three-step studies are viewed has shifted substantially. Ten years ago we were thinking primarily in terms of conflicts of pre-operational centrations within the pair or group of interacting children — an essentially cognitive analysis still. Today our concern is more with the way in which just the fact of interacting with others (inclusive of being confronted with different centrations) transforms the experience of the situation for the children. Moreover, we are conscious that not only in the 'interaction session' but also in the pre- and post-tests the child is in an interactive setting, and in these situations too the child's experience in the test is modulated in subtle ways by the conditions of his or her encounter with the experimenter. And we are alive to at least some of the ways in which the wider network of roles and relationships from which we draw our 'subjects' will impinge upon their readings of the situations we create for them (Hinde, Perret-Clermont, and Stevenson-Hinde 1985).

Conclusion

Where does all this work leave conservation? To some extent we have just used the conservation task as a convenient point of departure, or point of reference, for studies of the operation of interpersonal/contextual cues in testing and learning situations. But much more interesting is the way in which some of these cues (especially the notion of fairness at the outset of a game, or of equality of reward) *map on* to the conservation problem specifically, providing a rationale for it and supporting a correct reading of the questioner's intent. We would like to suggest that these various 'mappings', between the logic of the conservation task on the one hand and the practical social activities of exchanging and sharing on the other, may be important not just for the expression of an understanding of conservation but for the genesis of that understanding.

If for a moment we widen our perspective on 'the social context' we can see the child as being, in effect, an apprentice to his or her culture. The child is immersed in a language and a culture which are themselves grounded in practical and social human purposes. The concepts of amount, number, area, volume, weight, and so on exist in that language and culture because they have long served just such practical purposes, associated with sharing, distributing, or transacting various commodities. And the various conservations are *embodied* in these concepts, since they refer precisely to those properties which are conserved across particular kinds of transformation.

Conservation concepts can thus be thought of not as transcendent logical entities but as historically elaborated products of certain practical and social purposes (Light 1986; Russell 1978). The conservation of liquids task to which we have made such extensive reference in this chapter, is really neither a matter of logic nor of exact science. When we pour juice from one beaker to another we conveniently forget differential evaporation, or the residues left behind in the 'empty' beaker. We disregard such things because for practical purposes the amounts can be regarded as the same. In this case the 'practical purposes' concern the sharing out of the juice.

In general terms, then, our argument is that in mastering conservation the child's task is to gain access to certain subtle, culturally elaborated abstractions. Although these are embodied in language, they are not 'merely linguistic'. The language that we use cannot readily be sanitized or separated from the practical purposes to which it relates. Language is not just a matter of agreements in meaning, but also of agreements in doing (shared forms of life, in the Wittgensteinian sense). Thus the child's task in mastering conservation concepts is arguably only possible to the extent that he or she is able to share in the purposes and practices to which these concepts relate. We have seen that where children's interpretation of the meaning of the situation is supported in this way, they can often give correct judgements. Rather than worrying too much about the status of these precocious judgements as 'true' indicators of the 'presence' of conservation we should perhaps concentrate on what these modifications of the conservation task have to tell us about the way in which children can be inducted into such socially supported correct performances, which bridge from the familiar to the unfamiliar, from the known to the unknown (cf. Rogoff Chapter 6, this volume).

In this chapter we have reviewed two lines of research on conservation which have been prominent in the last ten or fifteen years. What we have taken from the British and American work of the late 1970s and early 1980s is a concern with interpersonal and discursive cues in the assessment context. What we have taken from the 'continental' work of the same period is a concern with social mechanisms of cognitive change. The more recent work which we have discussed illustrates both the convergence of these two lines of research and the emergence of an alternative conception of *what develops*. Here, in place of a Piagetian focus on cognitive development as a sequence of emerging logical competences, pragmatic, intersubjective agreements-in-meaning are seen as lying at the heart of the developmental process. Such agreements (established in and through the child's day-to-day interpersonal behaviour) are envisaged as both the source and the substance of conservation itself.

Acknowledgements

The author's wish to acknowledge the support of Fondation Fyssen, Paris (P.L.) and the Swiss National Foundation for Scientific Research (FNRS no. 1-738-0.83) (A.-N.P.-C.).

References

Ames, G. and Murray, F. (1982). When two wrongs make a right: promoting cognitive change by social conflict. *Developmental psychology* 18, 894–7.

Carugati, F., De Paolis, P., and Mugny, G. (1979). A paradigm for the study of social interactions in cognitive development. *Italian journal of psychology* 6, 147–55.

Doise, W. (1985). Social regulations in cognitive development. In *Social relationships and cognitive development* (ed. R. Hinde, A. N. Perret-Clermont and J. Stevenson-Hinde). Oxford University Press, Oxford.

Doise, W. and Mugny, G. (1981). *The social development of the intellect*. Pergamon Press, Oxford.

Doise, W., Mugny, G., and Perret-Clermont, A. N. (1975). Social interaction and the development of cognitive operations. *European journal of social psychology* 5, 367–83.

Doise, W., Rijsman, J., Van Meel, J., Bressers, I., and Pinxten, W. (1981). Sociale marketing en cognitieve ontwikkelling. *Pedagogische Studien* 58, 241–8.

Donaldson, M. (1978). *Children's minds*. Fontana, London.

Elbers, E. (1986). Interaction and instruction in the conservation experiment. *European journal of psychology of education* 1, 77-89.

Gessell, A. (1943). *Infant and child in the culture of today*. Harper, New York.

Girotto, V. (1987). Social marking, socio-cognitive conflict and cognitive development. *European journal of social psychology* 17, 171-86.

Glachan, M. and Light, P. (1982). Peer interaction and learning: can two wrongs make a right? In *Social cognition* (ed. G. Butterworth and P. Light). Harvester, Brighton.

Grossen, M. (1988). La construction sociale de l'intersubjectivité entre adulte et enfant en situation de test. Ph.D. thesis, Université de Neuchâtel.

Hargreaves, D., Molloy, C., and Pratt, A. (1982). Social factors in conservation. *British journal of psychology* 73, 231-4.

Hinde, R., Perret-Clermont, A.-N. and Stevenson-Hinde, J. (eds.) (1985). *Social relationships and cognitive development*. Oxford University Press.

Light, P. (1986). Context, conservation and conversation. In *Children of social worlds* (ed. M. P. M. Richards and P. H. Light), pp. 170-90. Polity Press, Cambridge.

Light, P., Buckingham, N., and Robbins, A. (1979). The conservation task as an interactional setting. *British journal of educational psychology* 49, 304-10.

Light, P., Gorsuch, C., and Newman, J. (1987). Why do you ask? Context and communication in the conservation task. *European journal of psychology of education* 2, 73-82.

Mackie, D. (1980). A cross cultural study of intra- and inter-individual conflicts of centrations. *European journal of social psychology* 10, 313-18.

McGarrigle, J. and Donaldson, M. (1975). Conservation accidents. *Cognition* 3, 341-50.

Mead, G. H. (1934). *Mind, self and society*. University of Chicago Press, Chicago.

Miller, S. (1982) On the generalisability of conservation. *British journal of psychology* 73, 221-30.

Mugny, G., Perret-Clermont, A.-N., and Doise, W. (1981). Interpersonal coordinations and sociological differences in the construction of the intellect. In *Progress in applied social psychology, vol. 1* (eds. G. Stephenson and J. Davis). Wiley, Chichester.

Nicolet, M. and Iannaconne, A. Norme sociale d'équité et contexte relationnel dans l'étude du marquage social. In *Interagir et connaitre* (eds. A.-N. Perret-Clermont and M. Nicolet). Peter Lang, Berne (in press).

Perner, J., Leekam, S., and Wimmer, H. (1984). The insincerity of conservation questions. Paper presented to B.P.S. Development Section Annual Conference, Lancaster, September, 1984.

Perret-Clermont, A.-N. (1976). L'interaction sociale comme facteur du développement cognitif. Doctoral thesis, University of Geneva.

Perret-Clermont, A.-N. (1980). *Social interaction and cognitive development in children*. Academic Press, London.

Perret-Clermont, A.-N. and Brossard, A. (1985). On the interdigitation of social and cognitive processes. In *Social relationships and cognitive development* (eds. R. Hinde, A.-N. Perret-Clermont, and J. Stevenson-Hinde). Oxford University Press.

Perret-Clermont, A.-N. and Mugny, G. (1985). Effets sociologiques et processes didactiques. *Psychologie sociale du développement cognitif* (ed. G. Mugny). P. Lang, Bern.

Perret-Clermont, A.-N. and Schubauer-Leoni, M. (1981). Conflict and cooperation as opportunities for learning. In *Communication in development* (ed. W. P. Robinson). Academic Press, London.

Piaget, J. (1932). *The moral judgement of the child*. Routledge and Kegan Paul, London.

Piaget, J. (1968). *Six psychological studies*. University of London Press, London.

Rijsman, J., Zoetebier, A., Ginther, A., and Doise, W. (1980). Sociocognitief conflict en cognitieve ontwikkeling. *Pedagogische Studien* **57**, 125–33.

Roux, J.-P. and Gilly, M. (1984). Aide apportée par le marquage social dans une procedure de résolution chez des enfants de 12–13 ans. *Bulletin de psychologie* **38**, 145–55.

Rose, S. and Blank, M. (1974). The potency of context in children's cognition. *Child development* **45**, 499–502.

Russell, J. (1978). *The acquisition of knowledge*. Macmillan, London.

Samuel, J. and Bryant, P. (1984). Asking only one question in the conservation experiment. *Journal of child psychology and psychiatry* **25**, 315–18.

Vygotsky, L. (1934/1962). *Thought and language*. MIT Press, Cambridge, MA.

Zhou, R. (1987). Marquage social, conduites de partage et construction de la notion de conservation. Unpublished PhD thesis, University of Provence, Aix-en-Provence.

8

The myth of cognitive diagnostics
ANGUS GELLATLY

Introduction

In this chapter I attempt to do four things. First, the term *cognitive diagnosis*, which is associated with studies of cognitive development, will be explained. Second, it will be shown that the fundamental ideas associated with the notion of diagnosis are essentially those which Johnson-Laird (1982, 1983) has dubbed the 'mental logic' view of reasoning, and share the same shortcomings. Third, I will claim that the very notion of cognitive diagnosis rests upon a misperception of the nature of medical diagnosis, and that it is, in fact, a myth. Fourth, I will argue that although shortcomings in the notion of cognitive diagnosis (mental logic) have been frequently pointed out, the myth still flourishes in many areas of psychology; it appears to have an insidious grip upon much of our thinking. For this reason and in order to reveal the nature of the myth and its many, often subtle, manifestations, reference will be made to and examples drawn from a variety of research topics within cognitive psychology.

These four aims, then, provide the principal segmentation of the chapter. However, before proceeding with the argument proper, two points are worth making about the way in which the cognitive versus social dichotomy enters into the present concerns.

The first of these is that the notion of cognitive diagnostics is rooted in a wholly individualistic tradition of thought. In this tradition, each child is thought to rediscover, or reconstruct, the knowledge of his or her culture. Sometimes the child is explicitly likened to a scientist building theories on the basis of experience; but in this case the image is always that of a lone scientist rather than that of a person socialized into a scientific community (cf. Kuhn 1962; Barnes 1982). Congruent with this imagery of isolated individuals is the habit of explaining cognitive performances as deriving from endogenous competence or ability, or the individual understanding of certain principles or rules. Cognitive development is seen as the acquisition not of concrete practices but of abstractions. On the basis of a particular performance a competence, or understanding of a rule, is attributed to the individual, and this is then taken to be the *cause* or *explanation* of the original performance. In the present chapter it will be urged that this approach to individual cognition is in error (*see also* the chapters by D'Andrade and by Light and Perret-Clermont in this volume). The line of argument to be pursued is that acceptance of the myth of cognitive diagnosis leads us to mistake concepts elaborated in talk — linguistic practices that are social constructions — for mechanisms of individual cognition. The result is that the concepts then come to be located in, or to be attributed to, individual people. More specifically, particular social practices that have been learnt in connection with, for example, problem solving, inference-making, or counting are confused with abstract principles that can, but need not be, used to characterize those practices. The myth of cognitive diagnosis, it will be argued, both sustains and is sustained by the individualistic approach to cognition.

The second point to be noted is that much of what follows has been influenced by the writings of sociologists of knowledge (such as Barnes 1982; Barnes and Edge 1982; Bloor 1976, 1983; Collins 1985; Pinch 1985). Their emphasis on the negotiability of the meaning of experimental results and, more especially, on the role of collective practices in the application of concepts and rules can provide a much-needed antidote to the individualistic tendencies so prevalent in much of cognitive psychology.

Cognitive diagnosis

The actual term 'cognitive diagnosis' is associated with the Piagetian literature on development, although as we will see the same basic idea recurs in a variety of research contexts. Ideally, the classic Piagetian tests of cognitive development were supposed to be diagnostic of cognitive structures that purportedly underlie — and, in some sense, generate — cognitive performances. Tests were supposed to diagnose transitivity, reversibility, a grasp of one-to-one correspondence, and so on. Successful performance on a test was intended to be indicative of the subject *having* the corresponding cognitive structure. In practice, however, it turned out that the diagnosticity of any particular test might have to be hedged as theorists found a need to invoke contrasts between, for example, true conservation and pseudo-conservation. In other words, a subject might pass one particular test of conservation yet still be judged not to have achieved true conservation because of failure on a different test.

Almost from the start, then, the Piagetian criteria of diagnosis were blurred. In recent years, this fuzziness has become increasingly noticeable, and indeed the diagnostic status of the classical Piagetian tests has been strongly challenged. Transitivity, conservation, and a grasp of one-to-one correspondence have all been claimed, on the basis of other evidence, for pre-operational children who generally fail the classical tests (e.g. Bryant and Trabasso 1971; McGarrigle and Donaldson 1974; Gelman 1978).

A point to notice about these developments is that despite the challenge to the diagnostic status of the original tests, the notion of diagnosis itself has often been retained. Frequently all that changes is that attributions of competence come to be made to much younger children, competences continuing to be located within individuals. For example, Gelman (1978, 1982) sees development as the child increasingly gaining access to an (in some sense) internal competence, with the result that it can be made manifest in a wider and wider range of circumstances. (We will return to this point later.) Similarly, Flavell (1985) devotes several pages of his book to the problems and complexities of cognitive diagnosis and to its supposed theoretical and educational implications. He concludes his discussion of the topic by stating: 'Finally, diagnosis is central to all psychological study, cognitive development or other'.

My own view is that Flavell's statement is absolutely correct as a representation of contemporary cognitive psychology; terminology may vary, but cognitive diagnosis *is* taken to be central to most areas of cognitive research. I shall argue that this is always a mistake. For the moment, however, I want to restrict the argument to the domain of cognitive development.

What we have seen in the last ten to fifteen years are three related responses to perceived shortcomings in the classical Piagetian tests viewed as diagnostic tools.

(1) A first response, associated for instance with Donaldson (1978), has been to stress the importance of the experiment as a social interaction. Initially emphasis was restricted to the manner in which social context influences the expression of a child's putative competences. Children were found to be more likely to give conserving responses following an 'accidental' transformation of one of two equal quantities than following an intentional transformation by the experimenter. The interpretation was that children responded to the whole behaviour, not simply to the crucial conservation question. Here the basic assumption was retained of competences residing within the individual and waiting to be diagnosed; only the sensitivity of the experimental test was queried.

Subsequently, however, the idea has begun to gain ground that social interaction does not simply facilitate or inhibit the expression of competences but is itself in some sense constitutive of them (*see* Light and Perret-Clermont, this volume). This latter is a conception that fits well with the views expressed in the present chapter.

(2) A second, and more prevalent, response to shortcomings in Piagetian diagnostics is associated with such persons as Bryant and Trabasso (1971; Trabasso, 1975), Gelman (1978; Gelman and Baillargeon, 1983), and others. This also involved the seeking out of more sensitive diagnostic tests to replace the classical tests, but the view was that social context is only one of many factors that may influence the expression of a competence, and the emphasis

has tended to be on information processing factors such as memory limitations. Once again, however, the idea was retained of competences residing within, awaiting expression and diagnosis. Which is not to deny that this second type of response also led to the questioning of what it might mean for an individual to *have* a competence or a rule. The lengthy deliberations of Flavell (1985) or Greeno, Riley and Gelman (1984) demonstrate this questioning. In some cases, indeed, questioning of just this sort resulted in yet a third response to the problems of diagnosis.

(3) The third response has been that of such people as Klahr and Wallace (1976) and of Siegler (1976, 1986), who have rejected the notions of diagnosis and competences in favour of production system or flow chart representations of decision procedures. This also is a position with which the views expressed in the present chapter are very much in sympathy. However, as will be illustrated later, even proponents of this approach to modelling cognition are prone to slip back unwittingly into thinking in terms of cognitive diagnostics.

The first of my four aims, to explain the meaning of cognitive diagnostics, has now been fulfilled. Along the way I have described how challenges to the diagnostic status of the classical Piagetian tests have led to a variety of theoretical responses; these have included questioning, and even rejection, of the notion of cognitive diagnosis, yet the notion still persists within the field of cognitive development.

The debate over mental logic

In this section I shall pursue the second of my aims, which is to show that, despite terminological differences, the basic ideas associated with the notion of diagnosis are not restricted to the field of cognitive development but can be found in theorizing in the rather different area of adult reasoning. My exposition will be a brief one and will draw heavily on Johnson-Laird's (1982, 1983) attempt to purge the psychology of reasoning of this fallacious thinking, which he refers to as the 'doctrine of mental logic'. By broadening the scope of the investigation it will also be possible to bring out features of the diagnostic/mental logic approach which show it to be based on a general misconception about the nature of cognition.

The doctrine of mental logic

There is a venerable debate as to whether formal logic is *descriptive* of cognitive processes of reasoning or whether it is merely *prescriptive* of what is deemed to constitute sound reasoning. The doctrine of mental logic, so dubbed by Johnson-Laird (1982, 1983), represents the former of these two views. It asserts that there is a logic of the mind that guides human reasoning, mentation that is not so guided failing to count as reasoning.

The mental logic account of reasoning has been explicitly espoused by Kant and by Boole, by Piaget (1953), and more recently by Braine and Roumain (1983), Rips (1986), Fodor (1980, 1983), and Henle (1962, 1981). As previously indicated, it crops up also in the writing of developmentalists such as Gelman (1978; Gelman and Baillargeon, 1983; Greeno, Riley, and Gelman, 1984) and Flavell (1985).

One way to see if people of differing ages, cultures, and education are possessed of a common mental logic is to set them formal problems such as syllogisms. If this is done, 'errors' in performance are very soon observed. It turns out that the likelihood of 'correct' responses is a function of number of years of formal schooling. However, mental logicians need not and do not take these findings as evidence against the existence of a universal mental logic. They rightly infer that the task as tackled by less schooled or unschooled (and sometimes by heavily schooled) subjects differs from the task intended by the experimenter. Both Henle (1962), who explicitly subscribes to the doctrine, and Scribner (1977), who does not, argue that 'incorrect' responses are to be explained as failure to remember premises, the importation or illicit conversion of premises, or refusal to accept the intended task. If the actual reasoning of subjects is examined, so the claim goes, it is found never to flout logic.

For mental logicians the next move in the argument is to posit an underlying mental logic (or competence) which can be masked by performance factors like those identified above. Evidence for a mental logic is adduced not only from reconstructions of reasoning on formal problems but also from everyday conversation and behaviour, and from examination of the psycholinguistics of logical connectives. For example, from the fact that people tend to paraphrase 'Get out of my way or I'll hit you' as 'if you don't get out of my way, I'll hit you' it has been argued that they have logical schemata for both OR and IF–THEN, and that they understand the logical relationship between the two (Braine and Roumain 1983). Without schemata, it is said, it would be impossible to comprehend statements containing the connectives. Similarly, the existence of an OR schema might be adduced from the exchange: 'Would you like tea or coffee?'; 'Not tea'; 'Here you are then, a cup of coffee'.

What the mental logician does is to cite a performance that can be judged to have the form of a particular schema, then attribute to the individual a representation of the schema which is then held to explain the original performance. This is obviously a circular procedure. Refutation is impossible because failure to exhibit schema-consistent behaviour when it might be expected can always be explained as some kind of performance failure rather than as lack of competence.

Some objections to the doctrine

While the task-as-understood account of 'incorrect' responses to formal problems is readily acceptable, the move from there to the positing of a mental logic is much less so. Mental logicians face the problem of how to determine in a principled fashion which behaviours require the invoking of a mental schema and which are to be dismissed as only logic-like; that is, having the appearance of logic while not in fact being based on logical processing. As mentioned previously, difficulties of this kind have been common in connection with studies of conservation and transitivity. Piagetians have often argued that when pre-operational children succeed on conservation or transitivity tests they must have made use of sub-logical processes such as memorization, guess-work, or labelling (e.g. Youniss and Furth 1973; Halford 1984). The problem is that such claims are *post hoc* and are motivated by the need to protect Piaget's theory from refutation. The following example illustrates some of the difficulties consequent upon this kind of reasoning.

Suppose an adult human learns that a goal, G, may be reached by either of two routes A and B. On subsequent occasions one of the routes is blocked and the subject is observed always to follow the other. On a mental logic account this might well be acceptable as evidence for an OR schema that guides behaviour; it seems directly comparable to the example above concerning the choice of tea and coffee. But now suppose that, instead of a human, a rat is taught to reach a goal box by running down either of two alleyways. When, on future trials, one of the alleyways is blocked the rat runs down the other. Is this now evidence for the rat having a mental schema for disjunction? More radically, suppose a rubber ball is propelled along a Y-maze, one or other arm of which is blocked on every trial. Would we then have reason to attribute a disjunctive schema to the ball?

The purpose of the example is not to argue that the behaviours of ball, rat, and human must be explained in terms of the same mechanisms simply because they can be characterized in terms of a certain resemblance. The point to be grasped is that it is a fallacy to attribute a schema, rule, or competence to an individual on the basis of a performance which happens to be characterizable in terms of that schema, rule, or competence. The example makes the fallacy transparent because there can be no *principled* reason for attributing the disjunctive schema to the human which does not equally apply to the rat and the ball. And while some might be happy to grant logical schemata to rats, surely no one would wish to do so for balls.

At this juncture it is tempting to enter into a discussion of the way in which resemblances and characterizations are created, a topic that has been examined by sociologists of knowledge (Barnes 1982; Bloor 1983). Such a digression is not, unfortunately, allowable in the present context. Instead we shall have to settle for accepting that logical schemata, or inference patterns, are part of our way of talking about things, not part of the cognitive processes of reasoning. Diagnosing schemata, rules, or competences on the basis of performance is simply wrong-headed (*see* Gellatly 1988 for a more detailed discussion).

Reasoning with mental models

If reasoning does not consist in the application of a mental logic, how is it achieved? The answer given by Johnson-Laird (1982, 1983) is mainly in terms of mental models.

Johnson-Laird allows, in fact, that people may engage in what is called truth-functional reasoning (Johnson-Laird 1983; Gellatly 1988). He argues, however, that where possible they prefer to reason through the construction and manipulation of mental models that represent important features of the relevant problem domain. The theory has been worked out in most detail for the case of syllogistic reasoning, and has even been implemented as a computer programme that solves syllogisms. My intention here is to give just a flavour of the theory by providing a rough description of how the theory applies to a single syllogistic problem. The aim is simply to ;demonstrate the possibility of alternatives to a mental logic account of reasoning.

Consider what conclusion may validly be derived from the following pair of premisses:

(1) None of the artists is a beekeeper
    All of the beekeepers are clerks

One way of proceeding is to imagine a number of actors in a room, all wearing one or more hats. Each hat is marked with one of the letters A, B, or C. To model the first premiss two distinct groups of people must be kept separate:

(2) artist
    artist
....
    beekeeper
    beekeeper

The next step is to extend the representation also to include interpretation of the second premiss. All individuals who are acting as beekeepers must be free to wear a clerk's hat also, but allowance must be made for the possible existence of clerks who are not beekeepers, indicated by the parentheses in the following representation, or model.

(3) artist
    artist
....
    beekeeper = clerk
    beekeeper = clerk
              (clerk)

Four possible conclusions relating artists and clerks may be read off this representation. These conclusions are: 'None of the artists is a clerk';

'None of the clerks is an artist'; 'Some of the artists are not clerks'; 'Some of the clerks are not artists'. However, to be sure that these candidate conclusions are in fact valid it is necessary to search for alternative models of the premisses that might render some or all of the conclusions false. For (1), though not for all syllogisms, a second model happens to be possible:

(4) artist
    artist = clerk
....
      beekeeper = clerk
      beekeeper = clerk

This model shows that the first two candidate conclusions from (3) are unwarranted, but it leaves both 'some of the artists are not clerks' and 'some of the clerks are not artists' as putative conclusions. Yet once again it is necessary to search for possible counter-examples. And, it happens, a third model consistent with the premisses of (1) is also possible:

(5) artist = clerk
    artist = clerk
....
      beekeeper = clerk
      beekeeper = clerk

This model excludes all conclusions except 'some of the clerks are not artists'; provided only that the class of beekeepers is assumed not to be an empty one.

Johnson-Laird proposes that people solve categorical syllogisms in something like this manner. Not by applying inference rules but by setting up models in which individual items are represented by tokens, by deriving potential conclusions, and by then seeking to falsify these. The idea of imaging actors with hats on provides one concrete illustration of how this might be done, but what counts in the theory is that the relational structure of a mental model matches that of the problem to be solved. The theory makes predictions about the relative difficulty of all possible categorical syllogisms depending upon whether the premisses permit of one, two, or three models. Because of increased load on working memory, more errors are expected the greater the number of possible models. These and other detailed predictions of the theory have been strongly supported by Johnson-Laird and Steedman (1978), Johnson-Laird and Bara (1984), and Johnson-Laird, Oakhill, and Bull (1986).

My purpose here has not been to give a detailed exposition of the theory of mental models but only to indicate how reasoning can occur without the application of inference rules. As it happens, many of the steps executed by Johnson-Laird's computer programme are in conformity with particular inference rules, or inference schemata. Indeed, mental logicians like Braine and Roumain (1983) criticize the notion of reasoning without rules or schemata by pointing to such instances; the schemata, they say, have been smuggled through the back door. But the point to be emphasized here is that although what the programme *does* can be characterized in terms of schemata, it does not *use* schemata or rules to carry out its procedures. We have arrived back at the circular argument, so dear to proponents of mental logic and cognitive diagnosis, whereby one goes from examples of behaviour that instantiate a particular schema to attribution of the schema to the individual (or programme). But, as we have seen, on this basis it becomes difficult to avoid attributing schemata to rats and rubber balls.

Attributions of competence: a social process

The notions of cognitive diagnosis and of mental logic refer to what are, for almost all intents and purposes, the same set of ideas. It is not surprising, therefore, that they tend to provoke the same structure of debate. In the former instance, dispute has centred on the diagnosticity of tests. For example, why should a child be attributed with the ability to conserve only if he or she passes the traditional Piagetian test rather than a test involving an 'accidental' transformation of the quantity to be conserved? Similarly, why attribute class inclusion to the child who can successfully compare the class of wooden beads to its sub-classes of brown and white beads, but not to the much younger child who succeeds only on the analogous task employing different materials, for example children versus boys and girls (Piaget 1952; Trabasso, Isen, Dolecki, McLanahan, Riley, and Tucker 1978)? A close parallel to this argument is provided for mental logic and reasoning by the examples cited earlier of the human, the rat, and the ball. Why attribute logical schema in one case but not others?

Elsewhere I have argued that attributions of competences such as conservation, class-inclusion, or transitivity can never be based solely on empirical criteria (Gellatly in press). Such attributions cannot but be theoretically motivated; they are tied in with the particular purposes of those party to the decision, and they acquire force only to the extent that a consensus prevails. The same claim has also been made for the identification of what shall count as an inference, and for the attribution of inference-making ability (Gellatly 1987, 1988). It is suggested that whether rats, or pre-operational children, make inferences is not an issue to be settled empirically but a matter of convention to be settled amongst interested parties.

If these arguments are accepted they could appear to reflect poorly on the enterprise of cognitive psychology, for it might be felt that a discipline worth its salt should be able to establish absolute diagnostic, or attributional, criteria. In the next section I will try to show that this gloomy conclusion need not follow. This will be done by fulfilling my third aim, that of showing that the notion of cognitive diagnosis (or the attribution of competences) rests upon a misconception of the nature of medical diagnosis. The argument will be that diagnostic criteria in medicine are no less dependent upon convention than are diagnostic criteria in cognitive psychology.

The nature of medical diagnosis

To make the argument of this section I shall draw extensively on Ludwig Fleck's (1979) book, *The genesis and development of a scientific fact.*

Though only translated into English in 1979, Fleck's book was first published in 1935. Fleck was a microbiologist specializing in bacteriology, and his book deals with the emergence of the modern concept of the disease entity, *syphilis.* The idea of the disease can be traced back to the fifteenth century. It emerged at that time from a variety of beliefs and facts about chronic illnesses and skin complaints, but its boundaries, nomenclature, and symptomatology remained highly unstable. The early idea of the disease subsumed a range of what are now considered to be very different conditions, including leprosy, smallpox, gonorrhoea, soft chancre, and tuberculosis, amongst others. With hindsight, it readily can be understood why treatment outcomes were unpredictable, given that some of these conditions respond to, for example, mercury compounds, whilst others do not. Additionally, the theoretical framework for understanding the disease was provided by theology and astrology, outbreaks of the disease being thought to be linked with the ascendancy of Saturn and Mars.

The theoretical position remained extremely confused throughout the eighteenth and nineteenth centuries, yet there was a continual search for a single common factor. The search was concentrated on the 'befouled' blood of the syphilitic, a notion that itself derived from the ancient theory of humours. Many claims as to the specific character of syphilitic blood were made and repudiated. Eventually, in the first decade of the twentieth century, came the identification of *Spirochaeta pallida* and the suggestion that this was the causative agent in the disease. The concept of the disease became organized around the discovery, and detection of the spirochaete became the criterion for the diagnosis of syphilis. It appeared that order and understanding had been imposed upon the previous theoretical chaos.

Fleck's book was written, however, to show that the story did not end at this neat conclusion. Complications soom became apparent, simplicity gave way once more to complexity. Carriers of the spirochaete were discovered who had not developed the clinical disease. Then there was room for debate as to whether *S. pallida* was a cause or a symptom of syphilis, and with the development of the science of bacteriology it became clear that no disease could be understood solely by reference to a single 'causative agent'. The clinical condition itself was later subject to further differentiation. The identification and classification of spirochaetes also proved problematic. For instance, *S. pallida* could only be distinguished from other classes of spirochaete through the use of animal tests and, in practice, not always then because of failures of experimental cultures and innoculations. Yet this meant the disease was being used to define *S. pallida*, rather than the reverse. Fleck concluded that the concepts of the disease and of its diagnosis were still evolving, and that they would continue to do so. There could be no natural stopping place because developments in a variety of interrelated fields of research might lead to conceptual adjustments.

Bloor (1983) argues that in this respect there is nothing exceptional about the disease concept of syphilis. The same picture of an oscillation between apparent theoretical simplicity and apparent theoretical complexity can be observed in the development of any scientific concept. For present purposes, however, Fleck's history is especially instructive because of the emphasis on diagnosis. Its impact is reinforced because a modern parallel that comes readily to mind is the currently evolving concept of AIDS. Once again there are carriers who have not developed the clinical syndrome; tests are not wholly reliable; at least two viruses are implicated, and these are associated with different prognoses; ideas about mechanisms of transmission have altered sharply within a few years and remain the subject of heated debate, and so on.

With AIDS the relativity of diagnostic criteria is also singularly transparent. For the clinician, on the one hand, clinical symptoms are likely to weigh as heavily as, or even more heavily than, blood tests as diagnostic signs. For potential sex partners, on the other hand, as well as for insurance companies, a positive blood test result may be as immediately significant as any clinical symptom. (Indeed, the legal and political implications of using blood tests as a diagnostic criterion are being bitterly contested.) Finally, for epidemiologists all kinds of diagnostic sign are likely to be relevant.

What these examples show us is that the diagnosis of disease is not an absolute matter; criteria change over time and they are dependent on the interests of those who make the diagnosis. The definition and diagnosis of disease rests on a network of theoretical distinctions in a variety of medical disciplines; it is influenced by legal and political interests and by factors such as the cost and availability of diagnostic tests and the purpose for which the diagnosis is made. In drawing our attention to the relativity of diagnostic criteria in medicine, Fleck reveals the tangle of theoretical complexities underlying them. These complexities have usually been obscured for two main reasons, the first of which is epistemological. The usual expectation of scientific facts and concepts has been that they should display stability and finality. It is just because disease entities and diagnostic criteria have been assumed stable, as a matter of course, that their shifting bases did not attract attention. As Kuhn notes in his introduction to the translation of Fleck's book, the very title, with its stress on the scientific fact as something which evolves, constituted a direct challenge to epistemological orthodoxy. And it is this which probably explains the long period of neglect through which it passed. The second reason for the obscuring of the complexities that underpin diagnostic criteria resides in the fact that in medical diagnosis the emphasis is at least as much practical as it is theoretical. For most people for most of the time what counts is the efficacy of the diagnosis, not the neatness and consistency of its theoretical base.

In cognitive psychology, by contrast, the focus of interest in diagnosis is overwhelmingly theoretical rather than practical, possible educational implications notwithstanding. It should come as no surprise then, following what we have seen of Fleck's analysis, that the diagnosis of cognitive competences cannot be grounded on absolute criteria, nor that one and the same test may be accorded different diagnostic status within different theoretical frameworks. It is in this sense, of absolute criteria, that cognitive diagnosis is, and will always remain, a myth.

The ubiquity of notions of mental logic and cognitive diagnosis

By this juncture in the argument a number of readers have probably grown restless. They may feel like throwing up their hands and protesting: 'Surely nobody really means that rules or schemata guide or generate behaviour in the sense which the author has been suggesting. All that people mean when they talk about rule-governed behaviour is that the behavioural output conforms to the rules, or the schemata'.

My account of the debates over cognitive diagnosis and over the doctrine of mental logic should have made it clear that such protests are mistaken. Many psychologists either believe explicitly, or else assume implicitly, that rules can guide behaviour. In fact, some of the most explicit statements of the view that behaviour may be rule-governed, rather than simply rule-conforming, have been made in connection with psycholinguistics (e.g. Chomsky 1965, 1980). Stabler (1983) has explicitly raised the issue in connection with psycholinguistics, and the statements of Rumelhart and McClelland (1985, 1987), on the one hand, and Pinker (1987; Pinker and Prince 1988), on the other, are clear evidence that radically opposed views continue to be held. Yet even if we eschew the debate in psycholinguistics, as lack of expertise forces me to do, examples of theorists appealing to the guiding function of rules, or principles, are only too easily discovered in other areas of cognitive psychology. They appear with varying degrees of explicitness in, for example, the writings of Braine and Rumain (1983), Flavell (1985), Fodor (1980, 1983), Henle (1962, 1981), Gelman and Baillargeon (1983), Greeno, Riley, and Gelman (1984), and Rips (1983; 1986).

An insidious feature of the notion of mental logic is that it tends to creep back into our thinking, even into the thinking of those who explicitly decry it. An example is to be found in Siegler (1986). Although not referring to it in those terms, Siegler explicitly disavows cognitive diagnosis. In his well-known studies of children's performance on balance scale problems, Siegler (1976) observed a developmental sequence such that children's reasoning about the problems could be characterized in terms of a succession of rules, with older children conforming with the more advanced rules. Siegler (1976, 1986) is very clear that these rules, expressed as a decision tree, provide a language for *representing* what children do but that the rules do not *guide* the behaviour. Yet, despite his explicit disavowal, Siegler sometimes slips into writing as though rules are internally represented.

Like Piaget, Siegler found in a range of tasks that children tend to fixate on a single dimension of an unfamiliar problem, as they do with weight on balance scale problems, or height in conservation of volume tests. Siegler (1986) points out that this does not mean children are incapable of considering more than a single problem dimension because in speaking they simultaneously take account of pronunciation, sentence formation, how to convey a desired meaning, how loudly they need to talk, and so on. Siegler suggests that speaking is a familiar task whereas typical laboratory tasks are unfamiliar. He proposes that children have a fall-back rule for unfamiliar tasks for which they lack detailed solution procedures. Siegler suggests the fall-back rule: 'If you lack direct information about how to solve a problem in which you need to judge which object has more x, then focus on a single seemingly most important dimension and choose the object with more of that dimension as having more x'. He goes on to say that: 'Conceptualizing 5-year-olds' one-dimensional problem solving strategies as reflecting such a fall-back rule suggests why children focus on a single dimension in some but not all situations'.

Now what is abundantly clear is that this rule is Siegler's rule; it is not a rule operated by young children. Children do not fixate on a single dimension because they have a rule that tells them to do so. Rather, it is because they tend to fixate on a single dimension of unfamiliar problems that Siegler is able to formulate a rule which characterizes their behaviour. The rule is not inside the individual children, it is part of our way of talking about what they do. The *causes* of this type of behaviour remain to be formulated, perhaps in terms of unfamiliar problems inducing heightened arousal that results in attentional rigidity.

The use of this example is not intended in any way as a denigration of Siegler, merely as a demonstration of how easy it is to slip into thinking in individualistic terms, into falling again for the myth of cognitive diagnosis. In Siegler's case this may amount to little more than an unfortunate style of expression, however, the debates over logic and reasoning and over the diagnosis of children's competences illustrate that the habit of thought can go very much deeper. In the remaining section of the chapter I shall document this fact with respect to Gelman's writings on children's understanding of number, particularly the understanding of the principle of one-to-one correspondence.

Understanding number

Piaget argued that pre-operational children did not *have*, or *understand*, the principles of number — including the principle of one-to-one correspondence. The basis of his assertion was their failure on number conservation, seriation, and class-inclusion tests. The occasionally observed counting behaviours of pre-school children were said to reflect no more than rote performance of a procedure involving recitation of a string of number names together with co-ordinated tagging of objects.

Gelman and Gallistel (1978) argued, however, that the performance of young children on a variety of counting tasks showed that they had, 'an implicit understanding of counting principles, which guides performance in counting as well as in the acquisition of skill in applying the counting procedure'. The principles they referred to were those of:

(1) One-to-one correspondence
(2) Cardinality
(3) Stable order
(4) Abstraction
(5) Order irrelevance

Gelman and Gallistel claimed that young children's counting behaviours do demonstrate implicit understanding of the one-to-one principle because:

(a) in counting they tag every item with only a single number word,

(b) they can adapt to unusual demands, like making the second item from the left in a line 'one',

(c) they correct errors of double counting or omission made by a puppet. The claim, it should be noted, is not simply that performance is *consistent* with the one-to-one principle but that it reflects an *implicit understanding* of the principle. It should be clear that what we see here is one more example of the same debate that always develops around questions of cognitive diagnosis. Piaget, for his own purposes, adopted conservative diagnostic criteria. Gelman and Gallistel, by contrast, opt for more liberal criteria and can report behaviours of young children which they are able to characterize in terms of the principles that interest them.

Greeno, Riley, and Gelman (1984) pursued the topic further in a paper which contains some very bald statements of a notion of mental logic. They argue that as a child's understanding of the one-to-one principle improves it becomes more explicit: not in the sense of being verbalizable, but in the sense that it increasingly underlies what the child does. They develop a model in which 'the counting principles are specified explicitly and *give rise* to suitable procedures that are consistent with the principles' (p. 96, italics added). They also say, 'To characterize . . . counting principles, we need to postulate a knowledge structure in which the principles appear in [more] explicit form' (p. 99), and 'The claim that children have this competence says that they have mental representations of the principles characterized in the analysis, and *the principles are used* in the children's thought and behaviour' (p. 138, italics added).

Greeno *et al.* have many interesting things to say about number, or counting, competence. It would be possible to quote sections of their article in which they seem almost to refute the notion of mental logic. Yet the tendency to think in terms of a mental logic obviously persists strongly and leads them to develop an implementable model of counting in which explicit principles are employed. These explicit principles have the same status as the putative mental schemata of Braine and Rumain (1983) or Rips (1983).

In discussing cognitive development in general, Greeno, Riley, and Gelman (1984) suggest that it consists of the individual acquiring increasing accessibility to, and explicit understanding of, conceptual structures that are initially implicit. This formulation, which they take from Rozin (1976), is a strong form of the notion of mental logic. The supposition that the development of counting skills consists in the elaboration of increasingly explicit principles of counting, for example one-to-one correspondence, is open to at least three objections. The first of these, already rehearsed repeatedly in the present chapter, concerns the problem of explaining behaviour in terms of hypothetical cognitive structures. The second, also familiar, pertains to the mistaking of social practices for mechanisms of individual cognition. The third relates to the assumption that principles can somehow define their own future applications.

The first objection can be illustrated as follows. Gelman and Gallistel (1978) formulate the principle of one-to-one correspondence as: 'Assign one, and only one, number to each object in the set to be counted'. As the statement of a principle, this seems reasonable enough. It is analogous to the statement of a logical rule, or schema, of the type: 'Given the premises "If p then q" and "p", conclude "q".' Without doubt one can observe many instances of people behaving in accordance with the one-to-one principle, just as one can for the logical rule. The difficulty lies in moving to the assertion that the principle, or the logical rule, in some sense *guided* the behaviours. The argument is inevitably circular because the principle and the rule were both induced in the first place from observations of what have been judged to be paradigmatic instances of counting and inference making. Essentially we are back at the problem of the rat and the rubber ball. Indeed, a parallel example can be given. For Gelman and Gallistel's five counting principles can all be said to be observed in the mechanical counting of, for example,

a turnstile 'clicker'. The clicker undoubtedly exhibits one-to-one correspondence, stable order, and cardinality. Since it is oblivious to the nature
of the items going through the turnstile, and equally to the order in which
they go through, it also exhibits abstraction and order irrelevance. Yet
surely no one would say the clicker was 'guided' by the principles. It has,
rather, been designed to exemplify them.

The second objection to an accessing account of the development of
enumerative skills is that, with its individualistic bias, it totally misses the
component of socialization. Children neither invent, nor give birth to, the
counting principles for themselves. They are taught and encouraged to
enumerate. 'Look! One doggy, two doggies, *three* doggies!' Counting, or
enumeration, was never something invented by a lone individual confronting
a pile of pebbles, nor has it ever been the making overt of existing but covert
cognitive processes. It must surely have developed as a social practice,
elaborated over time by people in interaction with one another, people with
rituals to perform and accounts to keep. As with the cooking of food or the
husbandry of animals, the universality of counting practices is a sign of their
utility, not of their being somehow immanent within each child. Children
learn to count not by coming to represent the five principles to themselves
but by being taught 'That's how we do it'.

As stated above, the third objection to the accessing account of the
development of counting skills has to do with the assumption that principles
can somehow define their own future applications; it also calls attention to
the dangerous habit of confusing the social with the individual.

Consider an average Western adult, skilled at counting and even able to
quote Gelman and Gallistel's formulation of one-to-one correspondence but
not a mathematician. Now suppose the question is asked: 'Are there more
whole numbers or more even numbers'?. It would be wholly reasonable to
assimilate this problem to the principle of class inclusion and to conclude
that there are more whole numbers. Mathematicians have decided, however,
that the question is to be answered with reference to one-to-one correspondence. Indeed, a system is defined as infinite when the whole of the
set can be put into one-to-one correspondence with part of the set. What
this example shows us is that the occasion for invoking a particular principle
is not self-evident but a matter of accepted social practice. It would make
little sense to claim that our non-mathematician, who answered there are more
whole numbers than even numbers, had a less explicit or accessible understanding of one-to-one correspondence than a mathematician familiar with
this example. Yet this is precisely the kind of argument offered by mental
logicians in the case of children who engage in counting behaviours but who
fail the standard Piagetian test of one-to-one correspondence. Gelman and
her associates follow Rozin (1976) in proposing that the young child has an
implicit sense of the one-to-one principle and that this becomes more explicit,

or accessible, in the course of cognitive development. And exactly the same argument has been made by Piagetians in regard to implicit and explicit transitivity (Gellatly 1987). Yet what our example demonstrates is that individuals do not elaborate, or get greater access to, principles; rather, they learn accepted social practices. They discover what is the accepted way of proceeding in particular circumstances and, maybe, what principles to invoke as justification (Barnes 1982; Bloor 1983).

Despite all of this, a mental logician such as Rozin or Gelman might claim that the learning of more and more accepted practices in which a principle can be descried is precisely what increased access, or increased explicitness, consists in. But in this case it would be hard to see what is gained by positing mentally represented principles over and above the learning of the accepted practices themselves. This is just another case of cognitive diagnosis. As usual, there are no grounds for claiming that behaviour is *controlled* by the principles supposedly being diagnosed; rather, the behaviour instantiates, or can be characterized by, the principles. It is only the myth of cognitive diagnosis that sustains such claims and causes us to postulate ghostly rules and principles in the machine.

Summary

In this chapter I have attempted to deconstruct the myth of cognitive diagnosis. It has been my contention that the myth has a wide currency in cognitive psychology, that it readily insinuates itself into much of our thinking. In some guises the fallacy on which it rests is easily spotted and repudiated, yet when it presents itself in other forms there can be total failure of recognition. It seems that the habit of mistaking social conventions or classifications for attributes of the individual mind is one to which psychologists—and perhaps all people—are peculiarly prone. Attempts to identify individual qualities of intelligence or creativity follow the same pattern (*see* Weisberg 1986). It may be that eternal vigilance is the price to be paid if such errors are to be avoided.

References

Barnes, B. (1982). *T. S. Kuhn and social science*. Macmillan, London.
Barnes, B. and Edge, D. (eds.) (1982). *Science in context*. Open University Press, Milton Keynes, UK.
Bloor, D. (1976). *Knowledge and social imagery*. Routledge and Kegan Paul, London.
Bloor, D. (1983). *Wittgenstein: a social theory of knowledge*. Macmillan, London.
Braine, M. D. S. and Rumain, B. (1983). Logical reasoning. In *Handbook of child psychology, vol. III Cognitive development* (eds. J. H. Flavell and E. M. Markman). Wiley, New York.

Bryant, P. and Trabasso, T. (1971). Transitive inferences and memory in young children. *Nature* **232**, 456–8.

Chomsky, N. (1965). *Aspects of the theory of syntax*. Mouton, The Hague.

Chomsky, N. (1980). *Rules and representations*. Columbia University Press, New York.

Collins, H. (1985). *Changing order: replication and induction in scientific practice*. Sage, Beverly Hills.

Donaldson, M. (1978). *Children's minds*. Fontana, London.

Flavell, J. H. (1985). *Cognitive development* (2nd edition). Prentice Hall, Englewood Cliffs, NJ.

Fleck, L. (1979). *Genesis and development of a scientific fact*. University of Chicago Press, Chicago.

Fodor, J. A. (1980). Fixation of belief and concept acquisition. In *Language and Learning: the debate between Jean Piaget and Naom Chomsky* (ed. M. Piatelli-Palmarini). Harvard University Press, Cambridge, MA.

Fodor, J. A. (1983). *The modularity of mind*. MIT Press, Cambridge, MA.

Gellatly, A. R. H. (1987). The acquisition of a concept of logical necessity. *Human development* **30**, 32–47.

Gellatly, A. R. H. (1988). Human inference. In *Human and machine problem solving* (ed. K. K. Gilhooly). Plenum, London.

Gellatly, A. R. H. (In Press) Influences on conceptions of logic and mind. In *Scientific knowledge socialized* (eds. I. Hronszky, M. Feher, and B. Dajka). Reidel, Dordrecht.

Gelman, R. (1978). Preschool thought. *American psychologist* **34**, 900–05.

Gelman, R. (1982). Accessing one-to-one correspondence: still another paper about conservation. *British journal of psychology* **73**, 209–20.

Gelman, R. and Baillargeon, R. (1983). A review of some Piagetian concepts. In *Handbook of child psychology, vol. III, Cognitive development* (eds. J. H. Flavell and E. M. Markman). Wiley, New York.

Gelman, R. and Gallistel, C. (1978). *The child's understanding of number*. Harvard University Press, Cambridge, MA.

Greeno, J. G., Riley, N. S., and Gelman, R. (1984). Conceptual competence and children's counting. *Cognitive psychology* **16**, 94–143.

Halford, G. (1984). Can young children integrate premises in transitivity and serial order tasks? *Cognitive psychology* **16**, 65–93.

Henle, M. (1962). On the relation between logic and thinking. *Psychological review* **69**, 366–78.

Henle, M. (1981). Another vote for rationality. *Behavioral and brain sciences* **4**, 339.

Johnson-Laird, P. N. (1982). Thinking as a skill. *Quarterly journal of experimental psychology* **34A**, 1–30.

Johnson-Laird, P. N. (1983). *Mental models*. Cambridge University Press, London.

Johnson-Laird, P. N. and Bara, B. (1984). Syllogistic inference. *Cognition* **16**, 1–61.

Johnson-Laird, P. N., Oakhill, J. and Bull, D. (1986). Children's syllogistic reasoning. *Quarterly journal of experimental psychology* **38A**, 35–58.

Johnson-Laird, P. N. and Steedman, M. J. (1978). The psychology of syllogisms. *Cognitive psychology* **10**, 64–99.

Klahr, D. and Wallace, J. G. (1976). *Cognitive development: an information processing view*. Erlbaum, Hillsdale, NJ.

Kuhn, T. S. (1962). *The Structure of scientific revolutions*. University of Chicago Press, Chicago.

McGarrigle, J. and Donaldson, M. (1974). Conservation accidents. *Cognition* **3**, 341–50.

Piaget, J. (1952). *The child's conception of number*. Routledge and Kegan Paul, London.

Piaget, J. (1953). *Logic and psychology*. Manchester University Press, Manchester.

Pinch, T. (1985). Towards an analysis of scientific observation: the externality and evidential significance of observational reports in physics. *Social studies of science* **15**, 3–36.

Pinker, S. (1987). *Fallacies in connectionist approaches to human language*. Paper read to the Experimental Psychology Society, Oxford, July 1st.

Pinker, S. and Prince, A. (1988). On language and connectionism: Analysis of a parallel distributed processing model of language acquisition. *Cognition* **28**, 73–194.

Rips, L. J. (1983). Cognitive processes in propositional reasoning. *Psychological review* **90**, 38–71.

Rips, L. J. (1986) Mental muddles. In *Problems in the representation of knowledge and belief* (eds. M. Brand and M. Harnish). University of Arizona Press, Tucson, AZ.

Rozin, P. (1976). The Evolution of intelligence and access to the cognitive unconscious. In *Progress in psychobiology and physiological psychology* (eds. J. M. Sprague and A. N. Epstein). Academic Press, New York.

Rumelhart, D. E. and McClelland, J. L. (1985). *On learning the past tenses of English verbs* ICS Report 8507, University of California, San Diego.

Rumelhart, D. E. and McClelland, J. L. (1987). *Parallel distributed memory systems: implications for cognition and development*. Paper read to the Experimental Psychology Society, Oxford, July 1st.

Scribner, S. (1977). Modes of thinking and ways of speaking: culture and logic reconsidered. In *Thinking: readings in cognitive science* (eds. P. N. Johnson-Laird and P. C. Wason). Cambridge University Press, London.

Siegler, R. S. (1976). Three aspects of cognitive development. *Cognitive psychology* **8**, 481–520.

Siegler, R. S. (1986). *Children's thinking*. Prentice-Hall, Englewood Cliffs, NJ.

Stabler, E. P. (1983) How are grammars represented? *The behavioral and brain sciences* **6**, 391–422.

Trabasso, T. (1975). Representation, memory, and reasoning: how do we make transitive inferences? In *Minnesota symposia on child psychology, vol.9* (ed. A. D. Pick). University of Minnesota Press, Minneapolis.

Trabasso, T., Isen, A. M., Dolecki, P., McLanahan, A. G., Riley, C. A., and Tucker, T. (1978). How do children solve class inclusion problems? In *Children's thinking: what develops?* (ed. R. S. Siegler). Erlbaum, Hillsdale, NJ.

Weisberg, R. W. (1986). *Creativity: genius and other myths*. W. H. Freeman, New York.

Younis, J. and Furth, H. G. (1973). Reasoning and Piaget. *Nature* **224**, 314–15.

9

Culturally based reasoning

ROY G. D'ANDRADE

Reasoning, or inference, is widely agreed to be a central cognitive process. People are able to solve a variety of problems: syllogisms, chess puzzles, cryptoarithmetic, analogies, mathematical problems, spacial rotation problems, etc. The issue that plagues the cognitive sciences is *how* they do it. One tenaciously held position is that people use *logic* to reason. As Adams states:

> Among the classic controversies that psychology has inherited from philosophy is that of whether human thought adheres to the laws of logic. On one side is the conviction that somehow it must. Reasoning is, after all, the only means we have for extending our knowledge beyond what we have learned explicitly. If we were insensitive to the laws of logic, we would have no basis, save empirical, for evaluating the necessity of our conclusions (Adams 1980, p. 745).

One implication of the position that people use logic to reason is that when there are differences between individuals — or groups of individuals — in their ability to solve various types of problems; these differences are the result of differences in some general capacity to reason. But if reasoning is not a matter of having available some general logic machine, rather a matter of being able to mentally manipulate certain specific representations, then differences between individuals are more probably due to how well formed these representations are. And how well formed particular representations are is likely to be due to differences in experience, in schooling, and in cultural background.

The idea that people use logic to reason has been investigated by psychologists in a number of experiments. Support for the hypothesis that people use logic for simple logical problems has been presented by Adams (1980) and Osherson (1975), while counter-evidence has been presented by Wason (1968), Johnson-Laird (1983), and others. One major type of counter-evidence is that people consistently fail certain simple and straightforward problems just because of the *content* of the problem. Since logic operates on a *formal* representation of a problem (all problems are reduced to variables and logical connectives), if people used logic and failed, this could only be because either they were unable to represent the problem correctly, or were unable to find a sequence of inferences to reach the desired conclusion. But people fail on problems which they both understand quite well and which have logical forms which — based on their performance on problems with the same logical form but different content — they should be able to solve easily. A classic example of this type of problem is presented in Wason (1968). One representation of this problem is as follows:

All labels made at Pica's Custom Label Factory have either the letter A or the letter E printed on the front of the label, and have either the number 2 or the number 3 printed on the back side. The machine never makes a mistake about this — it always puts the letter A or E on the front, and the number 2 or 3 on the back.

As part of your job as a label checker at Pica's, you have the task of making sure that *if a label has an E printed on the front, it has a 2 printed on the back.* You have to check this, because sometimes the machine makes a mistake and breaks this rule.

Which of the labels would you have to turn over to make sure that the label had been printed following the rule? Mark an X under the labels you would have to turn over.

| A | 3 | 2 | E |

Approximately 80 per cent of the undergraduates who try this problem fail to solve it correctly. The correct solution is to turn over the label with an E on it and the label with a 3 on it. The most common answer is that one should turn over the label with an E on it and the label *with a 2 on it.* In fact, it does not matter whether an A or an E is on the front a label with a 2 on the back — neither letter would break the rule.

There have been a great number of studies to discover why people have so much trouble with this problem (*see* Johnson-Laird 1983 for a review of these studies). Subjects who have gotten the Wason problem wrong often find it hard to believe that they have made a mistake — they often argue that they are following the rule in turning over the label with a 2 on the back because the rule mentions a 2, and that there is no reason to turn over the label with a 3 on the back because the rule says nothing about 3s. One can try to demonstrate that one should turn over the label with the 3 on it and not the label with a 2 on it by making up some simulated labels and showing subjects that a misprinted label is not with a 3 on its back side and an E on the front — although a few students generally remain unconvinced even then.

An interesting discovery was made by Johnson-Laird, Legrenzi, and Legrenzi (1972) about this problem; that is, if the problem is translated into a 'realistic' example, subjects generally get it right. A realistic example is given below:

As part of your job as an assistant at Kingsway, you have the task of checking sales receipts to make sure that any sale of £30.00 or over has been approved by the section manager. The amount of the sale is written on the front of the form, while the section manager's approval is initialled on the back of the form.

Which of the forms would you have to turn over to make sure that the sales clerk had been following the rule? Mark an X under the forms you would have to turn over.

1 chair £77	approved _____	1 lamp £12	approved £3C
_____	_____	_____	_____

Approximately 70 per cent of American college subjects get the correct answer on the realistic form of the test, using 'Sears' and dollars instead of 'Kingsway' and pounds (turn over the receipt which is for £77 and the receipt which is *not initialled*). A number of realistic forms have been developed, such as the original Johnson-Laird, Legrenzi, and Legrenzi (1972) format which uses a rule about the price of stamps and open versus closed envelopes, the Cox and Griggs (1982) format which uses a rule about age of drinking, and the Gilhooly and Falconer (1974) format which uses a generalization about modes of travel between cities.

One explanation for these results is that with some types of problem content subjects have difficulty in understanding the proper meaning of the *if–then* connective (Osherson 1975). In order to test this hypothesis, an experiment was conducted in which the two forms presented above were given in random order to 140 University of California at San Diego (UCSD) undergraduates. (Seventy-five per cent got the Kingsway/Sears problem right, while 17 per cent got the label problem right). Immediately after the label problem subjects were asked the following questions:

The rule 'If a label has an E printed on the front it should have a 2 printed on the back' can be rephrased without the changing the basic meaning of the rule. Which of the rules below is a correct rephrasing of this rule? Put a check next to the correct rephrasing.

____1. If a label has a 2 on the back it should have an E on the front.
____2. If a label has a 3 on the back it should have an E on the front.
____3. If a label has a 2 on the back it should have an A on the front.
____4. If a label has a 3 on the back it should have an A on the front.

Which of the next set of rephrasings is correct?

____1. No label should have an A on the front and a 2 on the back.
____2. No label should have an E on the front and a 2 on the back.
____3. No label should have an A on the front and a 3 on the back.
____4. No label should have an E on the front and a 3 on the back.

After the Sears problem the corresponding set of questions about rephrasing were also asked. The responses were as follows:

Correct answer	per cent giving correct answer
If a label has a 3 on the back it should have an A on the front.	36
If a receipt is not initialled on the back the sale should be less than £30.	77
No label should have an E on the front and a 3 on the back.	86
No receipt should show a sale of £30 or over and not be initialled on the back.	95

These results indicate that most subjects *did* understand the *if–then* connective in the label problem — at least to the extent of being able to correctly transform the rule into 'No label should have an E on the front and a 3 on the back'. However, only 36 per cent could transform the *if–then* rule in the label problem into what is called the *contrapositive* (given any proposition of the form *if p then q*, the contrapositive is the logically equivalent proposition *if not q then not p*). For the label rule the correct contrapositive transformation is 'If a label has a 3 *(not 2)* on the back it should have an A *(not E)* on the front'. For the Sears problem, by contrast, most subjects were able to answer *both* questions correctly, and so had managed both transformations.

Note that the problem of the contrapositive transformation occurs in the Wason problem when the subject has to decide whether to turn over the label with the 3 on the back ('if it is a 3, what should I do?'). In fact, subjects who got the initial label problem right were more likely to get the contrapositive transformation problem right; a phi correlation of 0.41 ($P < 0.05$) was found between correct answers on the contrapositive question for the label rule and correct answers on the label version of the Wason problem.

The difficulty with the Wason problem, then, *is not* simple confusion about the meaning of the *if–then* connective, rather an inability to do a contrapositive transformation of an *if–then* proposition which has *arbitrary* content. In order to test this hypothesis more directly a questionnaire was administered to undergraduate students at UCSD using the following general format:

Test questions
Please circle the number of the correct answer to each question.

1. GIVEN: If James is a watchman then James likes candy.
   SUPPOSE: We find out that James *is* a watchman.
   THEN:
   (a) It must be the case that James likes candy.
   (b) Maybe James likes candy and maybe he doesn't.
   (c) It must be the case that James does not like candy.

2. GIVEN: If Jim cut himself Jim would be bleeding.
   SUPPOSE: We find out that Jim *did not* cut himself.
   THEN:
      (a) It must be the case that Jim is bleeding.
      (b) Maybe Jim is bleeding and maybe he isn't.
      (c) It must be the case that Jim is not bleeding.

3. GIVEN: If this rock is a garnet then it is a semi-precious stone.
   SUPPOSE: This rock *is not* a semi-precious stone.
   THEN:
      (a) It must be the case that this rock is a garnet.
      (b) Maybe this rock is a garnet and maybe it isn't.
      (c) It must be the case that this rock is not a garnet.

4. GIVEN: If it is raining then the roof is wet.
   SUPPOSE: The roof *is* wet.
   THEN:
      (a) It must be the case that it is raining.
      (b) Maybe it is raining and maybe it isn't.
      (c) It must be the case that it is not raining.

Four logical types of problems are presented in this test. These types are:

> *Modus ponens* (Problem 1 above)
>   if *p* then *q*
>   *p*
>   *therefore q*
> *Modus tollens* (Problem 3 above)
>   if *p* then *q*
>   not *q*
>   *therefore* not *p*
> *Affirmation of the consequent* (Problem 4 above)
>   if *p* then *q*
>   *q*
>   *therefore* maybe *p* and maybe not *p*
> *Denial of the antecedent* (Problem 2 above)
>   if *p* then *q*
>   not *p*
>   *therefore* maybe *q* and maybe not *q*

Of these four forms, only *modus tollens* involves the use of the contrapositive; that is, in *modus tollens* the subject must conclude from *if p then q* and *not q* that *not p* follows, which is to say that from *if p then q* one must conclude that *if not q then not p*.

Using the general format presented above, a series of questionnaires using different problems were given to different samples of undergraduate subjects.

Table 9.1. *Results of if–then tests*

Modus ponens (If *p* then *q*. *p*. Therefore *q*.)	per cent correct	Sample size
Arbitrary content		
If James is a watchman then James likes candy.	96	50
If Jones is an artist then Smith is a baker.	91	60
If Roger is a musician then Roger is a Bavarian.	89	30
If *A* is true then *B* is true.	87	29
Affirmation of the consequent (If *p* then *q*. *q*. Therefore maybe *p*, maybe not *p*.)		
Arbitrary content		
If Howard is in France then George is in Italy.	82	30
If Oscar is a card player then Oscar is left-handed.	83	35
If *X* is true then *Y* is true.	80	29
Denial of the antecedent (If *p* then *q*. Not *p*. Therefore maybe *q*, maybe not *q*.)		
Coherent content		
If Jim cut himself then Jim would be bleeding.	82	50
If it is raining then the roof is wet.	80	29
Arbitrary content		
If *P* is true then *Q* is true. (*P* is not true.)	81	24
If *M* is true then *N* is true. (*M* is false.)	70	24
If Sally is a manager then Sally is a blond.	69	35
Modus tollens (If *p* then *q*. Not *q*. Therefore not *p*.)		
Coherent content		
If this rock is a garnet then this rock is a semi-precious stone.	96	50
If Tom was born is San Diego then Tom is a native Californian.	86	35
If Janet lives in San Cristobal then Janet lives in Mexico.	80	50
If Bill cut himself then Bill would be bleeding.	77	35
If it is raining then the roof is wet.	68	33
If John bought a present then John spent some money.	65	60
Arbitrary content		
If Janet went to town then Janet brought home some bread.	57	60
If Roger drank Pepsi then Tom sat down.	53	60
If Roger is a musician then Roger is a Bavarian.	52	50
If James is a watchman then James likes candy.	51	35
If *D* is true then *E* is true. (*E* is false.)	45	33
If Harold is a politician then Harold is from New York.	40	35
If *J* is true then *K* is true (not *K* is true.)	33	35

Each questionnaire had a variety of kinds of logical problems, some with arbitrary content and some with culturally coherent or realistic content. On any one questionnaire each premiss was unique, but across questionnaires the same premiss might be used in different logical problems. Thus 'If James is a watchman then James likes candy' was used on one questionnaire in a *modus ponens* problem and on another questionnaire in a *modus tollens* problem. The results are presented in Table 9.1.

These results indicate strongly that college students are generally unable to solve *modus tollens* problems when the content is arbitrary, but can solve *modus tollens* problems when the underlying relationship and objects constitute a realistic or culturally coherent schema. In general, college students can solve *modus ponens*, affirmation of the consequent, and denial of the antecedent problems whether the content is arbitrary or coherent (No 'coherent content' *modus ponens* and affirmation of the consequent problems were given to subjects. It is assumed that if subjects can do 'arbitrary content' problems they can do 'culturally coherent' problems.)

What then, makes *modus tollens* difficult? *Tollens* requires the subject to look at the state of affairs set up by the formula *if p then q* from the perspective of *not q*. (One could describe the same state of affairs with very different formulae, such as *either q or not p*, or *not the case that p and not q*.) Given the state of affairs set up by the formula *if p then q*, when one encounters *p* one expects to encounter *q*. Changing the topic to *q* means changing the perspective. Looking at the state of affairs from the position of *q* leads one to expect that maybe *p* will be encountered and maybe not. Changing to *not q* changes the perspective again. From the position of *not q*, one expects *not* to encounter *p*.

The argument here is that *tollens* is more difficult than the other problems because none of the other forms require a double shift in perspective. *Modus ponens* requires no shift, *affirmation of the consequent* requires only a shift to the perspective of *q*, while *denial of antecedent* requires only a shift from *p* to *not p*. *Modus tollens* requires both a shift in topic from *p* to *q* and a further shift from *q* to *not q*.

This argument rests on the assumption that changing perspective makes demands on the cognitive processing system, and that greater changes make greater demands. Thus *modus tollens* puts a greater cognitive load on working memory than any of the other three logical problems—too heavy a load for normal subjects.

But cognitive load cannot be the whole story, because people can do *modus tollens* when the content is realistic—that is, when the relation is embedded in a well formed schema. Why can people do *tollens* when the content consists of a well formed schema? What subjects say is that the answer is obvious—they can *see* that it must be so. Given that a garnet is a semi-precious stone, then if this rock is *not* a semi-precious stone it surely cannot be a garnet.

It is obvious — one can see it must be so. But exactly *what* do the subjects see?

Without getting into issues of imagistic versus propositional thought, something can be said about this type of *seeing*. Suppose one is told 'If Pablo is an artist then Tom is a baker'. One can hold in mind the proposition without developing a deep or elaborated representation of the state of affairs. If asked one could answer questions like 'Who are the persons talked about?' (Pablo and Tom), 'What occupations are mentioned?' (artist and baker), 'Which persons have which occupations?' (Pablo is the artist, Tom is the baker), and 'What is the relation between Pablo being an artist and Tom being a baker?' (If Pablo is an artist then Tom is a baker). However, there is no specific content to this contingency — marked by the *if–then* connective — although one might imagine reasons why the contingency should exist; perhaps some old person has a bad memory and always forgets whether it is Tom who is the baker and Pablo who is the artist, or vice versa. If asked if Tom is a baker, this forgetful old person might say 'Not sure, but if Pablo is an artist then Tom is a baker'.

However, normally one does not develop such an elaborate fantasy about the possible reason for the *if–then* connective in the sentence 'If Pablo is an artist then Tom is a baker'. The relation is represented only by a *contentless* notion of contingency. (A *contentful* notion of contingency would involve causal, temporal, spacial, or class membership relations of some particular type.) Contentless contingency representation is quite adequate for very simple reasoning and inference such as a *modus ponens* move: 'And I just remembered that Pablo *is* an artist, so Tom *must* be a baker'.

A *modus tollens* move is much more difficult, and in trying to reverse the perspective so that Tom's being a baker is the focus, and in trying to then represent how things would be when Tom is *not* a baker, the non-specific and *contentless* contingency between Pablo being an artist and Tom being a baker typically gets 'lost'. When subjects are asked why they chose the wrong answer on *modus tollens* problems like the Pablo and Tom problem, they often say 'But Tom's being a baker doesn't have anything to do with Pablo's being an artist!' In a sense that is true. However, Tom's *not* being a baker would have something to do with Pablo's *not* being an artist. In the attempt to shift perspective from p to *not q* the shift is not made completely, and the contentless contingency drops out of the mental representation.

The situation is quite different when the *if–then* connective maps onto a well understood real world relationship. Suppose one is told 'If this rock is a garnet then this rock is a semi-precious stone'. Here there is specific content to the contingency relationship. A garnet is a *kind* of semi-precious stone. Or, to put it another way, being semi-precious is a *property* of garnets. Suppose one is told that this rock is *not* a semi-precious stone. One then has to take the perspective of *not q*; that is, to represent how things are when the rock one has is *not* a semi-precious stone. And how is that? Well, one knows that garnets *are* semi-precious stones, and since this rock is *not* a semi-precious stone, it is not a garnet. The specific *property/kind of* relationship between semi-precious stones and garnets remains salient as the perspective shifts because it is part of the original state of affairs set up by the subject — part of the very understanding of what a garnet *is*. The report that subjects give of *seeing* that a rock which is not a semi-precious stone is not a garnet is based on the fact that the subject has maintained the specific *contentful* 'is-a' relationship between *p* and *q* while shifting perspective.

This hypothesis, that failure to solve *modus tollens* is caused by loss of the representation of the contingency between *p* and *q* which, in turn, is caused by the fragility of such representations when the contingency has no specific content, is similar to Cox and Griggs (1982) hypothesis that realistic content serves a memory cue for tasks like the Wason (1968) problem: 'performance . . . is significantly facilitated only when presentation of the task allows the subject to recall past experience with the content of the problem, the relationship expressed, and a counter example to the rule governing the relationship' (Cox and Griggs 1982, p. 497). However, the emphasis here is on the presence of a cultural schema by which the subject can represent the contingency between *p* and *q* rather than on any specific past experiences with such contingencies. In the problem about garnets and semi-precious stones, for example, it is doubtful that the good performance on this problem is due to *real* experience with garnets and semi-precious stones. It seems more likely that the good performance is due to the culturally well-defined schema for the *relationship* between being a garnet and being a semi-precious stone.

It is interesting that when students describe why they made a mistake on the realistic *modus tollens* problems, it appears that they often got the wrong answer because they added more to the state of affairs than was given in the problem. One subject, for example, explained that the reason why it *might* be raining even if the roof is *not* wet (given that 'If it is raining then the roof is wet') is that there *might* be a tree over the roof. It was pointed out to the student that since the problem explicitly asks one to *assume* that if it rains the roof *will* get wet, one must also assume that there is no tree blocking the rain. The student immediately saw that this was the case and groaned. The rapid and vivid perception of the mistake made here contrasts with the difficulty of getting subjects to see why they should turn over the label with a 3 on it. Perhaps it is easier to see that one has added something extra than it is to see that something is missing — it is hard to see what is not there.

If the findings presented here that people cannot do complex problems like *modus tollens* with arbitrary content are generally true, then so-called *formal* reasoning — which by definition is reasoning without respect to content — must be limited to the simple logical operations which people can do regardless of content, such as *modus ponens*. One major effect of this limitation in formal reasoning is to make complex reasoning appear *context bound*. That is, somebody may be able to do a certain problem in one domain, but not be able to do a problem with an equivalent logical or mathematical form in a different domain. However, if the analysis given here is correct, the reason for the differential performance has nothing to do with the context affecting someone, but simply relates to the fact that somebody has a certain well formed schema made up of certain content which allows a kind of processing that the same person cannot do with a formally identical but less well-formed schema made up of other content. Or, to put it another way, content is not something which lies on the 'outside' (the *context*) of the representation of a problem. This just seems to be the case when one assumes that the *problem* is something made out of a particular logical form, rather than something made out of specific content.

The position argued here about how people reason is similar to the position taken by Johnson-Laird (1983). However, more stress is placed here on the importance of having a well-structured cognitive schema which can be used as the template for a specific instantiation of a particular state of affairs rather than on the fact that subjects create instantiations. When subjects are given a sentence like 'If Roger is a musician then Roger is a Bavarian', they build some sort of instantiation or representation of the state of affairs described in the sentence. However, this instantiation is not well formed — without a schema about why musicians should be Bavarians, the representation of the contingency is too fragile to permit integration of the new information that 'Roger is not a Bavarian' into a new instantiation of the full state of affairs (that Roger is not a musician).

Similarly, using Johnson-Laird's syllogism problems (1983, p. 101), when subjects are given 'Some of the artists are beekeepers' they build some sort of instantiation of this state of affairs, but this instantiation is too fragile or too fragmentary to be fully integrated with the second premiss 'None of the beekeepers are chefs', in a way which would permit subjects to 'see' that it must be the case that 'Some of the artists are not chefs', (17 out of 20 subjects failed to draw the proper conclusion for this form). What Johnson-Laird shows is that with arbitrary material, subjects can reliably do those syllogisms which require a minimal amount of mental manipulation of the representations, such as *All the A are B, All the B are C*, therefore *All the A are C* (19 out of 20), but cannot do those syllogisms which require a moderate amount of mental manipulation.

However, from the perspective given here, if better formed schematic relationships could be found for syllogistic problems, there should be a real increase in the number of subjects who can do the harder syllogisms (like the example above). For example, given 'Some artists are temperamental types' and 'No temperamental type always keeps his temper', many college students should, I predict, be able to infer that 'Some artists do not always keep their temper'. The form in this example is the same as the form used in the artist–beekeeper–chef example, but the relationships between objects is — I believe — more coherent.

A general point to be made here is that the ability to reason is strongly influenced by culture, since an enormous number of any person's schemata come from their culture — are cultural models (D'Andrade 1981). Of course, not all well-formed schemata are cultural — we all have a great number of idiosyncratic non-cultural experientially based schemata. But, with respect to *social* worlds, the great number of *socially shared* schemata are cultural, since it is through culture that human groups organize their behaviour.

To the extent that a culture has good cultural models (good in the sense that the schema captures the real world contingencies and is well learned), a member of that culture will be able to reason well about the objects and events referred to by these models (Hutchins 1980). Undoubtedly, people differ genetically in their abilities to do almost anything. The argument here is that much of the observed difference between people, or between groups of people, in how well they solve problems which require reasoning, is due to the degree to which the contents of the problems are cognitively well structured, and that only a small amount of the difference between people is due to genetic differences. And, when differences in problem solving are found between groups of people, it is much more likely that this is the result of a difference in shared cognitive structures, or culture, between the groups than the result of a genetic difference in some kind of general reasoning ability.

In summary, one important way in which the social world influences cognition is through the mediation of culture. Cultural schemata are crystallizations of past individual solutions to problems of human adaptation and adjustment which are socially shared and transmitted. All too often the portrait given by psychologists of how people reason is that of an isolated individual with bio-logically given mental machinery taking in information and processing it. A more accurate picture would portray the individual as a dependent member of a group of people who interact by means of a culturally given means of communication — language — and who share a common stock of simple and complex schemata about the world learned in emotionally rich social inter-action with others, and who need these cultural schemata to comprehend, remember, and reason effectively about specific events and objects.

References

Adams, M. J. (1980). Inductive deductions and deductive inductions. In *Attention and performance VII*, (ed. R. S. Nickerson), pp. 745–61. Erlbaum Hillsdale, NJ.

Cox, J. R. and Griggs, R. A. (1982). The effects of experience on performance in Wason's selection task. *Memory and cognition* **10**; 496–502.

D'Andrade, R. G. (1981). The cultural part of cognition. *Cognitive science* 5, 179–95.

Gilhooly, K. J. and Falconer, W. A. (1974). Concrete and abstract terms and relations in testing a rule. *Quarterly journal of experimental psychology* **26**, 355–9.

Hutchins, E. (1980). *Culture and inference: a trobriand case study*. Harvard University Press, Cambridge,MA.

Johnson-Laird, P. N. (1983). *Mental models*. Harvard University Press, Cambridge, MA.

Johnson-Laird, P. N., Legrenzi, P., and Legrenzi, M. (1972). Reasoning and a sense of reality. *British journal of psychology* **63**, 392–400.

Newell, A. and Simon, H. A. (1972). *Human problem solving*. Prentice-Hall, Englewood Cliffs, NJ.

Osherson, D. (1975). Logic and models of logical thinking. In *Reasoning: representation and process in children and adults* (ed. R. J. Falmagne), pp. 81–91. Erlbaum Hillsdale NJ.

Wason, P. C. (1968). Reasoning about a rule. *Quarterly journal of experimental psychology* **20**, 273–81.

10

Musical literacy and the development of rhythm representation: cognitive change and material media

LIZA CATÁN

A number of research studies on rhythm understanding in children and musically untrained adults have indicated that rhythm representation has a developmental history. Bamberger (1975, 1980), Fraisse (1978), Longuet-Higgins and Lee (1982), Steedman (1977), Smith (1983, 1984) and Povel (1981) identified two types of internal rhythmic organization. A natural, untutored type of organization, based on perceptual clusterings of shorter beats, separated by subjectively lengthened pauses between the clusters, was observed in both child and musically untrained adult subjects. This type of rhythmic organization is frequently labelled 'figural representation'. Musically tutored, older subjects displayed a more conventional rhythmic organization, which grouped the beats of a rhythm according to metrical boundaries. The transition from 'figural' to 'metric' rhythmic organization was seen as 'progressive', in the sense of moving towards a final, desired end-point, and 'developmental', in that metric organization was viewed as a mature, or educated, achievement.

However, from a developmental point of view, these studies lack important explanatory elements. They do not sufficiently examine or account for early origins and transitional states, and they make only cursory reference to the broad debate on maturational/experiential versus learning/training theories of cognitive development to account for the differential distribution of figural and metric forms of rhythm representation. Thus they do not directly address the question of how the earlier figural type of organization is transformed into conventional 'metric' rhythm representations. Even where musical training is identified as the source of differentiation between subjects expected to produce figural and metric representations, there has been no attempt to identify which aspects of specialized musical training activate the change.

In this paper, I shall examine the role of one aspect of musical training, the acquisition of musical notation, and concentrate upon the role of one aspect of musical notation, the graphic medium, in the development of rhythm representation. The acquisition of notation may be broadly viewed as part of the process of becoming musically literate, that is, acquiring a means of writing down material that is almost universally processed by aural means, akin to the more widely researched process of linguistic literacy.

The contribution of literacy to the development of mature levels of cognitive functioning, characteristic of Piaget's formal operational stage of development, is well established (cf. Bruner and Olsen (1977–8), Goody, Cole, and Scribner (1977), Scribner and Cole (1981)). This line of work has taken place within the broad orientation of Soviet activity-theory, which places individual cognitive change and development in the context of a subject's engagement in complex psycho-social activities. Soviet theorists (e.g. Davydov and Radzikhovskii 1985; Leont'ev 1981; Zinchenko 1985) view 'activities' as the basic unit of psychological analysis. Thus the essence of research guided by activity-theory is the view that psychological development and functioning is fundamentally constrained by the social needs and uses operating at particular historical moments, and by available material, technological, and psychological resources. The Western experimental tradition has typically concentrated upon individual, and increasingly 'internal', cognitive phenomena, conceptualizing related historical, social, and material phenomena as settings or contexts, producing 'noise' in the manifestation of internal cognitive processes. However, Soviet theory treated these elements as integral to an account of psychological development and functioning. Thus from this point of view, the acquisition and practise of literacy is seen as composed of a broad, and in some senses, indivisible, complex of elements which cut across traditional conceptual divisions between the mental and the material, individual and social, internal cognitive structure and external material condition or behavioural manifestation (cf. Rogoff 1982, for a contemporary discussion of this issue). However, even within this broader approach, the notion that different material media—in this case, the graphic medium—have demonstrable cognitive-developmental functions, has not been widely explored.

In the first section of this paper, I shall introduce the claim that the use of material media may structure and re-structure cognitive organization in developmentally salient ways, and summarize some little-known work on material media which dates from the 1920s, through to the 1950s. This discussion will be placed in the context of recent 'cognitivist' work on external representation in a variety of graphic media, including drawings, paintings, maps, and diagrams. The assumption underlying recent work in this field, that graphic-medium representations are simply behavioural manifestations of underlying cognitive structures and activity will be critically examined.

Three microgenetic studies of rhythm representation, modelled on a 1928 literacy study of Luria's (cf. Luria 1928), will be summarized in the following section. They describe changes in rhythm representation that occur during the early stages of literacy acquisition, and examine the relative importance of the graphic medium at this stage.

In the final section, I shall return to the activity-theory account of developmental change, with a view to placing the findings from these studies of rhythm representation within broader, socially embedded notions of cognitive development.

The psychological relevance of graphic-medium representations

Contemporary 'cognitivist' views

Researchers working within a contemporary 'cognitivist' framework have shaped questions about the psychological significance of graphic representations into a polarized debate about their relation to internal, mental representations. From the cognitivst point of view, only the latter are of interest to the psychologist. At one end of the debate, it is argued that internal representations may be accessed via the external notational product. At the other, it is argued that constructive processes for internal and external representations are not analogous, due to particular difficulties involved in the mastery of graphic or notational techniques and conventions. However, on both sides, it is assumed that the medium is cognitively neutral, and the fact that representations occur in a variety of material media is accorded no cognitive significance. Indeed, the idea of a primary psychological interest in material media runs counter to basic assumptions about the essential mentalness and the internal nature of psychological functioning in contemporary cognitive psychology.

The assumption that graphic-medium representations are of use only as indices of, and means of access to, purely mental, internal cognitive processes and structures, has a respectable history in Piagetian and post-Piagetian cognitive–developmental research. Piaget and Inhelder (1956) used children's drawings as an indication of their developing knowledge of space. This use of drawings as indices underlies, also, a later body of work on graphic medium map representations. For instance, while examining children's invented map notations for evidence of cognitive reorganization, Karmiloff-Smith (1979) pointed out that 'the child's *internal* representation can never be tapped, but merely external manifestations of it (the study of external notational representations) may provide insight into child growth which strict measurements . . . may entirely miss' (p. 115). And Wolf *et al.* (1986) argued that while 'children's notations are not simply transparent records of the way they apprehend and organize information . . . Nevertheless (they) give us an observable behavioural record from which to infer possible changes in their underlying ability to organize information' (p. 14).

This assumption about the pyschological status of graphic representations generally, and notational representations in particular, underlies empirical procedures employed in the small corpus of recent cognitive–developmental literature on notational rhythm representation (Bamberger 1975, 1980; Wolf *et al.* 1986). Bamberger (1975) identified two strategies for internally representing simple rhythms, and claimed that 'Children's drawings of simple rhythmic figures . . . have provided the *clues* from which we have derived the strategies of representation' (p. 1). In a later report (Bamberger 1980), she described a bidirectional interaction between the internal representation of rhythm and the construction of notational rhythm representations. She elicited invented notations from musically untrained subjects 'to study the cognitive mechanisms contributing to the construction of basic musical coherence in apprehension' (Bamberger 1980, p. 172), and then used the invented notations of musically tutored subjects to conclude that knowledge of conventional notation shapes the progressive reorganization of *internal* rhythm representations. However, the processes governing such 'shaping', or the procedures whereby untutored subjects' notations come to bear some of the characteristics of conventional notations, were not explained.

Thus in recent cognitivist research, graphic representations of rhythms (notations) have been accorded the same status as any other behavioural manifestation. Smith (1983, 1984), for example, used a different manifestation—drummed reproductions of rhythms—to access untrained rhythm representation and to gain evidence of the shaping of internal rhythm representations by musical training. Again, figural versus metric rhythmic organizations were observed in trained and untrained subjects respectively. However there was no sense that the use of a new medium might influence subjects' organization of rhythm. Drumming, like notating, was assumed to tap preformed internal rhythm representations.

On the other side of the debate, there have been studies of graphic representation in general, and children's rhythm notations in particular, which aimed to clarify why external notations may not be viewed as 'simply transparent records' of internal cognitive organization. Cohen (1983) studied the development of young children's invented rhythm notations from the point of view that it is governed by their understanding of general principles of notational well-formedness. Kosslyn *et al.* (1977) and Freeman (1972) argued that the production of early graphic representations was principally governed, not by the emergence of general underlying cognitive structures, but by the gradual mastery of techniques and conventions peculiar to the use of the graphic medium. Wolf *et al.* (1986) did not find the fact of technique-related mastery to be incompatible with the claim that notations may be used to access more fundamental aspects of internal cognitive organization. Nevertheless, Kosslyn *et al.* (1977) used this type of evidence to claim that graphic-medium representations could not be used as evidence for mental representations: 'drawings are not a "royal road" to the child's internal representations' (p. 211).

Werner's and Luria's view of media

The approach to notational representations taken in this paper is based upon the work of Werner (1954), Werner and Kaplan (1957, 1963), and Luria (1928, 1932). As opposed to treating notations as manifestations of more cerebral, universal, individual cognitive abilities, it explores the claim that, at particular times, or under certain conditions, cognitive development depends crucially upon the use of particular material media, which form an integral part of a context of highly specific historical and social needs and possibilities.

The claim that material media play a central role in cognitive functioning appeared in Werner and Kaplan's research during the 1940s and 1950s. A paper entitled 'Symbolic mediation and thought organization' (Werner and Kaplan 1957) records that, in the course of research intended to investigate the relationships between thought and language, they were led to question the basic assumption that thought, or experience itself, should be conceived of as pre-formed, independently of expressions in the different media, such as verbal code, gesture, or pencil-on-paper:

We recognized that it is not tenable to talk of the relations of verbally formulated to unformulated experience; rather experience must be seen as necessarily mediated, i.e. experience coming into being and formed in terms of different material media (Barten and Franklin 1978, p. 478).

Thus they believed that the different media did not simply provide cognitively neutral materials in which pre-formed thoughts were expressed, since experience itself was formed through the representational use of media. Thinking was conceptualized as representation in a medium, and many media are material or have material aspects which actively influence cognitive processes and products: 'the medium molds the experience in terms of its own immanent properties' (Barten and Franklin 1978, p. 478).

Having made this fundamental philosophical shift, the focus of their research turned to a two-pronged investigation: 'a comparative analysis of media and . . . the related problem of a developmental analysis of mediation' (Barten and Franklin 1978, p. 480). The comparative analysis of media involved experimental demonstrations that the use of a particular medium — movement, graphic lines, or verbal code — resulted in very different cognitive-organizational processes and products. For example, when using the line schematization technique in which subjects were asked to formulate concepts such as 'joy', 'sadness', or 'anger' in the unfamiliar medium of schematic lines, it was found that they produced gesturally controlled symbols which encoded pre-verbal, idiocyncratic, bodily-based connotations of concepts — connotations that were excluded by the use of conventional media, such as spoken or written language. Thus the non-conventional use of the graphic medium manifested cognitive organizations that had been identified by many

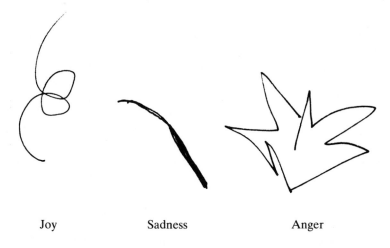

Joy   Sadness   Anger

Fig. 10.1.   Schematic lines from Werner and Kaplan (1957).

of the developmental psychologists of the time as 'primitive', or typical of the earlier stages of cognitive development (*see* Figure 10.1).

The developmental analysis of media followed from the comparative work. Werner and Kaplan claimed that some media, most notably those of movement and mimetic gesture, were essentially untutored resources. Bodily-involved modes of activity were believed to be utilized predominantly in the cognitive activity of young children, and by adults under regressive conditions as in dreams, drug-induced states, when exhausted or in novel situations. They argued that as the conventional media such as pencil-on-paper or paints-on-canvas become available, the possibilities and constraints of these new material media are exploited as a means of reorganizing experience, and their use evokes more abstract and generalized modes of cognitive organization. Thus they believed that important developmental shifts in representation occur as socialized, conventional media come to mediate cognitive functioning.

While Werner and Kaplan were the first to explicitly investigate the active cognitive role of the medium, it could be argued that their approach was limited by a lack of explicitness about the social embeddedness of conventional material media. This aspect of the problem was more thoroughly explored in the work of the Soviet socio-historical school. Of particular interest is Luria's 1928 literacy study, which formed part of Vygotsky's programme of research on the role of culturally evolved symbol systems in the development of 'higher psychological functions' (Luria 1979, pp. 46–50). The aim of Luria's study was to trace the impact of literacy — conceptualized as an integrated activity consisting of a writing system, graphic medium, social needs and use constraints, and pedagogic methods — upon the cognitive activity of previously non-literate children. Pre-literate child subjects were asked to devise ways of writing down spoken words and phrases, and told that their 'notes' were to be used to help them remember the original stimuli. When they baulked at the task, Luria encouraged them to continue and reminded them of its requirements. Thus the experiment modelled several important features of the emergence of literacy: he confronted his child subjects with a new material medium and also built into the experiment essential and inseparable features of the social aspects of literacy acquisition: a need to remember more than one can unaided, a teacher, a sense of pedagogic compulsion, and the basic task of transposing into the new graphic medium, material that had previously been organized through the medium of speech.

Despite the differences of emphasis in Werner's and Luria's work, Luria's demonstration of the actual course of cognitive reorganization during mastery of the pencil-and-paper medium shares many common observations with Werner's work using the 'line schematization' technique (cf. Werner 1954; Werner and Kaplan 1957, 1963). Despite, also, the incompatibility of 'classical' developmental theory and methodology with contemporary 'cognitivist' assumptions, both bodies of research on graphic-medium notation produced similar observational material. Both identified a pre-graphic, bodily-based mode of cognitive organization, which controlled the formation of the earliest notational symbols. Both Werner and Luria designated such modes 'natural'. Werner emphasized their mimetic qualities and called them 'natural symbols' (for example, an infant puffing out its cheeks when viewing an orange). Luria pointed out their frequently rhythmic quality (for example, scribbles that echo the spoken rhythms of sentences to be recalled). As their subjects engaged in socially constrained exploration and use of the graphic medium, they observed that dependency upon these untutored, mimetic modes of organization dropped gradually away, and the task of organizing material in the new medium became increasingly controlled by the properties of the medium itself. Luria, for instance, described how his subjects first used the spatial marking possibilities afforded by the medium to make marks whose position would aid in the recall of sentences. Later in the session, this property was exploited when they made longer strings of scribble to represent longer phrases and sentences.

The studies on the development of rhythm representation presented in this paper were designed to further explore this developmental sequence and provide an account of processes mediating the transition from untutored, gesturally controlled rhythm representation to representations that mark essential aspects of conventional rhythm notation. An examination of the role of the graphic medium in rhythm representation will form an integral part of this account.

Microgenetic studies of rhythm representation

The microgenetic method: general rationale

The three studies on the development of rhythm representation to be reported here employed a reconstructed version of the microgenetic experiment devised by Werner, Luria, and other developmentalists of the 1920s and 1930s. An account of its basic characteristics and major differences from more orthodox experimental methods may be found in Vygotsky (1978, Ch. 5), and a fuller version of its historical antecedents and reconstruction for present uses in Catán (1986, 1987).

The microgenetic method was originally developed by the Leipzig Gestalt school, to provide a means of studying developmental processes directly, as opposed to having to infer change from end-point data (or 'fossilized products', as Vygotsky later termed the evidence of orthodox experimentation). Its first label, *Aktualgenese*, indicated the aim of experimentally actualizing, or realizing, developmental processes, thus rendering them objects of investigation. The Leipzig school worked with naturally brief perceptual phenomena, developing 'primitivizing' techniques to evoke the earliest phases of change sequences. The techniques of *Aktualgenese* were elaborated by Werner to allow the study of processes that occur over more extended time spans, historically, and in the life of the individual, e.g. the historical evolution of literacy and its acquisition by the individual. Thus he devised tasks which retained salient aspects of the situation in which the process of interest occurred on the original levels of ethno- or ontogenesis, while enabling it to run its course over a single experimental session. These tasks were seen as miniaturized simulations of the historical or individual situations, which modelled original macro-developmental processes. Thus *Aktualgenese* became 'microgenesis'. The method was further extended by Vygotsky, Luria, and their coworkers, to examine change in psycho-social activities. In the Soviet work, aspects of the original macro-process to be modelled in the experimental micro-version were determined by a careful analysis of the social needs and conditions surrounding its emergence in the course of history and in current individual development. Thus microgenetic methodology aimed to activate artificial miniaturizations of socially constrained developmental processes (Leont'ev and Luria 1972).

These points will be illustrated with an account of the rationales behind the three microgenetic studies of rhythm representation to be reported in this paper.

Microgenetic methods and the study of rhythm representation

The first, baseline, study was designed to simulate the initial confrontation with a novel need to write down material that had not previously been conceived in terms of notational symbols. These fundamental conditions were re-created by working with children who were musically untutored and who had not therefore been taught about musical notation. It was assumed that, even though they would be familiar with the appearance of conventional music notation, they would not understand how it related to pitches and rhythms. Ninety-eight children aged between 6 and 13 years (average age 9.3 years) took part in this study.

The materials used in all three studies consisted of a pool of sixteen drummed rhythms based on nursery rhymes and folk-tunes (*see* Figure 10.2). They were performed on a drum simulator and recorded. These simple stimuli were used because, like the earliest notated musical pieces, the plainsong chants of the ninth and tenth centuries A.D., their rhythmic structure is controlled by a syllabic analysis of the spoken text; one note of music corresponds to a syllable of spoken text (Fig. 10.2). The use of novice subjects and syllabically controlled rhythms was intended to simulate salient aspects of the original circumstance in which musical notation emerged both historically and in the life history of the individual. However, the instructions issued to the children aimed, somewhat artificially, to channel them towards the initial use of the graphic medium independently of explicit social use constraints:

I'm going to play you some drumbeats, and I want you to think of a way of making marks on the paper that are like you think the drumbeats sounded. It's a sort of music writing, but not like the real music writing because you don't know about that. The main thing is that you listen carefully to the drumbeats and make marks that look like they sounded to you.

After listening to the drumbeats, they were asked to clap them back, in order to ensure that they had formed a basic representation of the rhythm upon which secondary, graphic-medium representations might build. The analogy here was to the dependency of phonetic and syllabic alphabets upon the representations of spoken language. They were then asked to think of ways of 'making marks that look like the drumbeats sounded'. Thus they were not told to notate for some purpose, but simply confronted with the task of transposing their pre-graphic rhythm representations into the pencil-and-paper medium. It was intended that this task would evoke a variety of notational solutions, and would provide the basic data for a notational typology and a sequence of notational transformations.

Two further studies were designed to simulate the social use constraints which had operated historically, during the early development of conventional rhythm notations. The first, *aide-memoire*, study was intended to simulate the task demands which prompted the emergence of the earliest 'neumatic' notations. Neumatic systems of notation were developed in ninth century Swiss monasteries, as memory prompts for choral performances of pieces

Baa baa black sheep have you any wool

5 6 pick up sticks 7 8 lay them straight

Here we go round the mulb'ry bush

Ding dong bell pussy's in the well

Jingle bells jingle bells jingle all the way

Goosey goosey gander whither shall I wander

Hush-a-bye baby on the tree top

Ach du lieber Augustin

D'ye ken John Peel with his coat so gay

Oranges and lemons say the bells...

Humpty Dumpty sat on a wall

Ride a cock horse to Banbury Cross

Half a pound of tuppenny rice

Little old man at the window stood

One in a taxi one in a car

Musical cliché

Fig. 10.2.   Non-pitch rhythms used in the studies of musical literacy.

that had already been learned by aural means. Because they were supplemented by aurally acquired memories, neumatic notations did not have to be sufficiently explicit to enable performers to generate a piece without already knowing how it went. Thirty-five children between the ages of 7 to 11 years (average age 9.8 years), participated in this study, and 12 out of the original pool of 16 rhythms were used. The children were asked to notate for the purpose of helping them to 'read', in the sense of clap back, the rhythms later on, which they did after every three trials. They were then invited to compare their notations with the original stimulus, to comment, and make alterations.

The third, 'scribe-performer', study was designed to model conditions surrounding the emergence of modal notations, which developed after improved communications between monasteries made it possible to send musical texts over considerable distances. This resulted in the separation of the roles of composer and performer, and hence the need for notations that were sufficiently explicit to generate the performance of unknown pieces.

This situation was modelled by using forty children aged 7 to 11 years (average age 9.8 years) working in pairs consisting of a 'scribe' and a 'performer'. The performer was absent while the scribe listened to and notated the rhythms, knowing that they would be used by the performer to clap back the rhythm. At intervals throughout the session, the performer would try to reconstruct the rhythm from the scribe's notation, and then both children were invited to compare the notation with the original stimulus, to comment and improve it.

Notational sequences and representational procedures: the baseline study

The procedures used in the original baseline study produced 98 protocols of the children's notations, plus the experimenter's handwritten notes of the session. These recorded the presence or absence of motoric components to the notations, alterations and comments that gave insight into the way the children were tackling the task, and their feelings about the adequacy of their notations.

The aim of the analysis of baseline study data was to establish a typology of the notations produced and a basic sequence of notational change. It was carried out in three phases. In the first phase, a notational typology was constructed on the basis of the formal features of the notations. A set of distinctive features was derived for each notational type, and individual protocols were analysed in terms of this typology. The reliability of the categorizations was checked by another rater's analysis of a quarter of the protocols. Discrepancies which the two raters agreed had been due to simple misapplication of the original set of features were discounted, after which they agreed upon 92 per cent of assignments of notations to type categories. The second phase of the analysis looked at the frequency with which, in the aggregated data, each notational type functioned as an instance of notational change, and then how each notational change functioned in relation to other notational types—whether it tended to start or end change sequences, and which notation it tended to precede and succeed. After the sequence had been established, sequential and formal information about the notations was expanded into a set of hypotheses about their representational functions and the procedures whereby subjects transformed one notational type into another. In the third phase, individual protocols were examined to see whether the individual sequences of notational change were in accordance with the hypothesized sequences; only 6 out of 80 change protocols were not in accordance with the predicted sequence.

This outline of the sequence of notational change will be based on a combination of the first two phases of data analysis. The various types of notation will be described in terms of their formal features, together with hypotheses about their representational functions and the procedures whereby they were constructed and transformed.

Motoric representations

The most basic and pervasive response to the notational task was that the children moved rhythmically, in time to the stimuli, as a spontaneous accompaniment to their listening. The form of the movements varied widely, from large, observable body movements, such as tapping or jiggling feet, moving the whole shoulder and torso area, tapping on the table, to more subtle movements that were observable only in principle, e.g. tensing muscles or tapping with the tongue on the roof of the mouth. An interesting feature of these body movements was that all the major features of the stimuli, such as the number of drumbeats and their relative duration, appeared to be accurately represented, and so the clapping and stamping bore a clear resemblance to the original rhythms. This spontaneity and accuracy contrasted with the tentative performance of the notational task, where many subjects misrepresented even the most obvious features of the stimulus, such as the number of drumbeats. Later, as the children realized that the task of notating would be facilitated by a clear memory of the rhythms, they developed the technique of 'fixing' them in memory before starting to notate, by replaying their rhythmic movements. They also replayed them while notating, as though to help them recall the stimulus and check what they had written. It thus appeared that these movements had a representational function, and that they provided the medium for pre-literate, already mastered, and automated ways of processing rhythm, which were in turn used as material on which to base the graphic recoding.

General support for this interpretation of the functioning of motoric representations came from the appearance of motorically controlled, early notational responses both in the baseline study (see below), and in a number of other studies on graphic-medium representations, e.g. Werner (1957), Luria (1928), Bamberger (1980), Ferreiro and Teberosky (1982). In the wider developmental literature, the notion of a pre-conceptual, bodily-based, developmentally early mode of cognitive organization that is kinaesthetically experienced and expressed in movement, has been described by Luria (1932), Piaget (1942, 1976) Werner and Kaplan (1963), and by a number of psychoanalytic theorists, e.g. Winnicot (1945), Milner (1950), Mahler (1968), and Gaddini (1987).

Action drawings

The first specifically graphic response to the task was produced by the strategy of replaying the original motoric representation while holding the pencil on the paper, producing a single line of marking (*see* Figure 10.3). By itself, the notation was inexplicit about many important aspects of the stimuli, but was supplemented by their full and accurate representation in the accompanying motoric representation.

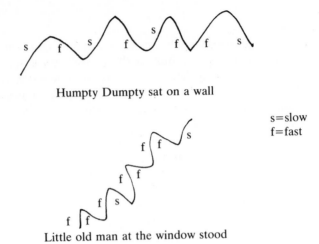

Humpty Dumpty sat on a wall

s=slow
f=fast

Little old man at the window stood

Fig. 10.3.   Motoric control — action drawings.

As in other studies of graphic-medium representations, Bamberger's (1980) youngest subjects also produced action drawings as rhythm representations. She described them as notations where 'the children actually "played", the rhythm on the paper with their crayons'. In the baseline study, as in Bamberger's, they appeared to comprise the most basic level of notational representation; although few were produced, they always functioned as starting notations, and all the subjects who produced them also attempted to notate during the presentation of the stimulus. This suggested that they were attempting to put as little distance as possible between their motoric and notational representations. It was hypothesized that action drawing notations functioned primarily to channel motoric representations into the activity of marking, and only secondarily to make marks that functioned as a free-standing representation of rhythm. Thus they appeared to be direct transpositions of motoric representations into the graphic medium, 'direct', because they were as yet unmodified by any specifically notational strategy of representation. Given that motoric representations appeared to be the basis on which action drawings were directly formed, it could be said that action drawings were generated, or controlled by, the underlying motoric representation. Action drawings, then, appeared to be the first graphic-medium representations of rhythm, where a relatively uniformative notation was generated and supplemented by an accurate, underlying, bodily-based mode of rhythm representation.

The beginning of notational control

This trade-off between the use of motoric and graphic media to represent rhythmic elements continued in the next phase of notational change.

All instances of action drawings were followed by notations which retained a clear motoric basis, but which were modified by exploiting the discrete marking possibilities of the graphic medium; subjects made a series of durationally undifferentiated marks to represent the number of separate drumbeats in the rhythm, with their varying durations still marked in the movements tapping out the stimulus on the paper (Figure 10.4). These notations no longer possessed the movement-based characteristic of continuity, and were thus able to correct the failure of action drawings to differentiate individual drumbeats. Thus it is possible that engagement with the graphic medium had presented the possibility of dividing up the motorically generated flow of movement into discrete drumbeat symbols. Nevertheless, these notations still did not differentiate between longer and shorter drumbeats, much less did they begin to address the main concern of conventional rhythm notation—the quantification of durational distinctions.

Detachment from motoric representation

The next step in the sequence consisted of a seemingly uniformative type of notation, where the motoric accompaniment was dropped, leaving the notation merely to record the number of drumbeats in the stimulus. Thus it retained the objective form of the previous notations, but was not generated by any mimetic body movements. The children simply drew a more or less correct number of symbols, often taking great care to count and check their number (Figure 10.5).

s   f   s   f   s   f   f   s

Humpty Dumpty sat on a wall

s=slow
f=fast

s   f   f   s   f   f   f   f   s

Little old man at the window stood

Fig. 10.4.   The beginning of notational control—discrete, undifferentiated, motorically controlled notations.

5, 6, pick up sticks, 7, 8, lay them straight

Fig. 10.5.   Detachment from motoric representation—discrete, undifferentiated notations.

This notation appeared to function as a watershed in the change sequence. One-quarter of the children did not progress beyond this point. One-half started with it and, despite the frequent occurrence of 'regressions' to earlier phases in the microgenetic sequence, children who started with this notation never regressed to generating notations by the direct transposition procedure. Thus there appeared to be a clear break between the use of the motorically generated, direct transposition procedure, and graphically-based representational strategies. The rest of the children passed through this type of notation before going on to develop more explicit, graphic representational procedures.

An occasional variant of this notational type gave some insight into the underlying representational procedure (Figure 10.6). This notation appears to indicate a simple counting error. However, subsequent questioning revealed that the subject had an accurate internalized representation of the number of drumbeats in the stimulus, and of their duration, but the only notational indication that some drumbeats were longer or shorter was that one symbol represented two shorter ones. The ratio of drumbeats to symbols suggests that the subjects were beginning to detach their rhythm representations from the underlying motoric representation, and internalize the representation of durational distinctions. Thus durationally undifferentiated notations functioned as a transitional phase between the use of motoric and graphically-based procedures.

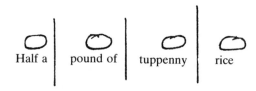

Half a   pound of   tuppenny   rice

Fig. 10.6.   Discrete, undifferentiated notations.

Increased notational control

As the motoric control of notations decreased, so durational distinctions were again externally marked but by graphic, rather than motoric, means.

The next notational type was produced by the procedure of using *spatial* durations to mark the different *temporal* durations; longer spaces between the symbols denoted longer attack-times between the drumbeats. However, the most usual variant retained some traces of the original motoric representation. The longer the pause between drumbeats, the longer the pause where 'nothing happens', and the hand moves further over the page before making a mark; the more crowded the drumbeats, the shorter the silent interval between them, and the less the hand moves across the paper (Figure 10.7).

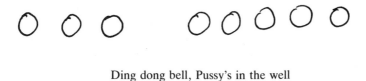

Ding dong bell, Pussy's in the well

Oranges and lemons say the bells...

Fig. 10.7.   Increased notational control—grouped notations.

Thus the shift to grouped notations illustrates the claim that, to devise a progressive solution to the problem of externally representing durational distinctions, subjects actively exploit the visual and spatial properties of the medium. In some cases, the direct transposition procedure was combined with visual–spatial symbolization, suggesting that the symbolic use of graphic space emerged from the pencil-on-paper channelling of the direct transposition procedure (Figure 10.8).

It may also be that the use of the graphic medium fostered this change by confronting subjects with an especially clear presentation of a problem requiring a progressive notational solution. Having constructed an external representation that could be completely detached from the bodily activity that originally produced it, subjects were able to recognize and reflect on the need for more explicit means to represent duration.

Bamberger also identified grouped notations, but interpreted them as the reflection of untrained perceptual organization, in which the last note in a perceptual group is subjectively lengthened. This type of grouped organization was seen as characteristic of the earliest notational types in Bamberger's work.

s=slow
f=fast

Humpty Dumpty sat on a wall

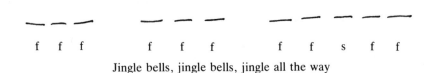

Jingle bells, jingle bells, jingle all the way

Fig. 10.8.   Grouped notations.

However, in the present study, grouped notations often appeared at a relatively late point in the change sequence, suggesting that grouping was a graphic-medium representational procedure that was worked towards, rather than a reflection of early, underlying perceptual organization.

Refinement of spatial representation

The next phase of notational change occurred as subjects began to utilize the possibility of varying the length of the space between symbols to achieve a more varied and accurate representation of temporal durations (Figure 10.9). Some of the older subjects became overtly concerned to mark accurately the varying lengths of the drumbeats in the spacing of notational symbols, and their comments reflected an awareness of the representational procedures they employed: 'If they're spaced out, they don't go as fast'. Again, the possibility of being able to reflect upon their graphic-medium externalizations

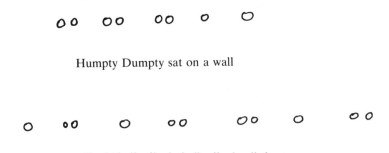

Humpty Dumpty sat on a wall

Jingle bells, jingle bells, jingle all the way

Fig. 10.9.   Refinement of spatial representations — grouped notations.

may have prompted them to move on from the simple longer/shorter distinctions of the earlier notations, to a more sophisticated awareness of the possible variety of fine durational discriminations.

Further notational control

The end-point of notational change in these musically untrained subjects consisted of notations in which spatially marked durations gave way to the use of different notational symbols to mark longer and shorter durations (Figure 10.10). While this representational strategy forms the basis of symbolization in conventional rhythm notation, in the baseline study, it was used only to

Baa, baa, black sheep, have you any wool

Ding dong bell, pussy's in the well

Fig. 10.10.   Further notational specification of duration.

mark a single qualitative differentiation between relatively longer and shorter durations. Only two subjects produced a quantitative rationale for their notations, explaining that a symbol represented a duration that was half, or twice, as long as another. So there was little evidence of a shift towards the orthochronic definition of duration characteristic of conventional rhythm notation, where each note value is twice the value of the next lower value note. Instead, when the children wished to differentiate a third duration in addition to simply making a distinction between longer and shorter drumbeats, they resorted to the earlier spatial grouping procedure (Figure 10.11).

Baa, baa, black sheep, have you any wool

Ding dong bell, Pussy's in the well

Fig. 10.11.   Further notational specification of duration — recording a third duration.

Summary

The change sequence can be summarized as a two-phase model, which accounts for the evolution of more adequate rhythm notations in terms of a gradual modification of motoric representations by graphic-medium representational procedures.

The first phase consists of notations that are generated by a motorically based procedure, which directly transposes underlying motoric representations of rhythm into the notational medium. These 'action drawings' are first modified through engagement with the discrete marking possibilities afforded by the medium, producing notations that represent the rhythm as a series of discrete drumbeats. These first externalizations are followed by a 'transitional' phase, where durational distinctions are detached from the control of motoric representations and internalized. The resulting notations, marking simply the number of drumbeats in the stimulus, presented subjects with the need to find an explicit *graphic* means for representing durational distinctions.

A second phase opens with the exploitation of the visual and spatial properties of the medium, which results in the development of a graphic-medium representational procedure. This procedure converts motoric representations into the spatial symbolization of duration times between drumbeats. The further refinement of spatial representations results in more precise and explicit notations. Finally, this clarity about the requirements of graphic symbolization prepares the way for the last notations, where all links with pre-literate motoric rhythm representation disappear, and duration is represented entirely by graphic resources.

Change sequences in the intervention studies

While the baseline study aimed to chart changes induced in rhythm representation by the introduction of a graphic medium, the *'aide-memoire'* and 'scribe–performer' studies were designed to elicit changes which occur when subjects notate for the purpose of remembering an already mastered rhythm, and then to devise notations sufficient for the generation of an unknown rhythm. It was expected that, with each additional social use constraint, more advanced, possibly orthochronic, types of notation would be produced, that different change sequences would occur, and that socially constrained conditions would encourage more rapid progress towards higher levels of the model.

Two types of data analysis were carried out. In the first, as in the baseline study, notations were assigned to type categories, and the ordering of each notational type within the change sequence noted. The second analysis consisted of a statistical comparison of the overall frequency of occurrence of each notational type in the three studies, and a further comparison of the frequency with which each functioned as an instance of notational change.

Contrary to expectation, the first phase of the analysis revealed no difference in the range of notational types produced in the three studies, and essentially the same sequence of change was found. There was no evidence of a progression towards more advanced conceptualizations of rhythm in the two socially constrained tasks. Nevertheless, a comparison of the proportion of change notations produced in the three studies showed that change occurred more frequently in both socially constrained tasks, more frequently of all in the 'scribe–performer' task. This suggests that the requirement of communication with another, and the opportunity to receive feedback from a partner afforded by this task, speeded up progress through the notational sequence.

Statistical comparison of the frequencies of occurrence of each notational type in the three studies revealed a shift in emphasis from the motoric to the graphic/notational aspects of rhythm representation in the intervention studies. A significantly lower number of early phase motorically controlled notations was produced. This trend away from motoric representation was complemented by an increased production of notations which attempted an explicit graphic representation of durational information. There was a significant increase in the use of spatial grouping as a representational procedure in the two intervention studies, both overall, and as instances of notational change. Especially when constrained to be explicit and systematic for another person in the 'scribe–performer' task, subjects produced a significantly increased number of the more explicit type of 'grouped' notations. Indeed, in many cases, these notations appeared sufficiently explicit to generate recognizable performances of the stimuli. There was also a significantly increased incidence of notations which completed the transition to purely graphic representation by inventing different symbols for longer and shorter durations.

The same trends appeared, also, in comparisons of the frequency with which notational types functioned as instances of change. Thus while motorically controlled notations frequently functioned as change notations in the baseline study, graphically controlled notations became the sole foci of change in the socially constrained tasks.

A final example of the trend towards graphically explicit notations was the significant decrease in the number of 'transitional' notations produced in the 'scribe–performer' study. It will be remembered that these seemingly uninformative notations consisted only of a more or less accurate representation of the number of drumbeats in the rhythm. They appeared with similar frequency in both the baseline and the *'aide-memoire'* studies, where the privacy of the task perhaps enabled the children to continue supplementing their notations with private motoric, or completely internalized, information about durational distinctions. However, the incidence of these notations decreased significantly in the 'scribe-performer' study, suggesting that the need to communicate with another prompted the emergence of more explicit notational externalizations.

The change from the conditions of the baseline to the two intervention studies may be viewed as a complete restructuring of the task. While the baseline study emphasized the personal and expressive, and the demand that rhythm be transcribed in a new medium, the intervention studies introduced the communicative uses of notation. The changes induced by the addition of historically salient social use constraints may be characterized as a narrowing of the range of notations produced and a rationalization of representational procedures. This takes the form of a greater reliance upon specifically graphic means for representing rhythm due, mainly, to the possibilities for externalization, complete specification, and hence communication that it affords. Thus the child is moved towards finding increasingly conventional, graphic means for representing salient characteristics of rhythm. Nevertheless, despite these important changes, the existence of the full range of rhythm representations under baseline study conditions suggests that, at least in the early stages of musical literacy, it is the initial exploration and use of the graphic medium that is the most salient factor prompting these developments.

Conclusion: why do rhythm representations develop?

In keeping with the emphasis of the classical developmentalists, who designed microgenesis as a specifically developmental experimental methodology, these studies of musical literacy focused on changes associated with the earliest origins and transitions of notational development. They produced evidence of a 'pre-history' of rhythm representation which may conceivably be seen as preceding and underlying the figural/metric distinction identified by other researchers. These changes were accounted for within the broad orientation of Soviet activity-theory, and were attributed to subjects' engagement in musical activities of a practical, socially defined nature. An attempt was made to separately identify the contribution of material/technological and communicative/social need aspects of these activities.

This type of account differs from those most frequently offered in the literature on developing rhythm representations. Bamberger (1980) explored the claim that 'age, and natural cognitive growth' provide the basic intellectual equipment for the transition to metric representations of rhythm, but concluded that specific musical training, especially training in the use of conventional notation, accounts for the distinction. She suggested that the acquisition of conventional musical notation might itself direct attention to the metric information in a rhythmic stimulus, and away from the broader, figural 'phrase shaping' aspects. However, this circular-sounding explanation has not been further explored. Other investigators have accepted the view that musical training underlies the development of rhythm representation, but have not completed this explanation with further analysis of the notion of 'training', or the identification the processes whereby training affects rhythm representation.

Wolf *et al.* (1986) looked at the development of rhythm representation from a perspective that is compatible with the activity-theory perspective developed in this paper. They produced statistical verification of a trend towards advanced rhythm representation between the ages of five and eight years, but pointed out that this trend occurred over a period of intense exposure to both the narrower skills and broader social uses of literacy across several domains of the formal school curriculum. Thus rhythm representation was seen as developing in the context of 'training', broadly defined as the total immersion of primary school children in the world of notational forms and purposes that characterize the different domains of literacy.

These considerations suggest that both the study of developing rhythm representation, and work on the effects of musical training, have been too narrowly conceived, in terms of very specific types of exposures to single factors. The work of Wolf *et al.*, and the studies reported in this paper, point to the view that, while it is possible to separate out and examine particular strands in the development of musical cognition, and the contribution of particular elements of musical activity, these aspects should always be viewed as integral parts of whole networks of broad, multi-aspected, and socially embedded activities. Thus consideration of material and social dependencies in musical cognition, many of which are highly specific to particular historical moments, are central to explanations of its development.

References

Bamberger, J. (1975). The development of musical intelligence in children's representations of simple rhythms. *MIT Artificial Intelligence Memo*, 342.

Bamberger, J. (1980). Cognitive structuring in the apprehension and description of simple rhythms. *Archives de psychologie* **48**, 101–19.

Barten, S. S. and Franklin, M. B. (eds) (1978). *Developmental processes: Heinz Werner's selected writings*. International Universities Press, New York.

Bruner, J. and Olsen, D. R. (1977–8). Symbols and texts as tools of the intellect. *Interchange* **8**, 1–15.

Catán, L. (1986) The dynamic display of process: historical development and contemporary uses of the microgenetic method. *Human development* **29**, 252–63.

Catán, L. (1987). *Literacy and cognition*. Unpublished D. Phil. thesis, University of Sussex, UK.

Cohen, S. (1983). *The development of notational skill in children*. Unpublished Ph.D. thesis, Stanford University, Stanford, CA.

Cole, M. (1985). The zone of proximal development: where culture and cognition create each other. In *Culture, communication and cognition, Vygotskian perspectives* (ed. J. Wertsch). Cambridge University Press.

Davydov, V. V. and Radzikhovskii, L. A. (1985). Vygotski's theory and the activity-oriented approach in psychology. In *Culture, cognition and communication: Vygotskian perspectives* (ed. J. Wertsch). Cambridge University Press.

Ferreiro, E. and Teberosky, A. (1982). *Literacy before schooling*. Heinemann Educational Books, London.

Fraisse, P. (1978). Time and rhythm perception. In *Handbook of perception, vol. VIII, perceptual coding* (eds. E. C. Carterette and M. P. Friedman). Academic Press, New York.

Freeman, N. H. (1972). Process and product in children's drawings. *Perception* 1, 123–40.

Gaddini, R. (1987). Early care and the roots of internalization. *International review of psychoanalysis* 14, 321–33.

Goody, J., Cole, M., and Scribner, S. (1977). Writing and formal operations: a case study among the Vai. *Africa* 47, 289–304.

Karmiloff-Smith, A. (1979). Micro- and macrodevelopmental changes in language acquisition and other representational systems. *Cognitive science* 3, 91–118.

Kosslyn, S. M., Heldmeyer, K. H., and Loclear, E. P. (1977). Children's drawings as data about internal representations. *Journal of experimental child psychology* 23, 191–211.

Leont'ev, A. N. (1981). The problem of activity in psychology. In *The concept of activity in psychology* (ed. J. Wertsch). Sharpe, New York.

Leont'ev, A. N. and Luria, A. R. (1972) Some notes concerning Dr Fodor's 'Reflections concerning L. S. Vygotsky's thought and language. *Cognition* 1, 301–18.

Longuet-Higgins, C. H. and Lee, C. S. (1982). The perception of musical rhythms. *Perception* 11, 115–28.

Luria, A. R. (1928/1978). The development of writing in the child. In *The selected writings of A. R. Luria* (ed. M. Cole). Sharpe, New York.

Luria, A. R. (1932). *The nature of human conflicts: an objective study of disorganization and control of human behaviour*. Liveright, New York.

Luria, A. R. (1979). *The making of mind: a personal account of Soviet psychology*. Harvard University Press, Cambridge.

Mahler, M. (1968). *On human symbiosis and the vicissitudes of individuation*. International Universities Press, New York.

Milner, M. (1950). *On not being able to paint*. The New Education Book Club, London.

Piaget, J. (1942). Les trois structures fondamenteles de la vie psychique: rhythme, regulation et groupement. *Revue Suisse de la psychologie* 1, 9–21.

Piaget, J. (1976). *The grasp of consciousness: action and concept in the young child*. Routledge and Kegan Paul, London.

Piaget, J. and Inhelder, B. (1956). *The child's conception of space*. Norton, New York.

Povel, D. J. (1981). Internal representation of simple temporal patterns. *Journal of experimental psychology: human perception and performance* 7, 3–18.

Rogoff, B. (1982). Integrating culture and cognitive development. In *Advances in developmental psychology, vol. 2* (eds. M. E. Lamb and A. L. Brown). Erlbaum, Hillsdale, NJ.

Scribner, S. and Cole, M. (1981). *The psychology of literacy*. Harvard University Press, Cambridge.

Smith, J. (1983). Reproduction and representation of musical rhythms: the effects of musical skill. In *The acquisition of symbolic skills* (eds. D. Rogers and J. A. Sloboda). NATO Conference Series 3, Human Factors 22. Plenum, New York.

Smith, J. (1984). Differences in memory and representation of rhythm with expertise. Poster presentation at the Inaugural European Conference on Developmental Psychology in Groeningen.

Steedman, M. (1977). The perception of musical rhythms and metre. *Perception* **6**, 555–69.

Vygotsky, L. S. (1978). *Mind in society*. Harvard University Press, Cambridge, MA.

Werner, H. (1954). Change of meaning: a study of semantic process through the experimental method. *Journal of genetic psychology* **50**, 181–208.

Werner, H. and Kaplan, B. (1957). Symbolic mediation and the organization of thought: an experimental approach by means of the line schematization technique. *Journal of psychology* **43**, 3–25.

Werner, H. and Kaplan, B. (1963). *Symbol formation: an organismic–developmental approach to language and the expression of thought*. Wiley, New York.

Winnicot, D. W. (1945/1956). Primitive emotional development. In *Collected papers*. Tavistock, London.

Wolf, D., Davison, L., Davis, M., Walters, J., Hodges, M., and Scripp, L. (1986). Beyond A, B and C: a broader and deeper view of literacy. In *The psychological bases of early education* (ed. A. Pelligrini). Wiley, London.

Zinchenko, V. P. (1985). Vygotsky and units for the analysis of mind. In *Culture, cognition and communication: Vygotskian perspectives* (ed. J. Wertsch). Cambridge University Press.

11

On the interaction of language and thought: some thoughts and developmental data

STAN A. KUCZAJ II, ROBERT H. BORYS, and MEAGAN JONES

> . . . *any number of impressions, from any number of sensory sources, falling simultaneously on a mind WHICH HAS NOT YET EXPERIENCED THEM SEPARATELY, will fuse into a single undivided object for that mind* . . . all things fuse that *can* fuse, and nothing separates except what must . . . The baby, assailed by eyes, ears, nose, skin, and entrails at once, feels it all as one great blooming, buzzing confusion (James 1890, p. 488, his italics and capitalization).

Although the available data on young infant's perceptual and cognitive capabilities demonstrates that William James erred when he characterized the infant's world as a blooming, buzzing confusion (*see* Banks and Salapatek 1983 and Harris 1983 for recent critical summaries of the relevant literature), the theoretical context in which James couched his speculation about the infant's experience is as pertinent today as it was 100 years ago. The amount of information available to the mind is vast and complex, and the manner in which children and adults make sense of it has long been a subject of concern in philosophy, linguistics, anthropology, and psychology. Most theorists concerned with this issue have agreed that a significant part of our interpretation of the available information involves the formation and utilization of concepts such as dog, relative, large, love, imaginary, proof, bright, intention, self, and so on (one notable exception to this generalization was the behaviorist school of psychology, which abhorred the notion of any sort of mental entity or process; *see* Watson 1913, for an example of this line of 'reasoning').

The almost universal acceptance of the importance of concepts in our understanding of the universe has not resulted in a general acceptance of any single theory of the nature and/or formation of concepts. To the contrary, there exists a myriad array of notions about both the nature of concepts and their formation. A critical examination of this literature is beyond the scope of this chapter, but the interested reader is referred to important edited works by Neisser (1987) and Rosch and Lloyd (1978). We shall limit our consideration of the problem of how we make sense of the world to one controversy that surfaces continually in the literature of concern — the effects of one's language on one's concepts.

Some historical background

The hypothesis that a speaker's language is related to his or her conceptual knowledge has a long history (Schaff 1973). Approximately 250 years ago, the German philosopher Herder proposed that the language of a culture shaped the concepts of the world held by that culture (Herder 1768). Herder's views have been summarized by Schaff as follows:

Language is . . . a treasure house and a form of thinking. It is a treasure house because the experience and knowledge of generations are accumulated in language, and it is a form of thinking because these are transmitted through language to the next generations in the process of upbringing. We think not only in some language but also *through the intermediary* of some language . . . The language of a nation fixes its experience and the various truths and falsehoods which the language transmits to coming generations, and thus the language molds their vision of the world . . . language determines the boundary and the outline of all human cognition (Schaff 1973, p. 9, his italics).

The view that language was instrumental in shaping human thought was also advocated by the German linguist Humboldt (1907). For both Herder and Humboldt, the language of a culture reflects the knowledge, values, and beliefs of the culture. The hypothesized interdependence of language and culture has implications for the role language is thought to play in a child coming to make sense of the world. In this view, a culture's language becomes the major socialization tool of the culture, socializing those who acquire it not only in terms of the society's mores, but also in terms of their accepted conceptual knowledge. Thus, language strongly influences thought, thought is reflected in language, and the conceptual differences that exist between cultures are assumed to be both caused by and reflected in the culture's language.

This theoretical stance places considerable emphasis on language as a mechanism for conceptual development and conceptual understanding, an emphasis that was echoed by Sapir and Whorf during the first half of this century.

The fact of the matter is that the 'real world' is to a large extent unconsciously built up by the language habits of the group. No two languages are ever sufficiently similar to be considered as representing the same social reality. The worlds in which different societies live are distinct worlds, not merely the same world with different labels attached (Sapir 1951, p. 164).

We dissect nature along lines laid down by our native languages. The categories and types that we isolate from the world of phenomena we do not find there because they stare every observer in the face; on the contrary, the world is presented in a kaleidoscopic flux of impressions which has to be organized by our minds — and this means largely by the linguistic systems in our minds. We cut nature up, organize it into concepts, and ascribe significances as we do, largely because we are parties to an agreement to organize it in this way — an agreement that holds throughout our speech community and is codified in the patterns of our language. The agreement is, of course, an implicit and unstated one, *but its terms are absolutely obligatory* (Whorf 1956, pp. 213–14, his italics).

The views represented in the above quotes have come to be known as the Sapir–Whorf hypothesis. The main points of the Sapir–Whorf hypothesis are quite similar to the views of Herder and Humboldt:

(1) The language of a culture strongly influences the manner in which members of a culture interpret information about their world.

(2) The differences that exist in the languages of different cultures result in corresponding differences in the world views of members of the cultures.

There is also another aspect of the Sapir–Whorf hypothesis that is important in the general context of the issues raised by William James in his assessment of the infant's world as a 'blooming, buzzing confusion'. James assumed that the infant's lack of experience with the world resulted in an inability to differentiate relevant parts of the world on the infant's part. Sapir and Whorf suggested that the differentiation of the information available in the world depended on the language to which the child was exposed. In their view, language directly influenced the conceptual content that one acquired by pointing to ways in which the world should be categorized, such categorization reducing the confusion that characterized the world of the young pre-verbal child. Thus, in regard to children's acquisition of the conceptual content necessary to comprehend their own experience, James emphasized the role of general experience with the world, whereas Sapir and Whorf emphasized the role of a particular sort of experience — language.

Before considering the implications of these views for developmental psychology, we should note that the Sapir–Whorf hypothesis has been interpreted in terms of both linguistic relativity and linguistic determinism (Brown 1958; Cole and Scribner 1974). The notion of linguistic relativity, sometimes referred to as the weak form of the Sapir–Whorf hypothesis, is based on a hypothesized covariance of language and thought. The basic tenet of linguistic relativity is that differences in language correspond to differences in thought. Of course, the causal connection is difficult to establish when two variables covary. Does language shape thought? Or does thought shape language? The notion of linguistic determinism, often referred to as the strong form of the Sapir–Whorf hypothesis, avoids this problem by postulating that language directly influences thought. Thus, linguistic relativity assumes that differences in thought are reflected in differences in language, whereas the notion of linguistic determinism assumes that differences in thought are caused by differences in language.

Implications of linguistic determinism and linguistic relativity for developmental psychology

The hypotheses advanced over the past 250 years by theorists such as Herder, Humboldt, Sapir, and Whorf have implications for developmental psychology, particularly those branches of developmental psychology concerned with language, cognition, and socialization. If linguistic determinism is correct, then the language that a child learns determines both the child's cultural values and the child's conceptual systems for understanding the world. If linguistic relativity is correct, then the language that a child learns reflects the cultural values and conceptual systems that the child will eventually acquire, although the language itself may not be the sole or even primary determinant of either socialization or conceptual development. Note that linguistic relativity and linguistic determinism both assume that different languages mean different cultural values and conceptual systems. Thus, the notion of culture-specific acquisitions and cultural differences is an inherent part of linguistic relativity and linguistic determinism, whereas the notion of universals is minimized (the only cultural and conceptual universals would be those also reflected in the languages of the world).

The view that language is a powerful socialization tool and that children acquire a particular world view as they acquire a language has its advocates in developmental psychology. Approximately 60 years ago, de Laguna (1927) suggested that

As language develops it acts like a sculptor, carving into sharper relief the features of the objective human world. What is at first vague in its outline . . . becomes gradually more distinct. The world is for the first time genuinely individuated. Objects stand out . . . At the same time likenesses and differences become distinguished and accentuated. As the world becomes individuated, it becomes classified (de Laguna 1927, p. 274).

De Laguna's position is similar to that advanced by Herder, Humboldt, Sapir, and Whorf. Language is viewed as an agent of socialization, providing the child with clues concerning appropriate conceptual categories, the precise nature of the appropriate categories varying from culture to culture. Cultural variation in categorization is marked by each culture's language and thereby transmitted from generation to generation via the linguistic code. This view of the relationship of language development and cognitive development has survived in various forms for over 250 years, and has its proponents in the current developmental literature (e.g. *see* Bloom, 1981; Ochs 1986; Ochs and Schieffelin 1984).

Although the notion that language plays a critical role in our construction of reality has both a long history and a number of advocates in contemporary psychology, it is far from a universally accepted hypothesis. Mervis (1987) has suggested that during the first few years of life words have very little influence in determining children's concepts of the world. According to Mervis, the 'linguistic input received by the child appears to have little importance either in determining that a category will be established or in determining the composition of a category' (p. 225). Instead, the young child is thought to form pre-linguistic concepts of the world, these pre-linguistic concepts influencing the child's first words rather than vice versa.

Mervis hypothesizes that the relative unimportance of linguistic input in children's initial category formation reflects young children's attentional biases. She suggests that very young children attend selectively to the language to which they are exposed, and are unlikely to attend to the labels for objects that do not interest them. Of course, this view of selective attention to linguistic input rests on the assumption that children can distinguish the labels for non-interesting objects from those for interesting objects, as well as being able to discriminate interesting and non-interesting objects. More important (at least from our point of view) is Mervis' suggestion that language plays little role in the initial formation of children's concepts of 'interesting' objects. As she notes, if a child finds an object interesting, it is likely that the child's interest in the object has led to the formation of a pre-linguistic concept. As a result, the first words of a child are most likely to be attached to already existing pre-linguistic concepts, rather than to cause the child to create a new concept.

The notion that words map onto concepts that have been developed non-linguistically is a common one (Bowerman 1981; Clark 1973; Huttenlocher 1974; MacNamara 1972; Nelson 1974; Wittgenstein 1953). In this view, cognitive development influences and constrains the meanings of words, rather than vice versa. For example, Clark (1977) suggested that children's acquisition of object word meaning was related to the obligatory classifier systems found in many of the world's languages.

Visual perception plays an important role (in) both . . . In both cases, objects are categorized primarily on the basis of shape, and the same properties of shape appear to be relevant in acquisition and in classifier systems. Roundness and length . . . appear to be very salient (Clark 1977, p. 460).

Based on her observations, Clark concluded that object word meaning acquisition in all languages and the classifier systems of human languages are similar to one another because both depend on a universal 'a priori, non-linguistic categorization process'. In other words, all children possess similar (if not identical) non-linguistic strategies for manipulating and organizing information concerning objects and their attributes, these strategies influencing both the ontogeny of object words and the evolution of classifier systems in human languages. Independent support for Clark's hypothesis comes from a study of the classifier systems of more than fifty languages by Allan (1977). Allan found more similarities than differences in the classifier systems of diverse languages, support for Clark's position but contrary to what might be expected based on the assumptions of linguistic relativity or linguistic determinism.

Other scholars have also argued that language develops as a function of more general cognitive processes, mental representational abilities (MacNamara 1972; Piaget and Inhelder 1969) or cognitive skills (Sinclair 1971). This line of reasoning reflects the belief that cognition determines language rather than vice versa. Thus, more general cognitive skills are thought to determine both the child's early concepts and the child's acquisition of object words. The support for this theoretical stance discussed to this point includes children's acquisition of pre-linguistic concepts, their subsequent mapping of words onto such existing concepts, and the similarity of classifier systems across human languages. Additional support is found in observations that the types of meanings expressed by the first words of children are more similar than different, regardless of the culture being studied (see Barrett 1985; Bloom 1970, 1973; Brown 1973; Schlesinger 1971). If this pattern continues to hold true as additional information is obtained about early word meaning acquisition from more cultures, then it would appear that children's early word meanings are more determined by universal cognitive underpinnings than by either their language or their culture. The influence of cognitive predispositions on word meaning development may also continue after children have acquired their first words. As children expand their lexicon, they exhibit non-linguistic preferences when they attempt to determine the meaning of novel words (Clark 1973; Kuczaj and Lederberg 1977; Kuczaj and Maratsos 1975; Kuczaj 1982; Markman 1987). For example, children exhibit a preference for the upper surface of an object, which influences their acquisition of words such as *top* or *bottom* (Clark 1980).

To sum up, empirical support for either linguistic relativity or linguistic determinism is sparse in the language acquisition literature, at least in so far as the versions that correspond to the Sapir–Whorf hypothesis are concerned. However, there are other possibilities concerning the influence that language has on thought (see Rice and Kemper 1984, for a more thorough discussion of these and related issues). One of these alternatives was advanced by the Russian psychologist Vygotsky.

Vygotsky's view

Vygotsky (1962) argued that the development of cognition and the development of language have different ontogenetic roots, such that there is a 'pre-linguistic' period in the initial phases of cognitive development and a 'pre-intellectual' period in the initial phases of language development. Although Vygotsky emphasized the independence of early cognitive development and early language development, he also emphasized the interdependence of language development and cognitive development once the two lines of development had converged, such convergence hypothesized to occur sometime around two years of age. Vygotsky acknowledged the significance of language for thought when he stated that 'learning to direct one's own mental processes with the aid of words or signs is an integral part of the process of concept formation' (1962, p. 59). The importance delegated to language by Vygotsky is aptly stated by Luria.

Vygotsky interpreted differences in one's reflections of reality as differences in the system of psychological elements that govern such reflections. In his view, language is the most decisive element in systematizing perception; insofar as words are themselves a product of sociohistorical development, they become tools for formulating abstractions and generalizations, and facilitate the transition from unmediated sensory reflection to mediated, rational thinking . . . 'categorical thinking' and 'abstract orientation' are the consequences of a fundamental reorganization of cognitive activity that occurs under the impact of a new, social factor — a restructuring of the role that language plays in determining psychological activity (Luria 1976, pp. 49–50).

Although Vygotsky stressed the importance of language for thought, he did not believe that language played much role in helping children to interpret and organize the world before the age of five years. In Vygotsky's opinion, younger children lack the cognitive skills necessary to take advantage of the directions provided by language.

language . . ., with its stable, permanent meanings, points the way that the child's generalizations will take. But, constrained as it is, the child's thinking proceeds along it's preordained path in the manner peculiar to his level of intellectual development (Vygotsky 1962, p. 68).

It seems likely that Vygotsky underestimated the importance of language for thought in preschool-age children. Although Mervis (1987) has emphasized the mapping of children's first words onto existing pre-linguistic concepts, she has also acknowledged that linguistic input can influence young children's categories. For example, adult labelling of an exemplar may result in the child including the exemplar as an instance of a category. Adult labelling may also help the child to decide to which category an object belongs when the child considers the objects to be a potential member of two (or more) categories. As such, linguistic input may help even very young children to modify existing categories, particularly when peripheral examples of the categories are involved.

As children get older, the role of linguistic input in classification and categorization increases.

(1) The older child realizes that adult use of a different label for an object included in a child category implies that a new category assignment would be appropriate (Kuczaj 1986; Mervis 1987).

(2) For the older child, adult use of a word to label an object for which the child has no category may lead the child to form a new category (Markman 1987; Mervis, 1987).

Thus, it seems likely that language influences preschool children's categorization, by cueing the child either to modify an existing concept or to create a new concept altogether (*see also* Bowerman 1981; Clark and Clark 1977; Kuczaj 1975, 1982).

In a discussion reminiscent of Vygotsky's views, Schlesinger (1982) noted that although different languages do categorize the world in different ways, there is more similarity than one might expect (*see* Heider 1972 and Rosch 1974 for discussions of colour terms relevant to this point). This led Schlesinger to conclude that there is considerable perceptual regularity in the world that 'constrains but does not fully determine the formation of concepts' (1982, p. 146). Similarities across languages reflect the constraints imposed by perceptual regularity, whereas differences across languages reflect flexibility outside of such constraints. Thus, children's initial pre-linguistic categories reflect general perceptual regularity, and are relatively unstable, whereas later categories become permanent once they are 'firmly anchored' to language forms. In Schlesinger's view, stable categories are the result of a convergence of perceptual regularity and linguistic input. Thus, early thought is characterized by plasticity, and language helps to mold more stable concepts (a view shared by Vygotsky 1962).

To sum up, there are a number of opinions in the existing literature concerning the relationship of language and thought. The following two studies represent attempts to gather developmental data in order to better determine which of the conflicting views has the most credence.

Study 1

Purpose

The present study had two purposes:

(1) To investigate the manner in which classificatory experience with objects influenced children's acquisition of words with which to name the objects.

(2) To investigate the manner in which previous exposure to names for objects influenced children's ability to classify the objects.

Procedure

There were a total of four conditions in Study 1. Two conditions were designated 'experimental' conditions. The first such condition, the 'grouping first' condition, involved the initial presentation of twelve novel objects, constructed such that adults agreed that the objects could be categorized into three groups of four objects each. In the 'grouping first' condition, children were first encouraged to engage in free play with the objects for a period of approximately 10 minutes. After this initial experience, children were given a grouping task. This task consisted of asking children to put the objects into transparent containers and to put the objects that were alike into the same container. To reduce the likelihood of children grouping similar objects by chance, children were provided with twelve containers.

Following the grouping task, children were taught novel names for one of the exemplars from each of the three groups (the term 'group' here denotes the adult-recognized groups, not the 'groups' that the children had just created). This was done by introducing the child to three puppets, telling the child that the puppets spoke a different language than the child, and that the child should try to learn how the puppets talked so that he or she could help the puppets talk to one another (this technique has been used successfully to help children learn novel words and affixes, e.g. Kuczaj 1979). After the child had chosen one of the three puppets and the experimenter had selected another of the puppets, the child was shown one of the objects and told that 'my puppet calls this a ____. Can you have your puppet say ____?' This procedure was then used for each of the other target objects (one from each of the groups) and subsequently repeated until the child had been exposed to each target object and its novel name on three occasions. Following this exposure session to the three novel names, children were asked to name each of the twelve objects by showing the child an object and asking what the puppet would call it, showing the child another object and asking what the puppet would call it, and so on, until the child had been asked to label each of the twelve objects. The children were then encouraged to play with the objects for another 10-minute period. Following this, children were once again shown the array of twelve objects and asked to put the objects into containers, the experimenter once again stressing that the child should put the ones that went together into the same containers.

The other experimental condition was the 'label-first' condition. The same tasks were used that had been used in the 'group-first' condition, but in a different order. In this condition, children were first shown a set of twelve novel objects organized in a random array. (One set of twelve objects was used in the 'label-first' condition and another set was used in the 'group-first' condition.) Immediately following this exposure, children were taught the novel names for one of the exemplars from each group, and were then asked to label each of the twelve objects. Children were then encouraged to play with the objects for approximately 10 minutes, and then asked to group the objects. Following this, children were taught the novel labels again (primarily as a memory refresher) and then asked to label the objects again.

The two experimental conditions can be schematized in the following manner:

(a) 'group-first': (1) exposure to array of objects, (2) play with objects, (3) grouping task, (4) taught labels, (5) labelling task, (6) play with objects, and (7) grouping task.

(b) 'label-first': (1) exposure to array of objects, (2) taught labels, (3) labelling task, (4) playing with objects, (5) grouping task, (6) taught labels, and (7) labelling task.

Thirty-six children volunteered to play with our objects and puppets. There were six males and six females in each of three age groups—three-year-olds, four-year-olds, and five-year-olds. All children were tested individually and were exposed to both conditions. The order of presentation of the two conditions was counterbalanced, as was the particular set of twelve objects used in a condition for a child.

The remaining two conditions were 'control' conditions, designed to mirror the two experimental conditions with one exception—the exclusion of either the grouping or the naming aspect of the condition. The 'grouping' control condition involved the initial presentation of one of the sets of objects used in the experimental conditions, after which children were encouraged to play with the objects for approximately 10 minutes. Children were then given the grouping task (as in the experimental conditions). Following this, children were shown three objects (one from each of the three groups), but not taught a name. Rather they were simply shown the three objects on three separate occasions. Children were then once again encouraged to play with the objects for approximately 10 minutes, and were then given the grouping task again.

The 'labelling' control condition involved the initial presentation of the other set of twelve novel objects, after which the children were taught the names for three of the objects (this procedure was identical to that used in the 'label-first' experimental condition). Following this, children were asked to name each of the objects (also as in the 'label-first' experimental condition). They were then encouraged to play with the twelve objects for approximately 10 minutes, taught the labels once again, and then asked to name the objects for the second time.

The control conditions can be schematized as follows:

(a) 'Grouping': (1) exposure to array of objects, (2) play with objects, (3) grouping task, (4) shown one object from each group (but not taught name), (5) play with objects, (6) grouping task.

(b) 'Labelling': (1) exposure to array of objects, (2) taught labels, (3) labelling task, (4) play with objects, (5) taught labels, (6) labelling task.

Thirty-six children volunteered to participate in the 'control' conditions. The sample of children was demographically identical to that of the sample for the 'experimental' conditions. As in the 'experimental' conditions, each of the thirty-six children received both conditions. The order of presentation of the two conditions was counterbalanced, as was the set of twelve objects used in each condition.

Results

We shall first consider the results from the grouping tasks. Table 11.1 shows the percentage of correct groupings (defined as those instances in which the child put all of the appropriate members into the same box). Comparing the percentage of correct groupings in the first grouping tasks for group-first and label-first conditions indicates that having been taught a name for one exemplar from each group (and perhaps having been asked to label each exemplar) seems to have helped children to group objects correctly (particularly for three- and four-year-old children) $F(1,30) = 6.76$, $P < 0.02$. The influence of having been taught a name for a category instance on subsequent grouping performance is also evident when we compare children's performance on the second grouping tasks in the control and group-first conditions. The children in the control conditions improved little if at all from the first grouping task to the second grouping task. In contrast, the children in the group-first condition improved dramatically from the first grouping task to the second grouping task, $F(1,30) = 29.03$, $P < 0.001$. The difference between these two groups reflects the difference between having been provided a label and not having been provided a label. However, the influence of having attempted to group the objects prior to being exposed to a name for one exemplar from each group on subsequent grouping is evident when we compare the second grouping task for the group-first condition with the grouping task for the label-first condition. Children in

Table 11.1. *Per cent correct groupings in study 1, categorized by age and condition.*

	Condition				
	Control		Group-first		Label-first
Age, years	First grouping	Second grouping	First grouping	Second grouping	First and only grouping
3	11.1	16.7	5.6	36.1	25.0
4	22.1	30.6	22.2	55.6	44.4
5	36.1	27.8	25.0	61.1	39.9

Table 11.2. *Percentage of objects correctly named in study 1, categorized by age and condition.*

	Condition				
	Control		Label-first		Group-first
Age, years	First labelling task	Second labelling task	First labelling task	Second labelling task	First and only labelling task
3	27.1	44.4	31.3	57.6	42.4
4	47.9	55.6	48.6	65.9	60.4
5	52.1	67.4	56.9	75.7	58.3

the group-first condition were much better at grouping the objects after having been taught names than were the children in the label-first condition, $F = 4.71$, $P < 0.04$. The difference between the two conditions was apparently caused by the grouping experience that the children in the group-first condition had prior to being exposed to the names. Thus, being exposed to names appears to help children to better group objects, but experience with grouping prior to learning the names makes the naming effect even more dramatic in the subsequent grouping conditions.

The results of the labelling tasks are summarized in Table 11.2. Comparison of the conditions (label-first and group-first) in which children were asked to name each of the objects for the first time suggests that prior experience with grouping the objects (the group-first condition) facilitated three- and four-year-old children's correct labelling of the objects; $t(11) = 2.61$, $P < 0.05$ for three-year-olds; $t(11) = 3.15$, $P < 0.01$ for four-year-olds. The effect of having been asked to group the objects on subsequent success on the labelling task is also evident when we compare the second naming task performances of the control condition and the label-first condition. Children who had been asked to group the objects were much more likely to name the objects correctly in the subsequent (second) labelling task than were children who had not been asked to group the objects, $F(1,30) = 27.83$, $P < 0.001$. In other words, children who had been allowed to play with the objects but had not been asked to group the objects (the control group) were not as likely to label the objects correctly as were the children who had been asked to group the objects. Nonetheless, the children in the control condition did improve in their performance on the second labelling task, $F(1,70) = 49.65$, $P < 0.01$, although the improvement was less than was observed for the children in the label-first condition. Thus, although grouping the objects did facilitate children's subsequent success in the labelling task, being allowed to play with the objects (the control condition) also improved children's labelling performance (perhaps having been asked to label the object prior to playing increased the children's tendency to look for similarity among the objects). Moreover, having been taught the names on two occasions also seems to have influenced children's success in naming the objects on the second labelling task. Thus, even though the three- and four-year-olds in the group-first condition correctly named more objects in the first labelling task (and only labelling task for them) than did the children in the control and label-first conditions, children in the control conditions correctly named about as many objects in the second labelling task as did the children in the group-first condition in the first labelling task, even though children in the control condition had not been asked to group the objects. Nonetheless, children who had been asked to group the objects after the first labelling task and who were then re-taught the labels were most likely to label correctly the objects in the second labelling task.

To sum up, the results of the first experiment demonstrate that:

(a) being exposed to names for objects facilitates classification of objects, and

(b) experience with objects helps children to determine the correct extension of labels, experience involving attempts to group objects seeming to be more influential than play alone.

Study 2

In study 1, the effects of categorization experience with objects on subsequent success in naming the objects and the effects of naming experience on subsequent categorization success was investigated. This was accomplished by asking children to group novel objects and to label the same objects with novel names that had been taught to each child. In study 2, we wished to further ascertain the significance of verbal labels by asking children to create names for the novel objects rather than by providing them with the novel names.

There were two conditions in study 2, each of which corresponded to one of the experimental conditions in study 1. The 'group-first' condition consisted of the initial exposure of the children to the set of twelve novel objects, encouraging the children to play with the objects, asking the children to group the objects, asking the children to label the objects, encouraging the children to play with the objects, and then asking the children to group the objects once again. In the labelling task, children were introduced to three puppets, and asked to choose one of the puppets so that the experimenter and the child could talk to one another in puppet language. After the child chose a puppet, the experimenter selected one of the remaining puppets and told the child that the puppets spoke a different language that the experimenter did not know. The child was asked to guess what the puppet called an object, and then asked to do the same for another object, and so on until the child had been asked to name each of the twelve objects.

In the 'labelling-first' condition, the child was first exposed to the array of objects, then asked to name the objects, next encouraged to play with the objects, then asked to group the objects, next encouraged to play with the objects once again, and finally asked to name the objects for the second time. As in the group-first condition, the labelling tasks consisted of asking the child to guess what the puppets would call each of the twelve objects.

Thirty-six children (twelve three-year-olds, twelve four-year-olds, and twelve five-year-olds; six males and six females in each age group) participated in study 2. Each child participated in each condition, and the order of presentation of the two conditions was counterbalanced.

Children's performance on the grouping tasks is summarized in Table 11.3. Comparing the results of the two first grouping tasks, it appears that being asked to create a name for an exemplar facilitated children's ability to classify the objects, $F(1,30) = 5.0$, $P < 0.04$. Note that although this effect held for the four-year-old and five-year-old children, being asked to create a label did not facilitate the grouping performance of the three-year-old children. This pattern is quite different from that observed in study 1, where being taught labels prior to the first grouping task markedly improved three-year-old children's performance on the grouping task. Children's performance in the second grouping task in study 2 indicates that being asked to group the objects and then being asked to create names for the objects facilitated the four-year-old and five-year-old children's performance in the second grouping task, $F(1,30) = 10.18$, $P < 0.004$. This effect is less dramatic than the one observed in study 1, but is present in study 2 nonetheless. Comparing the results of study 2 with those of the group-first condition and the appropriate control group in study 1, we see that the improvement in the second grouping task is small (or non-existent for five-year-olds) when no

Table 11.3. *Per cent of correct groupings in study 2, categorized by age and condition.*

Age, years	Condition		
	Group-first		Label-first
	First grouping task	Second grouping task	First and only grouping task
3	14	17	11
4	19	39	39
5	30	44	44

Table 11.4.   *Percentage of words in study 2 used to name two or more objects for a group but no objects from another group, categorized by age and condition*

Age, years	Condition		
	Label-first		Group-first
	First labelling task	Second labelling task	First and only labelling task
3	11	11	25
4	22	44	47
5	33	47	47

names are used, better when children are asked to create names for the objects, and best when children are taught a name for an exemplar for each group.

Before discussing the results from the labelling tasks, a brief consideration of scoring decisions is in order. Given that children were asked to create names for the objects, it is impossible to determine whether or not a word was used correctly. Instead, we elected to examine words that were used consistently and generally. 'General use' was defined as the use of a word created by the child to refer to more than one of the novel objects. 'Consistent use' was defined as the use of the created word to refer to only instances of one category. Thus, 'general and consistent use' involved the use of a word to refer to two or more objects from one category, but no use to refer to any other object. The results of the labelling tasks, based on these criteria, are summarized in Table 11.4. Looking at the results of the first labelling tasks, it is clear that having been asked to group the objects prior to being asked to create names for the objects enhanced children's ability to create 'general and consistent' names, $F(1,30) = 10.31$, $P<0.004$. Moreover, comparing performance on the first labelling tasks in study 1 with that in study 2 reveals that the general positive effect of prior grouping experience on subsequent naming performance is evident when children are taught novel names or are asked to create novel names.

Children's performance on the second labelling task in study 2 suggests that the grouping experience intervening between the first and second naming tasks improved children's performance on the second labelling task, $F(1,30) = 13.00$, $P<0.001$. Such improvement occurred for four-year-old and five-year-old children, but not for three-year-olds. Moreover, children's performance on the second labelling task was not better than that of the first naming task for the group-first condition. This pattern is different from that observed in study 1, where the intervening grouping experience seemed to improve three-year-old, four-year-old, and five-year-old children's subsequent naming performance, not only in comparison to their performance on the first labelling task in the label-first condition but also in comparison to their performance in the first (and only) labelling task in the group-first condition. This comparison suggests that providing children with a name for an object has a different effect than does asking children to create the name for an object. A control condition that was subsequently conducted involved asking children to create names for objects and then having them do so again without any grouping experience. In this condition, children exhibited little if any improvement in the second labelling task, this also being quite different from the pattern that was observed in the 'labelling' control condition in study 1.

Discussion

The results of study 1 and study 2 suggest the following conclusions:

(1) previous experience with novel objects helps children to determine the correct extension of a novel word used to refer to such objects;

(2) previous experience with naming novel objects (with a novel name) facilitates children's subsequent categorization of the objects;

(3) being taught a novel word and being asked to create a novel word seem to yield different effects, suggesting that the notion of words as *conventional* symbols is an important one.

Experience with the novel objects influenced children's success on the naming tasks in study 1 in one of two ways. Having been asked to play with the novel objects resulted in improved success in correctly naming the objects, suggesting that in the course of playing with the objects children were able to ascertain at least some of the similarities and differences among the objects. However, children who had been asked to try to group the objects prior to being asked to name them were more likely to correctly name the objects than were children who had only played with the objects. The grouping experience seems to have increased the children's natural propensity for dividing the world into those things that are similar and those things that are different, which in turn facilitated their correct extensional decisions in the naming task.

Having been taught novel names for one exemplar from each group and then being asked to name each of the twelve novel objects increased the likelihood that children would group appropriate objects together. Apparently, children use the appearance of a novel name for a novel object as a cue to search for the category of objects to which the name refers. When children hear a novel word used to refer to a novel object, they seem to assume that the word refers to a class of objects rather than to only an individual object. This assumption triggers the search for the basis for class extension, one result being improved performance on grouping tasks such as that used in study 1.

Being taught a novel word for a novel object yielded different results than did being asked to create a novel word for a novel object. Although children who were asked to create a name for a novel object were better able to group objects appropriately, compared with when they had not been asked to create a name, the improvement was less dramatic than that observed for children who were taught novel names for novel objects, particularly for three-year-old children. Moreover, the effect of having been asked to group the objects on two occasions (with a naming task intervening between the two grouping tasks) did not improve children's second grouping performance beyond that observed in the condition in which children were asked to group the objects for the first time after having been asked to create names for the objects. This pattern is quite different than that observed in study 1.

The effects of experience in grouping the novel objects on success in the naming task also differed when children were asked to create names rather than to learn new names. The most striking difference involved the performance of three-year-old children. In study 1, when three-year-old children were taught labels, then asked to group the objects, and then asked to name the objects for the second time, their performance on the second naming task was far superior to that on the first naming task. In contrast, there was no such improvement when three-year-old children were asked to create names in study 2.

The differences in task performance between attempting to learn a novel name and attempting to create a new name may reflect differences in the status that children grant the two types of names. When children hear a novel label used to refer to an object, they seem to assume that the name labels a category of objects, an assumption that triggers a number of consequences in regard to the formation of an object category and word extension. In contrast, when they are asked to create a new name for an object, this disposition to search for categories rather than individual instances seems to be diminished, leading to less consistency in the children's extension of the novel names. This difference is most evident in three-year-old children. Four-year-old and five-year-old children's creative naming success benefits from previous grouping experience with the objects, regardless of whether the grouping experience occurs before any attempt at naming or after the first attempt at naming. Three-year-old children benefit from grouping experience only if they have not yet attempted to create names for the objects. This pattern suggests that if three-year-old children are first asked to group the objects, this initial attempt at classifying objects increases the likelihood that they will attempt to use the names they create to refer to classes of objects. However, if they are first asked to name the objects, they are unlikely to use their created names to refer to classes of objects, a tendency that is not overcome by subsequent attempts to group the objects. This may also be the reason that naming did not improve the three-year-old children's grouping success in study 2. They were unlikely to use names in a general fashion, which in turn failed to improve their ability to discern the relations among the objects necessary for successful grouping.

All in all, the data obtained in study 1 and study 2 suggest that conceptual development and semantic development are intertwined rather than isolated or related in such a manner that one invariably influences the other. This is not to say that conceptual development depends on language. By the time that children begin to attach meaning to their first words, they have already created a rich conceptual system that helps them to understand the world. Although it is not clear exactly how many of the first words learned by children are attached to previously formed concepts, there is no doubt that the existing conceptual framework affects the initial development of the lexicon (Bowerman 1981; Clark 1973; Huttenlocher 1974; Mervis 1987). However, it seems likely that the development of the lexicon also results in changes in children's conceptual systems (Bowerman 1976, 1981; Clark and Clark 1977; Kuczaj 1975, 1982). Children's non-linguistic experience does not always contain appropriate and efficient information about the conceptual distinctions encoded by a language (Schlesinger 1977). Linguistic input provides valuable information about such distinctions and thereby influences children's conceptual development (Bowerman 1976; Kuczaj 1975, 1982).

The view that language development influences conceptual development in the ways outlined above does not necessarily entail influences of language upon our perception of reality, as has been suggested by Herder, Sapir, and Whorf, among others. Nor does the notion that language development influences conceptual development necessarily mean that language determines the ontogenesis of cognitive concepts and processes. In addition to the fact that children acquire considerable information about the world prior to learning any words, the world itself is structured in particular ways (Gibson 1966; Rosch 1977; Rosch, Mervis, Gray, Johnson, and Boyes-Braem 1976), and it is unlikely that language could alter this basic structure. Nonetheless, it is possible that language, other cognitive propensities, and the available information interact to yield both culture-specific and universal concepts (Bowerman 1981; Church 1966; *see also* Rice and Kemper, 1984).

Specifically, exposure to novel words alerts children to look for the similarities and differences among objects that must be determined in order to establish the correct extension of a word and a category. If the novel word is used to refer to a new category of objects, then exposure to the word will lead the child to formulate a new object category. If the novel word is used to refer to an exemplar from an existing category, then the word may be attached to the already existing category. Even in such a case, linguistic input is likely to assist the child in determining the proper extension of the word. Word meaning is not an instantaneous process, but instead one in which children gradually determine the correct extension of the word (Clark 1973; Kuczaj 1986; Vygotsky 1962). Children must pay attention to the way in which a word is used by others to determine its correct extension, and so linguistic input plays an important role in the modification and consolidation of children's pre-linguistic concepts and the concepts that are initially acquired as a result of exposure to a novel word. The results of study 1 demonstrate that being provided with a novel label for an exemplar of a novel concept facilitates children's subsequent grouping of the novel objects, suggesting that the novel word did in fact cause children to look for similarities among the novel objects. However, previous experience with the objects, particularly previous attempts to group the objects, increased children's subsequent success in correctly naming the objects, suggesting that children may more readily determine the correct extension of a novel word if it can be attached to an existing concept, however tentative the existing concept may be. The interaction of language development and conceptual development seems to be one of interdependency, at least once children have begun to acquire their lexicon. Although language seems likely to influence conceptual development in the ways described above, the extent to which language can exert its influence on the developing conceptual system is unknown. Once we have better determined both the ways in which language can influence conceptual development and the ways in which it cannot, the interrelationships of the two developing systems will be better known. Then, and only then, will we be able to determine the significance of language in the ontogenesis of that remarkable container and creater of human experience—the human mind.

References

Allan, K. (1977). Classifiers. *Language* **53**, 285–311.

Banks, M. and Salapatek, P. (1983). Infant visual perception. In *Handbook of child psychology: infancy and developmental psychology, vol. 2* (eds.) M. Haith and J. Campos. Wiley, New York.

Barrett, M. (1985). *Children's single-word speech.* Wiley, New York.

Berlin, B. and Kay, P. (1969). *Basic color terms.* University of California Press, Berkeley, CA.

Bloom, A. (1981). *The linguistic shaping of thought: study of the impact of language on thinking in China and the West.* Erlbaum, Hillsdale, NJ.

Bloom, L. (1970). *Language development: form and function in emerging grammars.* MIT Press, Cambridge, MA.

Bloom, L. (1973). *One word at a time: the use of single-word utterances before syntax.* Mouton, The Hague.

Bornstein, M. (1973). Color vision and color naming: A psychophysiological hypothesis of cultural difference. *Psychological bulletin* **80**, 257–85.

Bowerman, M. (1976). Semantic factors in the acquisition of rules for word use and sentence construction. In *Directions in normal and deficient child language* (eds. D. Morehead and A. Morehead). University Park Press, Baltimore.

Bowerman, M. (1981). Cross-cultural perspectives on language development. In *Handbook of cross-cultural psychology Vol. 4* (eds. H. C. Triandis and A. Heron). Allyn and Bacon, Boston.

Brown, R. (1958). *Words and things.* The Free Press, New York.

Brown, R. (1973). *A first language: The early stages*. Harvard University Press, Cambridge, MA.

Church, J. (1966). *Language and the discovery of reality*. Vintage Books, New York.

Clark, E. (1973). What's in a word? On the child's acquisition of semantics in his first language. In *Cognitive development and the acquisition of language* (ed.) T. Moore. Academic Press, New York.

Clark, E. (1977). Universal categories: On the semantics of classifiers and children's early word meanings. In *Linguistic studies offered to Joseph Greenberg: On the occasion of his sixtieth birthday*, (ed.) A. Julland Anma Libri, Saratoga, CA.

Clark, E. (1980). Here's the top: Nonlinguistic strategies in the acquisition of orientational terms. *Child development* **51**, 329–38.

Clark, H. and Clark, E. (1977). *Psychology and language*. Harcourt Brace Jovanovich, New York.

Cole, M. and Scribner, S. (1974). *Culture and thought*. Wiley, New York.

de Laguna, G. (1927). *Speech: its function and development*. Indiana University Press, Bloomington, IA.

Gibson, J. (1966). *The senses considered as perceptual systems*. Houghton-Mifflin, Boston.

Harris, P. (1983). Infant cognition. In *Handbook of child psychology: infancy and developmental psychobiology, vol. 2* (eds. M. Haith and J. Campos) Wiley, New York.

Heider, E. (1972). Universals in color naming and memory. *Journal of experimental psychology* **93**, 10–21.

Herder, J. (1768). Fragmente über die neuere deutsche Literatur. Abänderungen und Zusätze der zweiten Ausgabe der Fragmente. Erste Sammlung. Reprinted in *Herders Werke*. Gustav Hempel, Berlin.

Humboldt, W. (1907). *Gesammelte Schriften*. Berlin.

Huttenlocher, J. (1974). The origins of language comprehension. In *Theories in cognitive psychology: the Loyola Symposium* (ed.) R. Solso Erlbaum, Hillsdale, NJ.

James, W. (1890). *The principles of psychology, vol. 1*. Holt, New York.

Kuczaj, S. (1975). On the acquisition of a semantic system. *Journal of verbal learning and verbal behavior* **16**, 589–600.

Kuczaj, S. (1979). Evidence for a language learning strategy: On the relative ease of acquisition of prefixes and suffixes. *Child development* **50**, 1–13.

Kuczaj, S. (1982). The acquisition of word meaning in the context of the development of the semantic system. In *Verbal processes in children* (eds.) C. Brainerd and M. Presley. Springer-Verlag, New York.

Kuczaj, S. (1986). Thoughts on the intensional basis of early object word extension: Evidence from comprehension and production. In *The development of word meaning* (eds. S. Kuczaj and M. Barrett). Springer-Verlag, New York.

Kuczaj, S. and Lederberg, A. (1977). Height, age, and function: Differing influences on children's comprehension of younger and older. *Journal of child language* **4**, 395–416.

Kuczaj, S. and Maratsos, M. (1975). On the acquisition of *front*, *back*, and *side*. *Child development* **46**, 202–10.

Luria, A. (1976). *Cognitive development: its cultural and social foundations*. Harvard University Press, Cambridge, MA.

MacNamara, J. (1972). Cognitive basis of language learning in infants. *Psychological review* **79**, 1–13.

Markman, E. (1987). How children constrain the possible meanings of words. In *Concepts and conceptual development: ecological and intellectual factors in categorization* (ed. U. Neisser). Cambridge University Press, New York.

Mervis, C. (1987). Child-basic object categories and early lexical development. In *Concepts and conceptual development: ecological and intellectual factors in categorization* (ed. U. Neisser). Cambridge University Press, New York.

Neisser, U. (1987). *Concepts and conceptual development: ecological and intellectual factors in categorization*. Cambridge University Press, New York.

Nelson, K. (1974). Concept, word, and sentence: interrelations in acquisition and development. *Psychological review* **82**, 267–85.

Ochs, E. (1986). Introduction. In *Language socialization across cultures* (eds. B. Schieffelin and E. Ochs). Cambridge University Press, New York.

Ochs, E. and Schieffelin, B. (1984). Language acquisition and socialization: three developmental stories and their implications. In *Culture theory: essays on mind, self, and emotion* (eds. R. Shweder and R. LeVine). Cambridge University Press, New York.

Piaget, J. and Inhelder, B. (1969). *The psychology of the child*. Basic Books, New York.

Rice, M. and Kemper, S. (1984). *Child language and cognition*. University Park Press, Baltimore, MD.

Rosch, E. (1973). On the internal structure of perceptual and semantic categories. In *Cognitive development and the acquisition of language* (ed. T. Moore). Academic Press, New York.

Rosch, E. (1974). Linguistic relativity. In *Human communication: theoretical explorations* (ed. A. Silverstein). Erlbaum, Hillsdale, NJ.

Rosch, E. (1977). Human categorization. In *Studies in cross-cultural psychology, vol. 1* (ed. N. Warren). Academic Press, New York.

Rosch, E. and Lloyd, B. (eds.) (1978). *Cognition and categorization*. Erlbaum, Hillsdale, NJ.

Rosch, E., Mervis, C., Gray, W., Johnson, D., and Boyes-Braem, P. (1976). Basic objects in natural categories. *Cognitive psychology* **8**, 382–439.

Sapir, E. (1931). Conceptual categories in primitive languages. *Science* **74**, 578.

Sapir, E. (1951). *Selected writings of Edward Sapir in language, culture, and personality* (ed. D. Mandelbaum). University of California Press, Berkeley.

Schaff, A. (1973). *Language and cognition*. McGraw-Hill, New York.

Schlesinger, I. (1971). The production of utterances and language acquisition. In *The ontogenesis of grammar* (ed. D. Slobin). Academic Press, New York.

Schlesinger, I. (1977). The role of cognitive development and linguistic input in language acquisition. *Journal of child language* **4**, 153–69.

Schlesinger, I. (1982). *Steps to language: toward a theory of native language acquisition* Erlbaum, Hillsdale, NJ.

Sinclair, H. (1971). Sensorimotor action patterns as a condition for the acquisition of syntax. In *Language acquisition: Models and methods* (eds. R. Huxley and D. Ingram). Academic Press, New York.

Vygotsky, L. (1962). *Thought and language*. MIT Press, Cambridge, MA.

Watson, J. (1913). Psychology as the behaviorist views it. *Psychological review* **20**, 158–77.

Whorf, B. (1956). *Language, thought, and reality*. MIT Press, Cambridge, MA.

Wittgenstein, L. (1953). *Philosophical investigations*. MacMillan, New York.

12

Ostensive learning and self-referring knowledge

BARRY BARNES

Although psychologists, philosophers, and social scientists all share an interest in the nature of knowledge, only psychologists have made detailed empirical studies of how knowledge is transmitted and acquired. Yet the study of how knowledge is acquired may immensely enrich our understanding of what is being acquired. If we wish to understand how concepts are related to the objects, events, and processes in our physical environment, and the role they play in our interaction with that environment and with others in that environment, then we should be prepared to give detailed attention to how concepts are learned.[1] Empirical studies of the acquisition of concepts may be relevant not just to the problems of psychology but to those of sociology and epistemology as well.

One procedure that plays an important part in the initial acquisition of concepts is ostension. Ostensive learning, learning which involves pointing and saying or analogous demonstrative practices, has an essential role in establishing connections between concepts and the world. Recently, there has been a tendency to play down the importance of ostensive learning. Partly this may represent a reaction against earlier thinking wherein its importance was exaggerated. Psychologists have rightly been stressing the role of practical manipulative activity in the learning process, and of social interactions and collective experience. Partly, too, it may represent recognition of the enormous difficulties involved in characterizing ostension and in demonstrating how it can have clear and unambiguous results: the indefinite character of ostension is notorious, especially amongst epistemologists and philosophers.[2] None the less, for all that ostension is not all-important it remains important, and for all that its investigation is not easy it is possible and should be undertaken.[3]

Even the most rudimentary insights into how ostensively-based learning proceeds may lead to valuable conclusions. For example, it is evident empirically that many acts of ostension are required before competence in the use of any given concept is acquired: the concept must be associated with a whole set of particular instances. This simple point about ostensive learning suggests a way of understanding the relationship between various systems of classification and hence separate bodies of knowledge. In different cultures, the concepts used to refer to natural objects and processes may be learned as unique clusterings of ostended particulars, so that different systems of natural-kind concepts may be sustained and transmitted, all equally viable as representations of natural order, all equally reasonable bases for the description of the natural world. Thus, if it is recognized that systems of classification are learned in the last analysis ostensively, one is led to a conventionalist view of classification.

The notorious indefiniteness of ostensive learning may itself be taken as another example of a simple empirical finding with profound consequences. Let it be the case that when a concept is learned by ostension its 'meaning', or correct use, cannot be clearly and unambiguously fixed. And let it be accepted that the learning of empirically significant concepts does indeed rely upon ostension. We may then infer that the future use of these concepts is not fixed in advance, but has, in a sense, to be improvised. Possessors of the concepts will at no time be fully clear as to what their concepts mean, in the sense of their being able to anticipate the future use of the concepts in all conceivable circumstances. Thus, if the indefiniteness of ostensive learning is recognized, one is led to a finitist view of classification. The existing conventions for applying concepts must be thought of not as determinants of the future application of these concepts but as precedents which are referred to as people decide upon the future application of the concepts. This distinction, between understanding convention as determinant and understanding it as precedent, is of great significance in the social sciences, and the importance of establishing which is the correct view can hardly be overstated.[4]

Encouraged by these examples, I shall continue to discuss ostensive learning in extremely simple terms in this paper. I wish tentatively to suggest that ostensive procedures only very slightly different from each other may transmit two different kinds of knowledge which I shall call 'normal' and 'self referring' knowledge.[5] I shall go on to identify distinctive characteristics of bodies of self-referring knowledge and to emphasize the particular importance of these characteristics in the context of the social sciences. If the argument stands, then it will identify a third rudimentary feature of ostensive learning with a profound sociological and epistemological significance.

Some basic features of ostension

Let me adumbrate (perhaps I should say caricature) what is involved in ostensive learning. We must have a teacher and a learner interacting in some specific context or situation. The context will be a physical environment, containing physical objects, events, processes, and a social environment of communicating persons. The teacher, endeavouring to teach the concept C, points to objects in the physical environment and refers to them as instances of C, that is, the teacher points, and at the same time utters the noise properly associated with C. He or she may also point to other objects and make the noises for not-C. The learner watches the teacher and begins also to point to objects and call them Cs. Teaching is successfully completed when the learner is able to point out Cs as well as the teacher, that is, when other members in the context recognize the learner's linguistic competence as equal to that of the teacher and hence themselves.

Behaviourally, there may be little or nothing more to say about ostensive learning. Therefore I must set aside behaviourism in order to continue. What must the learner do in order to learn the concept C? Intuitively, it seems that the learner must do two things: somehow, identify a particular object as the ostended object, as the thing which is a C, the thing which is pointed at or otherwise singled-out from the backdrop of the environment, and, somehow, consciously or unconsciously, get a sense of what it is which makes the ostended object the kind of object it is, namely a C. Both these two things are extraordinarily difficult to describe and discuss. To attempt to do so is a good way of recognizing the virtues of behaviourism. I shall persist, nonetheless.

The teacher points to an object. Somehow, the learner successfully identifies the object. Let us say the object is a ball and the learner identifies the ball. The learner becomes aware of a volume in space which is the ball, and is bounded off from the rest of space which is not the ball. He or she identifies a volume which, so far as we can tell, is the correct volume, the volume pointed out by the teacher and recognizable as the 'right' volume by any competent observer.

How though does the learner recognize that the ball is indeed a ball? What is it which makes the ball a ball? Let us say that the learner simply looks at the ball and notes its spherical shape, the sort of shape he or she has noted before is possessed by other balls. By noting the shape of the ball the learner confirms the original identification of the ball. The ball is initially a ball because it seems to be pointed out as a ball by the teacher. The ball is confirmed as a ball because it is spherical, like previous objects pointed out as balls by the teacher.

Let us say that the learner attends first to the matter of searching out the object, and secondly to the matter of searching out its nature. The ball is found, and its spherical, ball-like nature is identified. To speak thus is to gloss over many recognized difficulties, but these difficulties will not concern me here since I wish only to make a simple, very general point which should stand even if exception is taken to the way I have described ostensive learning. The point is this: we generally assume that the nature of an object lies within itself, that when an object is identified, as a volume in space, as it were,

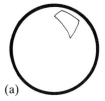 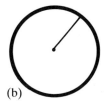

(a)   (b)

Fig. 12.1. Sphere (ball). Knowledge about the ball, the object (a), is obtained by examining its internal properites in order to discover its nature (b).

that which makes it the object it is will lie within its boundaries. Thus, a ball may be identified as an object, and then identified as a ball, as spherical, solely and simply by looking at the volume of space which is the ball. Once an object is identified and separated from context, the assumption is that the nature of the object can be ascertained without further reference to context, that the internal properties of the bounded object will then suffice.

Recall now the indefinite character of ostensive acts, and the fact that they always take place in an extended physical and social environment. Given these points there is no particular reason for the assumption that learners will always seek the nature of an object by scanning what lies within its boundaries. They could equally well look beyond the boundaries of the object, to what lies in the context of the ostensive act.

To scan within the boundaries of an object in search of its nature is the paradigm case for us, and makes good sense of what is involved in learning, and confirming our learning, of concepts referring to many everyday material objects. To scan outside the boundaries of an object for its nature is an anomalous case as far as our current understanding is concerned. But it is just as realistic a possibility as the first, and is critically involved in the acquisition of concepts used to refer to social statuses and other features of 'the social order'. The paradigm case makes sense of how we acquire much of our natural knowledge, knowledge which is used to refer to entities independent of itself. But the anomalous case, I wish to argue, is equally important, if only because it makes sense of our acquisition of social knowledge, self-referring knowledge which is acquired as we constitute ourselves as a society. The referents of our knowledge of the social order have a nature which lies beyond themselves: it is necessary to look outside them to recognize what they are.[6]

Self-reference

At this point some illustration is necessary to give instances of objects whose nature lies beyond themselves and of knowledge which refers to itself. Let me do this by moving step by step away from the paradigm case. 'Ball' will

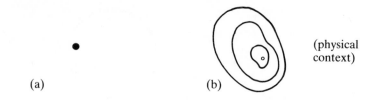

(a)   (b)   (physical
                                                   context)

Fig. 12.2.   Summit. Knowledge about the summit (a) is obtained by examining the
nature of what lies outside it (b).

continue to serve as a concept used to refer to everyday material objects. We know that the ball is spherical. On the one side, there we are, with our knowledge of the ball. On the other side is the ball, entirely separate from us. To check whether our knowledge is or is not correct we move to the ball, observe it, measure it, rotate it. The shape of the ball is unaffected by what we believe about it; it is there internal to the ball, to be investigated as a phenomenon external to us. If the shape is indeed found to be that of a sphere this shows that our knowledge is correct, that we are indeed properly informed about the nature of the ball (Fig. 12.1).

This is perhaps our commonest paradigm of knowing. We have a shared belief about some separate, distinct, independently identifiable thing, and if the internal nature of that thing is as we believe it to be then our belief is correct. But not all our beliefs about the objects in our physical environment are like this. Suppose we believe that the rock in Figure 12.2a is the summit of a mountain. Once again there we are, with our knowledge; and there, separate from us, is a thing or object which can be pointed out, the summit. But now it is no longer the internal nature of the object itself which makes it a proper referent of our belief: now it is the relationship of that object with things outside itself. Suppose that some vandal hammers the top from the Matterhorn and makes off with it. Should the headlines read 'Vandal steals Matterhorn summit' or 'Vandal lowers Matterhorn summit!' The newspapers may take their choice, but what is certain is that the Matterhorn would not subsequently be known as a mountain without a summit. The weather may indeed have scraped an inch or two from the Matterhorn over the last century or so, without depriving it of its summit. A summit is that part of a moutain which exists in a certain relationship with all its other parts. To check that something is a summit is not the same kind of process as checking that it is a sphere: with the latter one looks to the internal nature of the thing itself—one looks at or inside the thing; whereas with the former one looks outside the thing itself, to its relationship with its context. Our belief that what we are pointing to is a summit is valid only if what we are pointing to relates to its context in a specific way. Summits are objects the nature of which lies outside or beyond themselves. In the ostensive learning

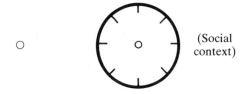

Fig. 12.3.   Target/leader. Knowledge about a target (a physical object) or a leader (a social entity) arises from the nature of the context that surrounds it.

of 'summit' the learner must look outside or beyond the summits being viewed in order to see what makes them what they are (Fig. 12.2).

Summits are physical objects, quite separate from us, but objects which are what they are only because of circumstances outside themselves. There are other physical objects just like summits, but objects of a nature defined not by a context of *physical circumstances* but by a context of *human activity*. The list of such objects is endless: auguries and omens, cups and reliquaries, jewellery; more mundanely, pollutions, rubbish; at a yet more practical level, erasers and pencil-sharpeners, reagents and solvents, targets and weapons, vermin and weeds. All these are independent entities which can be pointed to and identified, picked up and examined, described and measured; yet they are what they are only because of how we routinely act in relation to them. The learner must look to the social context as he or she acquires them by ostension.

With objects of this kind it is no longer a matter of us and our belief here, and the object and its nature there. It is no longer even a matter of us here, and object in context there. We now *are* the context which makes the object what it is. Consider the example of a Target (Fig. 12.3). It is a target because we believe it to be a target, and hence treat it as a target. Physical object though it is, a target is a target only to the extent that it is believed to be such and treated as such. In ceasing to believe that an object is a target, we dissolve away its nature as a target. In coming to believe that an object is a target, we constitute the context which makes it a target, and hence we constitute it as a target. Our believing self-refers and consequently it self-validates: we validate what we believe by referring to what we believe.

Here at last is a simple stereotypical example which captures something of the nature of our knowledge of our own social order. Social objects, if we may call them that, are often very much like the objects we call targets. They are identifiable as objects, as substantial bounded entities, but their nature is constituted externally by our beliefs about them: our beliefs constitute that which makes them what they are. John is the leader of the gang. He is the leader because the members know him to be the leader, and routinely act on the basis of what they know. Whoever the leader is, he is

Fig. 12.4.   ICI share. Objects such as ICI shares need not be represented because their nature lies in rings of belief and action that surround them.

the leader, in just the way that whatever is the target is the target. Both the physical and the social object are the objects that they are because of the context of knowledge and action which surrounds them (Fig. 12.3).

All concepts denoting a social status or position appear to be analogous to 'target' and 'leader' in this respect. Status terms denote objects the natures of which are constituted by the surrounding context of knowledge and action. Beliefs about the status of individuals in society are accordingly not fully independent of that to which they refer. To come to believe something about the status of an individual is to do two things at once: it is to accept a *claim* about that person's status and at the same time to contribute to the *constitution* of his or her status.

Given that the nature of a social object is constituted by what surrounds it, the actual physical manifestation of the object itself may be dispensed with. Only the hollow ring of belief and action is necessary. Consider shares in ICI, or the value of a share in ICI, or the voting power of a share (Fig. 12.4). Here are three hollow rings of belief and action: neither the share, nor its value, nor its power, need exist or be manifested as tangible objects. It is only our shared general familiarity with material objects and how to treat them, and their mnemonic convenience, that induce us occasionally to set marker objects at the centre of such hollow rings; and then it is important not to confuse the marker with what is marked, the share certificate with what is certified, the paper banknotes with the value of the share.

When a social object is pointed out one quickly looks out from the object if one seeks to check the correctness of the designation. What one looks toward is the generally accepted designation of the object, and the generally accepted way of acting in relation to it. An object is validly designated if that is how it is generally designated, and/or if action in relation to it is action routinely associated with that designation. A social object is constituted as a social object to the extent that it is believed to be such an object. Analogously, a social structure, considered as an array of social objects with recognized properties and recognized connections, is constituted of belief in its existence. Those who live in it encounter it as actions which flow from their belief that it (or its constituents) does indeed exist.

Society as a distribution of knowledge

Where a set of people continue to interact in something close to an ordered, routinized pattern we are inclined to speak of the existence of a society. Let us take a society to be a persisting system of routine practice. There are several ways of accounting for the existence of such systems and relating them to characteristics of the individual people who constitute them. Economists and political scientists tend to regard human activity as informed, calculative, planful and goal-oriented, and to see societies as constituted of activities of just this kind. Sociologists are sometimes more inclined to stress non-rational commitments to values, norms, or rules and to imagine that norms generate actions from individuals rather as inserted programmes generate output from computers and similar devices. Both of these positions face well-known fundamental difficulties, and indeed there is no extant approach to the general understanding of social order which does not face such difficulties. A discussion of the various alternative views and their relative merits would be out of place here. Instead I shall simply note my own inclination to a version of the 'economic' point of view. Social life, I suggest, is the product of interacting, informed, calculative human beings, operating with a developed awareness of what they are about, acting in ways which they calculate are in best accord with their interests as they perceive them.[7]

If society is indeed constituted by informed, calculative human beings, then routine practice must be the product of what these human beings know, and what these beings know must itself be confirmed and given credibility by the persistence of the routine practice which their knowledge produces. What people know must dispose them, on the whole, to persist with routine. The persistence of routine must, on the whole, confirm what people know. Accordingly, we may characterize a society as a persisting distribution of knowledge instead of as a persisting set of routine practices. The one characterization is as good as the other: either will suffice since each implies .the other. Individuals in a given society will know what the routines are. They will know how routines persist in the calculative, knowledgeable actions of other people. They will have a systematic and detailed knowledge of routine practice and its basis. And this knowledge, along with everything else they know, will lead them to act so that routine continues, so that their actions are part of the phenomena through which others know what is routine and are themselves able to act in ways which take account of its existence. If people are presumed to possess the capabilities and dispositional characteristics of knowledgeable, calculative agents, and if such people are able to sustain a social order, then there must be some distributions of knowledge among individuals which prompt individuals to act in ways which largely confirm and reconstitute the original distribution. These distributions are possible societies: every actual society is one such distribution.[8]

How people act depends upon what they know. Anything which is known may affect how people act. Therefore, everything which people know is constitutive or their existence as a society. To the extent that they are differentiated, knowledge of society and knowledge of nature both constitute 'society'. Considered as knowledge, a society is everything its members know, just as, considered as practice, a society is everything its members do. It is profoundly mistaken to imagine that natural knowledge is not a part of society, just as it is mistaken to imagine that technical and material practices are not a part of society.

A society is everything its members know, including everything they know about nature, about each other, about each others 'knowledge of nature and of each other, and so on. Such a body of knowledge will be used by its possessors to make references of innumerable kinds, but always including references to each other as possessors of knowledge. What is known will be something which is referred to in using the knowledge itself: the use of a body of knowledge will always involve the specification of the content of the knowledge, its basis, and its distribution, as referents. The system of knowledge which constitutes society is always *self-referring*.

Because it is a self-referring system members do two things when they learn what is known in their society. They become *informed* about all the entities and processes to which the knowledge is used to refer. And they become *constituted* or reconstituted as referents, as entities which may be referred to using that very same knowledge. It is easy to overlook the constitutive or performative dimension of learning when a single individual is concerned, but if we think of the entire membership of a society together this dimension becomes vividly apparent. In learning what a society knows the members as a whole thereby constitute the society itself as a distribution of knowledge, much of which knowledge will be *about* the society itself, and hence valid and 'consonant with social experience' only when it has been learned. Where knowledge is self-referring it must also be self-validating. A membership must learn it in order to become what it correctly describes.

The knowledge which is society is a self-referring system. Part of the system is what people know of 'the social structure', of social objects and social rules or norms applicable to such objects. This knowledge is almost entirely self-referring and is certainly the most intensely self-referring component of the knowledge which is society. As I have already tried to show, social objects are what they are by virtue of being known to be what they are. Analogously, social norms are rules applicable to social objects by virtue of being known to be so applicable, and how they apply is how they are known to apply. Social structure exists in no other way than as knowledge of social structure. Social structure exists as a sublime, monumental, self-fulfilling prophesy.[9] Thus, whereas knowledge of nature may refer, in the last analysis, to entities and processes beyond itself, knowledge of social structure (or social order) refers in the last analysis to knowledge, and hence precisely to itself. And whereas knowledge of nature may be confirmed or disconfirmed by processes involving reference to state of affairs which exist independently of the knowledge, knowledge of social structure must be confirmed or disconfirmed by processes involving reference to states of affairs which exist only because the knowledge is generally presumed to be true.

Society and knowledge of society

It may be that to think of society as a distribution of knowledge, and knowledge of social order as knowledge of knowledge, is counter-intuitive. Society and the structure of society seem to have a real independent existence. We feel able to learn about them in the same way that we learn of tangible material objects and their structures. And we may reasonably feel that we have learned more of them over time, or that we have corrected our earlier knowledge of them by more extended and careful observation. But how can knowledge be acquired and corrected if it is not knowledge of some external independent entity?

These problems resolve themselves if we are careful to distinguish between what collectives know and what individuals reckon to know. Consider first the matter of the external existence of society. My view is that society is a distribution of knowledge which sustains and is sustained by the practice of the members among whom it is distributed. Knowledge and practice here must be considered as properties of a membership, standardized by inter-subjective interaction within the membership. As such they transcend the individual member. Every member may perceive them as externally given. Yet there is nowhere for them to be situated other than in the membership itself.

Durkheim (1950) states that, like material objects, social facts are external to the individual. And so they are, almost. Every individual in John's gang recognizes John as its leader by noting what the others do and inferring what the others know. Every individual, when reflecting upon John's putative leadership, looks outward at a near-complete ring of confirming action, action confirming existing knowledge that he is indeed the leader and hence continuing to constitute the status he is known to possess, that of leader.

Strictly speaking, every member looks out on a different external context. That all these slightly different contexts around the social position may be brought together as perceptions of essentially 'the same' context allows an agreed social order to be created and sustained. The 'error' in individual perception involved here is so extremely small as to be for all practical purposes no error at all (Fig. 12.5). The individual who accepts the 'external' social fact of John's leadership will be making no mistake, even though a tiny part of what constitutes John's leadership is not external to that individual

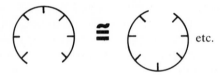

Fig. 12.5. Rings of knowledge and action that surround social objects such as 'leader' are slightly different for each individual who perceives that object. But the differences between individual perceptions are so small as to be negligible.

at all but internal, being nothing more nor less than his or her own knowledge of John's leadership. For many practical purposes individuals may neglect their own specific contributions to the social reality in which they believe. The gang member may take the leader as externally given, provided the gang is not too small; the share seller may take the share price as externally fixed, provided the holding is not too large.

What must be remembered, however, is that no matter how minute is the contribution of any given individual to the constitution of a social object, the nature of that object will nonetheless be *wholly* and *entirely* constituted by the totality of the individuals in the relevant collectivity. The gang leader is constituted as such by gang members' knowledgeable actions. The share price is constituted by knowledgeable market transactions. However many the individual pieces into which the hollow ring of knowledge and practice around a social object is broken, it remains such a ring, nothing more.

Consider now how it can be that we may learn more of the structure or order of a society, or correct what we think we know of it. Again it is necessary to distinguish between individual members and the membership among which knowledge is distributed. As an overall system, knowledge of social structure self-refers. There are no objects beyond its existing domain of application waiting to be discovered, nor any existing social objects with features other than those they are already known to possess. Yet individuals may nonetheless rightly feel dissatisfaction with the accuracy or the extent of what they count as their own knowledge, and may rightly seek to correct mistakes therein or to add to it and extend its scope. For individuals may be systematically incorrect in their beliefs about each other, or ignorant of pattern and order in their own beliefs. But knowledge, standardized, institutionalized belief, is determined by reference to individual belief, i.e. to what individuals reckon they know. As the one changes so must the other. Knowledge of social structure may accordingly be modified, extended, and corrected as individuals adjust what they reckon they know, and so in consequence may 'social structure' itself.

Individual members are right to feel that what they know of the structure of their own society is amenable to correction and elaboration just as their knowledge of nature is so amenable. People can indeed learn more about their society just as they can learn more about their physical environment. But there is a critical difference between the two kinds of learning. Ideally, to learn about the physical environment is to take account of more information about an independent realm, which realm remains unchanged by the learning process. We may proceed, confident that the acquisition of knowledge makes no difference to that which is known. But to learn about our own society may be to change that society, since in learning we ourselves change, and we are part of our own society. An act of learning in this case may both take account of the nature of society and change the nature of society. The act may alter knowledge of society and at the same time alter the referents of that knowledge; indeed it *must* do so. It is both an act of learning and an act of reconstitution of the phenomenon being learned about. It is at once cognitive and performative. Learning involves the adjustment of what members know, but society just is what members know.

Consider the cyclic character of fashion in clothing. A few people, opinion leaders at the top of the social hierarchy, may seek to dress distinctively, differently from everyone else. The rest of the society may seek to dress like those just above them in the hierarchy. If at a given point in time the opinion leaders know what is generally being worn, then they will set in motion a wave of activity which will eventually invalidate that knowledge. They will dress at variance with the norm, whereupon their new mode of dress will pass down the social hierarchy and become a new norm. As they themselves correct their increasingly inadequate knowledge, so they will increasingly tend to vary their dress yet again, inaugurating new waves of change, so that the familiar cyclic pattern in fashionable dressing is established and sustained. A recurring oscillation in social practice is established, associated with a continuing small degree of inadequacy in social knowledge. Note too that once it is established the oscillation itself becomes a complex social object, available for examination and reflection. A new layer of knowledge may be built up, as it were, by scanning what exists already. And the new knowledge may inspire new practice: explicitly formulated knowledge of the cyclic tendencies in dress routines does indeed inspire a significant range of economic activities in our society.

In the above example change in knowledge changed its referents and thereby eventually invalidated the knowledge (in both its initial and its changed form). Learning was implicated in the invalidation of what was learned. This, however, will by no means always be the case. It may be that as members we cannot learn about society without changing society. But that does not mean that learning necessarily invalidates itself. Knowledge and referent may change together, and yet the knowledge may remain valid throughout — satisfactorily related to its referents throughout. More and more people may learn that Geldof is a celebrity. Such learning changes the society wherein it occurs, and indeed alters the ring of knowledge and action surrounding Geldof which constitutes his celebrity in the society. But such learning does not invalidate what is learned or in any way lessen the celebrity of Geldof: on the contrary. The point being emphasized here is indeed a trivially obvious one. New members, after all, learn what their society knows, including what it knows of itself. Thereby they change the distribution of knowledge which is their society. But far from invalidating the knowledge they learn, their learning is actually what allows that knowledge to persist as valid knowledge: their learning reproduces and reconstitutes the society they are learning about; in learning they become confirming instances of what they learn. Everything changes; and everything stays the same.

Knowledge of social order and knowledge of natural order

Knowledge of social order refers overwhelmingly to itself and represents the most intensely and immediately self-referential component of the knowledge which is society. Knowledge of natural order is by no means devoid of self-reference loops, but ideally it is used to refer to entities independent of itself. Intuitively, it seems that we should be aware of a difference in kind between the two forms of knowledge, but we are not. Indeed, in some cultures there may be no terminology with which to make a distinction between the two kinds of knowledge, and in others it may even not be possible to discern any clear differentiation of kinds.

Some of the reasons for this have already been rehearsed. Social order is largely external to the individual, like natural order. Social objects may be just as material and tangible as natural objects: John the gang leader is just as substantial as the spherical ball, and once designated he is identified and re-identified by his physical characteristics just like the ball — indeed, recognition of John's physical form is crucially important in the continuing routine treatment of him in terms of his social status as gang leader.

It is important to remember too that natural order, however much it is differentiated from social order, purified of self-reference loops, corrected, and improved by observation and empirical investigation, remains, like social order, a system of conventions. Natural order is always an ordering constructed by people and used to make sense of nature, never an ordering insisted upon by nature itself and imposed upon people by it. The mere fact that social order has a conventional character does not serve to differentiate it from orderings of other kinds.

Probably the best way to understand the relationship between natural order and social order, both what distinguishes them and what allows them at times to run together indistinguishable, is to revert to considering how they are learned. Ostensive learning must be central in both cases. I have suggested that looking inside the ostended object for its nature is central where natural objects are concerned, and looking outside is central where social objects are concerned. But first of all it must be acknowledged that both kinds of looking may be involved in the learning of a concept. (Think of the teaching of 'jewel' or 'vermin' or 'pencil-sharpener'. How important are the intrinsic characteristics of ostended paradigm examples and how important is the context surrounding them?) And secondly it must be recognized that the actual behavioural act of ostension is visibly the same in both kinds of case. The ball is pointed out as a spherical ball; John is pointed out as the leader of the gang. Learning about nature and learning about society are the same kind of process: they feel the same; they can be run together; indeed they are the same.

The very same competences and procedures which allow us to learn about our physical environment and respond appropriately to it also allow us to learn about society, respond appropriately to it, and thereby keep it in existence as something we have learned about and know how to respond to. There is the possibility of a marvellous economy of explanation here: people have to be assigned learning capabilities in order to account for how they cope as organisms in a physical environment, and those very same learning capabilities may be what is necessary both to account for how people cope as agents in a social environment and how they constitute that environment in the course of coping with it.[10] Further empirical study of ostensively-based learning may help to show whether this is more than a possibility.

Notes

1. Philosophers use 'concept' in a specific, technical way. It is important to note that this is not the way in which the term is used in this paper. As philosophers use the term there are no concepts. I am much happier with psychologists' accounts of how concepts are acquired, save that some psychological texts hold that when a concept is 'fully' or 'completely' acquired it is a concept in the philosophical sense. My own view is that a concept is 'fully' acquired when the agent learning it is able to use the associated term as well as anyone else, even though at this point it cannot be said that a concept is possessed in the philosophers' sense. Needless to say, since I do not mean by 'concept' what philosophers mean I cannot speak of what concepts refer to, or of how they are used to refer to things, in quite the way that philosophers do, and must instead point to ostension as a paradigm of the referential use of concepts.
2. Quine (1960) offers a particularly useful account of the indefinite character of ostension.
3. Note how in the famous passages in the *Philosophical investigations* (1953), where Wittgenstein emphasizes the insufficiency of ostensive learning, simply conceived of, he none the less takes care to remind us of its continuing importance.
4. For an extended discussion of the sociological significance of the themes of these last two paragraphs *see* Barnes (1981, 1982) and Bloor (1983). For a philosophically oriented treatment see Hesse (1974, 1980).
5. I speak of two kinds of knowledge for simplicity; they should be regarded as idealized extreme cases. What is crucial is the notion that two kinds of response to an ostensive act may be involved in processes of knowledge acquisition.

6. The line of argument set out in this paper did indeed originate from an exploration of the idea that social structure is known by people rather than imposed upon people and that conforming social action is calculated from what is known rather than compelled by external coercion or internal commitment. *See* Barnes (1988) where a less developed version of what is set out here will be found in Chapter 2, Section 3.

7. What is commonly taken to be the 'economic' view of social life includes many claims which I myself do not accept and fails to take account of other claims which I regard as valid and important. My perspective is 'economic' in that it takes people to be knowledgeable, calculative, and goal-oriented. It does not assume that individuals are invariably self-interested. Nor does it ignore the role of inherited knowledge and culture in social life, as 'economic' approaches sometimes tend to do.

8. Again it is important to note that the term 'knowledge' is not used in its philosophical sense but in its sociological sense. What is known is not that which is correctly or justifiably believed but that which is generally believed or generally held to be justified as belief. What is known is what is standardized or institutionalized. Note also that knowledge should not be considered simply as a set of verbal formulations. Representations and competences may also count as knowledge: know-how is part of what the members of a society know.

9. This important notion was introduced into the social sciences over thirty years ago by Robert K. Merton (1968), albeit mainly in order to understand some of the insidious consequences of the diffusion of erroneous belief. The idea was generalized by Krishna (1971), and is used in a fully general way in Barnes (1983). See also Henshel (1978).

10. I do not wish to imply that the cognitive competences which sustain social order are all in some way extensions or derivations of those which sustain natural order. It is the simultaneous utility of these competences in relation to interactions with both the social and the physical environment which is striking. The point being made is consistent with views which give priority to the social context in the development of some competences, as in Whiten and Byrne (this volume).

References

Barnes, S. B. (1981). On the conventional character of knowledge and cognition. *Philosophy of the social sciences* **11**, 303–33.

Barnes, S. B. (1982). *T. S. Kuhn and social science*. Macmillan, London.

Barnes, S. B. (1983). Social life as bootstrapped induction. *Sociology* **17**, 524–45.

Barnes, S. B. (1988). *The nature of power*. Polity Press, Cambridge.

Bloor, D. (1983). Wittgenstein: *a social theory of knowledge*. Macmillan, London.

Durkheim, E. (1950). *The rules of sociological method*. (Translated by S. A. Solovay and J. H. Mueller.) University of Chicago Press, Chicago.

Henshel, R. L. (1978). Self-altering predictions. In *Handbook of futures research* (ed. J. Fowles). Greenwood Press, Westpoint.

Hesse, M. B. (1974). *The structure of scientific inference*. Macmillan, London.

Hesse, M. B. (1980). *Revolutions and reconstructions in the philosophy of science*. Harvester Press, Brighton.

Krishna, D. (1971). 'The self-fulfilling prophecy' and the nature of society. *American sociological review* **36**, 1104–7.

Merton, R. K. (1968). The self-fulfilling prophecy. In *Social theory and social structure*, 3rd edition. Free Press, New York.

Quine, W. V. O. (1960). *Word and object*. M. I. T. Press, Cambridge, MA.

Wittgenstein, L. (1953). *Philosophical investigations*. Blackwell, Oxford.

13

Learning through enculturation
H.M. COLLINS

Introduction

Enculturational and algorithmical learning

We do not know how we manage to learn. There are various ideas such as positive and negative reinforcement, ostensive definition, the building of new concepts from old by logical extension, hard-wiring of the brain for certain aspects of knowledge (such as linguistic structures, the ability to recognize elementary orientations and movements), and so forth, but these are all inadequate and insecure. One might say that the science of learning was still in the pre- , or multi-paradigmatic stage. The evidence for this is that brand-new speculative 'theories' of learning can still grow out of nothing and yet not be completely implausible.

One example (which I do not mean to endorse or condemn) can be found in Rupert Sheldrake's (1985) book *A new science of life*. Sheldrake springs upon us the theory of 'morphogenetic fields'. Amongst his ideas is the notion that things become easier for individuals to learn if they are already well known in the rest of the world. For example, certain ambiguous pictures, such as the well known 'Dalmatian dog' within a background of black and white splodges, are relatively easy to recognize because they have already been seen and recognized by many other people. He says that once many people have learned something, a *morphogenetic* field is created which we all share in some way, even though we have not learned the thing ourselves. To share in the morphogentic field we do not need to be in *social* contact with those who are already accomplished, much less do we need to have them teach us how to do it: it is just a matter of living on the same planet. Thus, he says, it should be easier for a novice to learn to recognize the ambiguous Dalmation dog than to learn to recognize another 'equally confusing' representation that was newly invented and therefore not widely known.

Sheldrake's idea is plausible enough for his book to have been reviewed in *Nature* and dangerous enough in its plausibility for the reviewer to suggest that the book should be burned. That the theory of morphogenetic fields is taken this seriously, I suggest, is because existing explanations of learning do not exclude it by their own overwhelmingly greater plausibility. Each has its own major problems. Consider, for example, ostensive learning. The trouble with ostensive learning, however, much it touches on common sense, is that the naïve learner cannot learn by ostension what is being pointed at and how the object is to be distinguished from its background. Learning by ostension leads to a regress. To illustrate, there is an apocryphal story about the naming of Toronto. This tells of the early Canadian explorers who came across a huddle of tepees on the northern shore of Lake Ontario. They stretched out their hands, pointed an index finger in the direction of the village, and made interrogative grunts and enquiring nods of their native guides. 'Toronto' came the response. The sting is that 'Toronto' means 'fingernail' in the local dialect! True or not, the story illustrates the fundamental paradox of ostensive definition. One has first to see the world in the same way as everyone else before one can learn to see it in the same way. If we do not start off with some unexplained and common capacity for cutting up the world into the same primitive 'lumps', then we cannot learn what the lumps are by having them pointed out to us. This is because we will not know what is being pointed at (Hesse 1974; Barnes 1976).

Sheldrake's typical examples could have been chosen to make this very point. Even if we allow that some primary brain wiring allows us to separate a real Dalmatian dog from its background by virtue of the fact that it moves all of a piece while the background stays still, this does not explain how we can learn to recognize a pictorial representation of such a dog, especially when it comprises a set of dots amongst other dots and splodges deliberately designed to obscure it. It is hard to find the sense in which this splodgy, printed 'dog' is 'the same as' the living, breathing, moving version, and therefore it is not clear how the ability to recognize a real Dalmation can be extended to confusing pictures of dogs, or indeed to any pictures of dogs, or even to other real dogs. Morphogenetic fields is as good an explanatory candidate as any.

Having made some logical space for speculation, I now want to discuss a 'theory' which is nearly as general as morphogenetic fields, but which does have a longer pedigree. This 'theory' says that we can recognize Dalmatian dogs and the like because we have 'skills' that we learn by sharing cultures, or 'forms of life' (Wittgenstein 1953; Bloor 1983). In other words, by living in society we develop the foundations of our ability to learn, without explicit or visible teaching—society is the basic knowledge-bearing unit, not the individuals within it. The theory fits well with the routine observations that people living in different sorts of societies develop different kinds of skill— they have different cognitions in different social worlds—and that people who are not members of a society that embodies a certain skill have immense difficulty in learning that skill.[1] I will now briefly sketch some more of the observable and potentially observable consequences of this *enculturational* model of learning and compare it with the more familiar *algorithmical* model, where we learn from explicable series of instructions, pointing etc., where all transmissions of information can be readily inspected.

Consequences of the enculturational model

In the early 1970s I found that scientists who wanted to build Transversely Excited Atmospheric pressure lasers (TEA-lasers) did not succeed if they used only written sources of information even when the authors tried their best to make certain that the documents contained every relevant fact and heuristic (Collins 1974, 1985a). What is more, these scientists were unable to build the laser even after they had engaged in prolonged conversation with 'middlemen' who knew a great deal about the devices, but had not yet built one for themselves. Even where a scientist had prolonged contact with a successful laser builder this would not guarantee success; such prolonged contact was a necessary but not a sufficient condition for knowledge transfer. If a scientist was to succeed in building a laser from a set of instructions, he (they were all men) had first to become a full blown expert himself. This he could only do by serving something close to an apprenticeship with an existing expert. Those who did not possess the skills themselves could not act as satisfactory masters to apprentices. Laser builders seemed to need to become socialized.

This state of affairs was only *evident* because the skill in question was very new — people were still developing the foundations of more formal learning. Novice scientists who were in receipt of even large quantities of written and other formal instructions still had insufficient experience to provide the interpretations of the information that would have made it practically useful. They were insufficiently 'enculturated' to learn from an 'algorithmical' recipe for laser building. To get to the point where the instructions made sense they had first to learn skills of interpretation — the skills of cutting up the world in the right way — through interaction with the mini-culture of TEA-laser builders.[2]

At first sight, many familiar areas of expertise do not seem to follow this pattern. Consider cases where we do use a written list of instructions in order to accomplish some task that we were otherwise incapable of doing — where the algorithmical model seems to work without problem. The use of a recipe is a good example. I have a recipe for port wine soufflé. Since I have no face-to-face communication with the author of the cookery book I cannot learn skills from her after the manner of an apprentice, nevertheless, at the end of the day, the recipe will enable me to make the soufflé. However, this is because of existing skills that I bring to the interaction.

For example, the recipe contains the following instruction: 'Beat the egg whites until stiff and then fold in'. To manage this I have first to contribute my knowledge of what all the words mean and this includes knowing that 'a white' is not white but is transparent — at least until it is beaten when it becomes white. I must know how to get the white from the egg by cracking it and separating it from the yolk and the other bits which may well be white (the membrane inside the shell and perhaps the shell itself). I must then know how and with what to beat the egg. If I am not an experienced cook I probably would not succeed in making the whites 'stiff', since unless you know what to expect one might appear to beat for an awfully long time without making much appreciable difference. When one starts to beat eggs it seems most unlikely that they will ever be so stiff that the bowl can be turned upside down without them falling out, but that is what stiff means. Then I have to know the special meaning of 'fold' in the context of cooking. In short, I will have to be a fairly accomplished cook at the outset to be able to make use of this instruction. How did I become so accomplished? The answer is 'through apprenticeship'. The 'tacit knowledge'[3] involved in cooking a soufflé has not been transferred via the written recipe but via face-to-face contact—in this case, with my mother.

The enculturational model of learning has very important but overlooked implications for a number of areas. For one thing, it tells us why we go to conferences. There is more to understanding how other academics think and act than reading their articles. It tells us why we need apprenticeships, visiting fellowships and, at a different level, why we need practical laboratory classes when we teach science. Learning to become part of an initially alien form of life is learning to do something, not just to remember something. It shows us why it is hard for an isolated, and thus independent, scientist to know if he or she has properly replicated a novel experiment: mastery of a culture (and its associated practices, for example, laboratory practices) can only be tested by social interaction and this leads to 'The Experimenter's Regress'. (To be independently certain that an experiment has been done correctly one must see if it produces the right sort of result, but to know what the right sort of result is, one must correctly perform an experiment, or believe what others tell you about what the correct result should be! See Collins 1985*a*, Chapter 5.) It tells us why we have a method called 'participant' observation in sociology and anthropology. Finally, it provides some predictions of what sort of intelligent computer programs might succeed (Collins 1985*b*, 1987).

Knowledge and artificial intelligence

I have argued through my examples that the 'algorithmical' model of learning, which works by the provision of bits of information and sets of rules to the learner, only works by being embedded within the mysterious process of 'enculturation'. Algorithmical learning only works because we are already encultured in the tacit skills needed to recognize and interpret. Ostensive definition works well for learning the names of things, but only so long as we can already recognize the things. The problem is 'entitativity', as

Donald Campbell (1973) puts it. We have no solution, I argue, outside of ideas like morphogenetic fields, unexplained primitive abilities to perceive the universe in lumps, or the almost equally mysterious 'culture'—though culture has more obvious and immediate manifestations.

One potential consequence ought to be a limit on the ability of 'intelligent' machines. If a machine cannot learn by enculturation then it ought not to be able to learn lots of things that we take for granted. Knowing even the most massive load of information and rules ought not to be equivalent to learning skills and abilities through enculturation. We cannot programme these skills into a computer because we do not know what the process of socialization comprises. To become enculturated a machine would have to be socialized—perhaps after the fashion that the ape-language people bring up chimpanzees within their own family setting. Outside of this sort of 'method' we are no nearer to making a socializable computer than making a computer that is sensitive to morphogenetic fields, or capable of learning from ostensive definition.[4]

What can computers not do by virtue of the fact that they cannot be socialized? To reach toward an answer to this question I will describe a thought experiment. The thought experiment involves a machine designed to imitate human conversational abilities (Block 1981). It is a machine of finite but almost inconceivably huge capacity and processing power, designed to store all possible written human conversations that can be completed in a finite time. This machine is not socialized but, at first sight, it seems to contain as much as a socialized human can put into it. The problem is to discover what it cannot do by virtue of its social isolation in spite of its containing such a huge knowledge base. The question is asked by comparing the machine to a human in a Turing test-like situation.

Block points out that if one communicates with a machine via a typewriter keyboard there is a finite number of possible exchanges that can be made in a fixed time. For example, if the time limit is an hour, and the speed of typing is that of a practised human—say sixty words per minute—then there will not be more than about 20 000 symbols interchanged during an hour (the numbers are my elaboration on Block's basic idea). There are about 100 possible symbols that can be typed—upper and lower case letters, the space and other punctuation marks, the digits and other symbols on the top row of the typewriter keyboard and, we will say, a 'return' symbol to signify the end of a conversational turn. This means that in an hour the number of strings of symbols that can be interchanged is about $100^{20\,000}$, or $10^{40\,000}$. This is a very large number and to think about it puts us straight into the realm of fantasy (compare the number of elementary particles in the observable universe—about 10^{125}). However, it is a finite number that nevertheless includes *everything* that has ever been written, and could ever be written, in an hour using typewriter keyboards. A small subset of these $10^{40\,000}$ strings is the set of all hour-long, reasonable, typed conversational interchanges. I say it is a small subset, but in absolute terms it is, no doubt, still a very large number, probably vastly in excess of the number of particles or even quantum transitions that there have ever been (about 10^{150}).

In our thought experiment, a 'programmer' selects from the large printed list of possible interchanges of symbols, the subset of sensible conversations and arranges that these are stored in the memory of a computer. Without going into detail, the computer is able to use this memory store to produce conversational responses to anything sensible that an interrogator might ask. All sensible questions are anticipated in the memory, and all possible answers are equally anticipated so that they can be called upon as necessary. There are some subtle technical problems which I will not deal with here, but suffice it to say that for such a design to work, the programmer must be able to separate the sensible conversations from the nonsense. If this can be done, the machine will be able to take part in any of those conversations. The extent to which the machine will produce sensible responses is just the extent to which the programmer provides sensible responses within the accepted strings. Let us turn to the problem of separating the strings into sense and nonsense.

As I have said, the programmer must *not* fill the computer's memory with the *whole* set of $10^{40\,000}$ strings, or the machine's conversational repertoire will be dominated by nonsense. Excluding some nonsensical strings is not difficult. For example, there is a string in the original set which comprises 20 000 'x's another comprising 20 000 'a's and another comprising 20 000 commas. All of these and their equivalents can be eliminated. The same applies to interchanges that comprise only a large majority of 'x's, commas, and so forth. Next there are the set of strings that consist of ordinary talk about, say, the weather, or about more esoteric topics with which the programmer is familiar or in which he or she is an expert. These conversations can be included without problem. The programmer does not have to invent these conversations, merely winnow them from the chaff of nonsensical strings in which they are initially mixed.

Another category of conversations will include attempts by an imaginary partner to talk of things that the programmer does not understand. Suppose the imagined conversational partner says, 'Give me the name of a disease of sheep' while the programmer knows nothing of sheep farming. Suppose one *possible* reply to the question is 'A disease of sheep is bloat'. The programmer will not know that such is a reasonable reply and will reject all the many potential conversational strings that contain this statement along with the strings containing all the truly unreasonable replies such as 'A disease of sheep is dandelions', 'A disease of sheep is syphilis', and 'A disease of sheep is xcx,,xd'. (All of these will be found repeated many times among the long list of $10^{40\,000}$ strings.) That the programmer rejects a string containing a reasonable reply merely reflects his or her ignorance in the matter of sheep. Since the machine is intended to mimic a human being rather than an omniscient being this is just as it should be. The machine's conversations will mimic the programmer's conversational ability, not the ability of a perfect being. Of course the programmer will include conversational strings which contain replies to the 'sheep question' along the lines of 'Sorry I cannot name a disease of sheep because I know nothing of farming'.

As we can see, in demarcating the set of conversations that the programmer can imagine, he or she is indirectly feeding knowledge of skills into the computer's memory. If the programmer were a skilled sheep farmer, then the extent to which the imaginary computer would respond to questions and take part in conversations about sheep farming would be exactly the extent to which that programmer could respond and take part. Indeed, such a machine would be an almost ideal expert system. Now, note that the programmer, as well as transferring to the machine the skill of sheep farming, also appears to be indirectly transferring *the skill of conversation* to the computer's memory. This is crucial to my argument.

The great advantage of this imaginary machine is that skills are transferred without the programmer having to know what they consist of. We seem to have found a way of transferring tacit rules without having to articulate them. It appears to be a way of teaching a machine everything we know about conversation without having to *know how to* teach it. This, then, seems to be about the best we can do without teaching the machine through normal socialization — the best we can do in the way of teaching by imparting a mass of what we can articulate. Is this as good as real socialization?

Now imagine the programmed machine in a Turing test-like situation. An interrogator is going to talk to the machine or ask questions with the intention of discovering its conversational inadequacies with respect to human beings. To simplify matters we will think only about what conversational inadequacies it has when compared with its own programmer, and we will assume its programmer was a competent, imaginative, but otherwise fairly normal human being.

So long as the interrogator asks questions concerning matters of fact or concerning those aspects of skilled performance that can be described in words, the machine will perform as well as its programmer. For example, suppose the interrogator asks 'Do you play golf?' If the programmer plays golf then the machine will probably answer 'Yes'. The interrogator might then ask 'What does it feel like when you 'hit from the top' rather than accelerating through the ball?' The machine would reply along the lines 'Well, the contact between ball and club feels, kind of, solid and wooden and hard, rather than sweet and effortless.' The machine could only reply in this way if the programmer had played golf but, given this, the machine could say everything there is to be said about golf so long as it could be expressed by typing for an hour or less. Since virtually everything that can be said about golf can be said in less than an hour (I do not mean it could all be said in one hour, but that it could all be said in units of time an hour or less in length) it is certain that the machine would not be flummoxed by a golf question that would not flummox its programmers.

The trick is that we are only asking the machine to appear accomplished in a written examination. Though it will pass a written test of golfing skills we have not asked it to demonstrate its skills on the golf course. There is no disputing that a computer could, in principle, perform well in any test of articulateable knowledge. The question is, does our knowledge comprise more than we can articulate? To use our machine to help us think this one through we need to imagine it practising a skill, not just talking about it.

Now, as I have indicated, there is a skill that the machine does appear to demonstrate practically even in the Turing test-like setting, namely, conversational skill. Has it been taught conversational skill or just a mass of information about all possible conversations? If these two are indistinguishable, that is, if the machine could demonstrate conversational skill having been taught only a mass of information, then we would be on the way of dissolving the mystery of learning; it could be, at least in principle, an essentially algorithmic process of very great, but finite complexity. There would, after all, be no principled need for morphological fields or mysterious processes of enculturation. I believe, however, that this machine has not been taught the skill of conversation, but its practical failings remain to be demonstrated.[5]

The problem is the inability of the programmer to anticipate all 'sensible' conversational moves in an open universe without including the larger part of the $10^{40\,000}$ strings and thus swamping the machine's conversational abilities with nonsense. In a Turing test the inadequacies of the imaginary design would become apparent if the human interrogator confronted the machine with a mis-spelling such as 'Do you play glof?', or with a deliberate piece of phonetic transliteration, such as 'Doo yoo plai goalf?', or with a deliberately Goon show-like statement such as 'Needle Niidel Noo!' These might be thought of as creative moves in the art of typed conversation which overstep the boundaries of existing writing conventions. Nevertheless, a human conversational partner could deal with these quite competently even though they had never been seen before. The difficulty for the programmer would be whether to include or exclude such possibilities within the list of sensible conversations. As soon as all strings of nonsense become included in the repertoire of the machine, the number of permissible strings explodes catastrophically, for there are far more potential 'creative' possibilities than conventional strings (even though few will ever be actualized).[6] If the machine can only work provided the programmer can separate sense from nonsense at the outset, then the machine will fail because the boundary of what can and cannot be said is under revision from moment to moment in human conversation.[7]

Part of learning a skill through the process of enculturation is learning how to extend or revise the boundary of the skill in unanticipated ways; this is one of the things that we do without knowing how. We have seen the problem that it causes for anticipating conversational moves — deciding whether a creative conversational move is sufficiently 'the same as' existing conventions to be assimilated within them — but the same problem arises for all processes of recognition. All involve decisions such as what is to count as 'the same' as what went before in one respect or another. That is why learning to recognize a real Dalmatian dog by ostension, even if it works, does not show us how we recognize pictures of Dalmatian dogs in confusing backgrounds, nor new Dalmatian dogs, nor even the same Dalmatian dog a moment later against a different background. All these involve the same sort of unanticipated extension of our recognition skills as coping with creative use of language. It is why we are stuck with black-box ideas like skill and enculturation. Fortunately we can use these black boxes in our scientific exploration of transmission of knowledge because the ideas have observable consequences.

Summary

I have argued that we do not know much about learning. Models of learning such as ostensive definition are just as mysterious as models such as morphogenetic fields. One familiar process that is associated with learning is 'enculturation', though it is as 'black boxish' an idea as any other. Nevertheless, the 'enculturational model' of learning can be shown to be at least a necessary foundation for an 'algorithmical' model. Some of the ramifications of enculturational learning have been described. In particular, the idea is very significant for expert systems and other intelligent machines. By examining a promising, imaginary design of intelligent machine, a point of principle about the limits of unsocialized machines has been made which reflects on our ideas of learning.

Acknowledgements

Many useful comments were made on the last section of this paper by participants of the conference which gave rise to this book. Unfortunately space and time have not been sufficient to develop the argument in the kind of detail that would do justice to all of them within this paper. I would like to thank Angus Gellatly for very useful editorial suggestions and encouragement during the completion of this draft of the paper.

Notes

1. Individuals can, in principle, re-invent a skill without learning it and then participate in the skill using society. Isolated societies may re-invent skills and the whole set of social practices that goes with them.

2. For example, they had to learn to recognize what counted as 'a short wire', among TEA-laser builders (Collins 1985 Chapter 3).
3. Michael Polanyi (1958), coined the term 'tacit knowledge'. Polanyi tends to use it rather more widely than I would wish to. For example, included in tacit knowledge is the scientist's ability to foresee hypotheses that will turn out to be fruitful.
4. Members of the 'artificial intelligentsia' sometimes make misleading statements which appear to impute human abilities to machines when the machines are capable of mimicking only the surface features of the equivalent human activity. Essentially, metaphors are being mistaken for reality. For example, there have been many computers designed to 'learn'. Recently there has been a fashion for 'machine induction' (*see* Bloomfield 1986 for a critical account). For an interesting account of the profligate way designers of intelligent programmes use terms belonging to the vocabulary of human cognition *see* McDermott (1981).
5. Compare John Searle's (1980) argument. Searle starts by hypothesizing a machine that *is indistinguishable* from a human in a Turing test and proceeds to argue that there is a conceptual difference between what the machine does, and what we mean by 'understanding'. (Block's 1981 article was actually written with the same intent.) My aim is to show that if the machine cannot 'understand', then it *cannot be indistinguishable* from a human. Human performance depends on understanding.
6. To anticipate one objection, if the machine is to mimic a human being, it will not be enough for it simply to reply with a 'do not understand' type answer to all creative moves by its human interrogator. One thing the interrogator might say is, 'Now you conduct the rest of this conversation as though you were the interrogator — let us see what kind of creative moves you are capable of! Actually, if the machine is to mimic a human's conversational skills, it needs to be able to do this kind of thing spontaneously. Thus if the machine is to mimic a programmer who is capable of using language creatively, it must be able to use language in the same way.
7. All being well a more detailed version of this argument will appear in Collins, H. M. *Artificial experts: social knowledge and intelligent machines*. MIT Press, Cambridge, MA [In preparation].

References

Barnes, S. B. (1976). Natural rationality: a neglected concept in the social sciences. *Philosophy of the social sciences* 6, 115–26.

Block, N. (1981). Psychologism and behaviourism. *The philosophical review* XC, 5–43.

Bloomfield, B. (1986). Capturing expertise by rule induction. *The knowledge engineering review* 1, 30–6.

Bloor, D. (1983). *Wittgenstein: a social theory of knowledge*. Macmillan, London.

Campbell, D. (1973). Ostensive instances and entitativity in language learning. In *Unity through diversity: a festschrift for Ludwig von Bertanlaffy* (eds. W. Gray and N. D. Rizzo), pp. 1043–57. Gordon and Breach, New York.

Collins, H. M. (1974). The TEA-set: tacit knowledge and scientific networks. *Science studies* 4, 165–86.

Collins, H. M. (1985a). *Changing order: replication and induction in scientific practice*. Sage, Beverley Hills and London.

Collins, H. M. (1985b). Where's the expertise: expert systems as a medium of knowledge transfer. In *Expert systems 85* (ed. M. J. Merry). Cambridge University Press.

Collins, H. M. (1987). Aritificial intelligence, expert systems and the behavioural co-ordinates of action. In *Artificial intelligence: philosophical and sociological perspectives* (ed. B. Bloomfield), pp. 258–82. Croom Helm, London.

Hesse, M. (1974). *The structure of scientific inference.* Macmillan, London.

McDermott, D. (1981). Artificial intelligence meets natural stupidity. In *Mind design* (ed. J. Haugeland), pp. 143–60. MIT Press, Cambridge, MA.

Polanyi, M. (1958). *Personal knowledge.* Routledge and Kegan Paul, London.

Searle, J. (1980). Minds brains and programs. *The behavioural and brain sciences* **3**, 417–24.

Sheldrake, R. (1981/1985). *A new science of life: the hypothesis of formative causation.* Paladin, London.

Wittgenstein, L. (1953). *Philosophical investigations.* Blackwell, Oxford.

14

Ecological psychology as a theory of social cognition
JIM GOOD and ARTHUR STILL

In this chapter we propose that J. J. Gibson's ecological psychology can provide an approach to social psychology (and particularly social cognition) that has many advantages over the *cognitivist* approaches that are currently favoured. It describes a social world that is experienced directly, and not merely as a cognitive representation. To gain some grasp of the potential achievement of ecological psychology in this respect it is necessary to place it within an historical context, in order to understand the problems it sets itself and the alternative it replaces. This alternative is cognitivism, a modern form of the body/mind dualism that originated with Descartes (Reed 1982; Still 1986*b*); it is a *theory* of cognition, but should not be identified with it, since ecological psychology is also a theory of cognition (Reed 1986*b*). In what follows we describe how pragmatism arose as a challenge to dualism, and prepared the ground for ecological psychology. We briefly outline the main features of ecological psychology, and attempt to identify aspects which need modification or extension to take account of the role of language, social interaction, and situational knowledge in social cognition.

The development of cognitivism

Before the mid-nineteenth century, that is before Darwin and the general acceptance of organic evolution, mind was generally treated in Cartesian or Lockean fashion as an entity or mechanism existing more or less independently of the physical world, though attached to a physical body (an automaton) and receiving inputs in the form of sensations or impressions. Its structures and workings were speculated upon by philosophers and others, but did not figure largely in the world described by naturalists. To the natural theologians of the early nineteenth century, for instance, mind was present, but only implicitly, as an appreciative observer. After Darwin, this traditional dualist treatment was gradually undermined. It became necessary to account for consciousness and mental events in naturalistic terms, either as a product of biological evolution, to be understood in terms of its adaptive potential within a niche; or as an emergent property of organized matter (or sometimes as both).

If the mind is an emergent property of the brain, then no radical departure is required from the traditional dualist vocabulary of mentalism. The structures of mind are taken to mirror, in some sense, the structures of the brain, and one of the tasks of structuralist psychology is to map these structures onto each other. In principle, once the feasibility of the project is accepted, it does not raise any special logical problems, and traditional dualist descriptions of mind can be retained. Thus within the modern system of mapping from hardware to software (as in the computer), everyday mental predicates are freely used, and current cognitivist theories, such as that of Johnson-Laird (1983), may be seen as sophisticated versions of the kind of explanation aimed at by Hartley in the late eighteenth century, or by the structuralists, such as Titchener, of the late nineteenth century.

Such explanations, in their modern form, pay lip service to the requirements of biological evolution, but no serious attempt has been made to face the problems of placing the embodied mind within an evolving system that includes organism and environment as equal partners. This failure of the cognitivist approach is no surprise to its critics, who regard these problems as insuperable within such a framework. Naturally enough, cognitivists concentrate upon problems to which they can offer plausible solutions, and therefore leave questions of evolution to footnotes and postscripts. Thus Johnson-Laird, in his epilogue to the final chapter of a book full of experiments and computational methods, writes that 'Consciousness may originally have emerged [in evolution] as a processor promoted to be an operating system and to monitor other processors so as to override pathological configurations.' Consciousness is thus reduced to 'a property of a certain class of parallel algorithms'. He continues, 'Computers can be conscious, though no direct behavioural evidence for their consciousness may ever be obtained' (Johnson-Laird 1983, p. 477). But if, as this seems to imply, there may be no observable effect of consciousness on behaviour, it is hard to see how it can ever have provided the selective advantage that is claimed.

The challenge of ecological functionalism

Serious concern for biological plausibility has been left to the other, more evolutionary approach, which examined consciousness in terms of its adaptive potential in the natural world. By the turn of the century this approach had become dignified as a school or movement, commonly called 'functionalism'. Recently 'functionalism' has come to be used in a misleadingly different way to refer to modern cognitivist theories (e.g. Johnson-Laird 1983). We therefore prefer 'ecological functionalism' (suggested to us by Paul Light, personal communication) to distinguish it from these theories. As a movement in philosophy rather than psychology, ecological functionalism is usually referred to as 'pragmatism'. It emphasizes the mutual interdependence of organism and environment, and in this respect may be called 'mutualist'.

Characteristically, ecological functionalism led to a more radical shift than did structuralism in attitudes towards the mind, and many attempts have been made to construct a vocabulary to support its shift away from dualism. The most notorious of these attempts was behaviourism, whose forceful programme tended to overshadow the earlier and more thoughtful theorists in this tradition (James 1912; Dewey 1929*a*; Mead 1938; see also Still 1986*a* for an account of the problems faced by Tolman in trying to keep hold of the tradition in the face of behaviourism). To some extent it even undid their achievements when it became dominated by stimulus–response psychology in the 1930s. For such a psychology, instead of abandoning Cartesian dualism altogether, tried to shelve its problems by focusing upon one aspect only, the Cartesian automaton, and temporarily ignoring the other aspect, the mind. Thus behaviourism, in spite of its antecedents, was part of the modern project of laboratory psychology within a Cartesian framework; this project has now switched attention back to the mind, ignoring the truly fundamental critique of the framework by ecological functionalism (this history is documented in detail in Good and Still 1986; Still 1986*b*).

Prominent amongst the earlier, and truly radical functionalists were the three great psychological pragmatists, James, Dewey, and Mead, each trying to do justice, within an evolutionary framework, to the complexities of psychological life, and each formulating, with more or less emphasis, three fundamental principles:

1.   Anti-essentialism

Consciousness is not something whose essence can be captured and displayed, but must be understood as arising out of the relationship between organisms and their environments.

Consciousness connotes a kind of external relation, and does not denote a special stuff or way of being. *The peculiarity of our experiences, that they not only are, but are known, which their 'conscious' quality is invoked to explain, is better explained by their relations—these relations themselves being experiences—to one another* (James 1904, 1912, p. 25, italics original).

'Consciousness' is but a symbol, an anatomy whose life is in natural and social operations (Dewey 1899, 1973, p. 162).

2.   Priority of action over thought

Knowledge arises out of action in the world, not from the passive contemplation.

The assumption of 'intellectualism' goes contrary to the facts of what is primarily experienced. For things are objects to be treated, used, acted upon and with, enjoyed and endured, even more than things to be known. "They are things *had* before they are things cognized" (Dewey 1929a, p. 21, italics original).

Later Dewey (1929b) aptly referred to intellectualism as the 'spectator' theory of knowledge.

3.   Mutualism

The organism and its environment (a unity artificially split as 'physical' and 'social') can only be understood as part of a system. Hence they are not logically distinct, and each implies the other. Mead wrote of the 'mutual interdependence' or organism and perceptual field, and continued,

This is expressed in the term 'perspective'. In biology the dependence of the organism upon its field has been the dominant standpoint . . . However, this overlooks the fact that the environment is a selection which is dependent upon the living form. . . . The conception of a world that is independent of any organism is one that is without perspectives. There would be no environments (Mead 1938, pp. 164–5).

The stumbling block for ecological functionalism, with its commitment to mutualism, has been its failure to develop the kind of physical embodiment of its structures that stimulus–response psychology (or its cognitivist counterpart, input–output psychology and information-processing) has, from its own point of view, so successfully realized in the experimental psychology laboratory, with its distinct independent and dependent variables. Dewey criticized the stimulus–response paradigm with damning cogency in 1896, by pointing to the impossibility of identifying a distinct stimulus and response in natural behaviour. Outside the laboratory stimuli and responses continuously modify each other in their mutual interdependence, to form 'a kind of behavioral loop' (Gibson 1979, p. 42). By forcing upon laboratory subjects the distinction between stimulus and response, or independent and dependent variables, cognitivism has developed a psychology which accords with its mechanistic and dualist preconceptions, rather than with those empirical demands of Darwinian biology that arise from the study of organisms in their natural habitats.

J. J. Gibson and ecological functionalism

Pragmatist and functionalist criticisms of cognitivism were neglected but not forgotten, and recently a number of approaches to language, perception, and cognition have converged on an analogous non-mentalistic approach to social knowing. These include the explicitly pragmatist (Rorty 1982; Shalin 1986), the dialectical (Markova 1986), and the Wittgensteinian (Coulter 1983; Bloor 1983). Yet the paradigm has remained unscathed, and continues to dominate academic psychology. There may be many reasons for this, but one is quite straightforward. Criticism needed to be followed by a viable alternative for the burgeoning empirical discipline of psychology, and neither the older pragmatists such as Dewey or Mead, nor their more recent descendants, have succeeded in providing this.

It is this failure of the pragmatist tradition to provide a framework for empirical psychology to replace the behaviourist stimulus–response or cognitivist input–output scheme, that makes the ecological psychology of J. J. Gibson so significant for our present purposes. For Gibson has established the empirical base that has been lacking in the pragmatist critique of dualism, and has shown how this can be used to found a cognitive psychology that accords with the three tenets suggested above. Instead of trying to establish a psychology based upon 'stimuli' or 'inputs' defined in the terms of physics, to which meaning is added by the organism's cognitive constructions, Gibson goes straight to a level of description which 'points both ways, to the environment and to the observer' (Gibson 1979, p. 129). This description is in terms of information structures, which are present in the ambient arrays of suitably equipped and active organisms, and which specify the surrounding surfaces and objects. Generally, these information structures only emerge as properties of transforming, rather than stationary arrays, and therefore they are not available to an observer who relies upon a static retinal image—for this can only pick up the information in stationary arrays. A cogent demonstration of this was an experiment by J. J. and E. J. Gibson in which observers watched a screen on which were projected the shadows of three-dimensional objects. While the object (and therefore its shadow) was stationary, judgements about the three-dimensional shape and orientation of the object were inaccurate. When the object moved, inducing a transformation of the two-dimensional shape on the screen, three-dimensional shape and orientation became apparent. The authors concluded:

. . . a motion consisting of a perspective transformation sequence can determine both a definite rigid shape and a definite change of slant in perception, for a wholly unfamiliar object, without the need of any presumption whatever about the probable shape of the object based on memory (Gibson and Gibson 1957, p. 137.

Thus, a retinal image which, like a camera, only contains static information, is woefully inadequate for specifying the surrounding objects and events of our experience, and must be massively supplemented by memory and other processes of cognitive or computational elaboration. Gibson's greatest insight was to recognize that by replacing the stationary observer with an active perceiver, access is obtained to dynamic information that *is* adequate for specifying an environment and does *not* need to be supplemented in order to account for our experience of being in the world. He invited us to think of eyes, not as cameras, but like hands, which pick up information by active exploration of surfaces. In the classic paper contrasting active and passive touch, he concluded:

... vision and touch have nothing in common *only when they are conceived as channels for pure and meaningless sensory data*. When they are conceived instead as channels for information-pickup, having active and exploratory sense organs, they have much in common. In some respects they seem to register the same information and to yield the *same* phenomenal experience (Gibson 1962, p. 490, italics original).

Through active exploration the organism picks up this information, which specifies those properties of the surroundings that support possible activities ('affordances'), as well as the position and orientation of the organism itself in relation to these supports.

The awareness of the world and the awareness of the self in the world seem to be concurrent. Both event motion in the world and locomotion of the self can be given by vision, the former by a local change in the perspective structure and the latter by a global change of the perspective structure of the ambient optic array (Gibson 1979, p. 187).

What is perceived therefore is the possibility of action in relation to the organism's present state, and Gibson spent much of his working life developing experimental paradigms to demonstrate this theory that accords so well with pragmatist requirements laid down by Dewey and others.

Very misleadingly, Gibson's theory has been presented merely as an alternative theory of *perception* (e.g. Bruce and Green 1985). Instead it is, more generally, a theory of *cognition* which concentrated upon perception because it is there that the traditional and erroneous preconceptions have most firmly established themselves. It is a *pragmatist* theory of cognition, based upon an ontology articulated in terms of the organism's active exchange with its environment, rather than on cognitive elaboration. In this ontology, experience is framed within *persistence* and *change* in place of the traditional categories of *being* and *form*, or *space* and *time* (Reed 1986a gives a full account of this new ontology).'Persistence and change in our surroundings and our relationship to them are experienced directly, while the traditional categories are constructions from this experience. This part of the theory is fully worked out in Gibson's last book, but much still remains to be done towards an adequate account of human cognition, one that takes seriously the full complexity of social behaviour.

Towards an ecological approach to social cognition

An important start has been made by Reed (1986b) through the notion of representational systems, which is based partly upon his reading of Gibson's notebooks and lecture notes on social psychology. Through social interaction, marks, counters, or sounds can come to develop a set of interrelations which amounts to a system apparently independent of any particular human usage. For instance, based on bartering activities, tallies or coins serve in place of the objects bartered, and lead to a system of monetary values. Such systems are apt to be reified, and come to have a seemingly independent existence around which the activities themselves are eventually seen to revolve. They also generate their own 'abstract' social activities, which involve the manipulation of representations, and the beginnings of human cognitive processes. Language, which amongst other things provides a means of sharing and drawing attention to ecological information, plays an essential part in this. It provides a unique source for the development of representational systems: sometimes specialized, as in the technical vocabulary of, for instance, law or botany; sometimes more general, as in the everyday discussions of people's actions, motives, beliefs, etc., known as 'folk psychology' (Stich 1983). By studying such representational systems, we may come to understand, in nominalist fashion, the development of talk about the self and others. Nominalism does not necessarily empty its referents of all contents. The word 'self' may not refer to a simple entity, but at a level necessary for understanding action, the 'self' and the 'other' are given immediately as dual aspects of the information that 'points both ways', to environment and to organism.

This more primordial level of awareness suggests another way in which ecological psychology may develop a theory of social cognition. J. J. Gibson spent much of his life studying the exploratory activities and the information structures that underlie our experiences as inhabitants of the so-called *physical* world. Less well known is his interest in social psychology, which he taught for 15 years at Cornell. Although he published only three papers in this field, he was well aware that

The richest and most elaborate affordances of the environment are provided by other animals and, for us, other people . . . When touched they touch back, when struck they strike back; in short they *interact* with the observer and with one another. Behavior affords behavior, and the whole subject matter of psychology and of the social sciences can be thought of as an elaboration of this basic fact. Sexual behavior, nurturing behavior, fighting behavior, cooperative behavior, economic behavior, political behavior—all depend on the perceiving of what another person or other persons afford, or sometimes on the misperceiving of it (Gibson 1979, p. 135, italics original).

It is not surprising, therefore, that those influenced by Gibson have recently extended his search for informational invariants underlying social experience (Knowles and Smith 1982; McArthur and Baron 1983). McArthur and Baron (1983), for example, raise the question of the information available in the structured stimulation that exists in our social environment and which we may utilize in perceiving others. In a wide-ranging discussion they illustrate the applicability of the approach to emotion perception, impression formation, and causal attribution, and consider the implications for an understanding of errors in social perception. Here we will confine ourselves to considering some of the prospects and problems for ecological psychology in two areas of social cognition. The first is a study of the information in movement that specifies intentionality and the nature of encounters between two people, the second is communication between doctors and patients who are dying. Only the first was designed to explore the ecological approach. The latter, however, supplies a test case for looking at its usefulness in understanding a complex everyday situation. It is included here in order to highlight some of the problems which an ecological approach to social cognition will have to solve.

Intentionality and social affordances

The Gestalt social psychologist, Solomon Asch, was one of the first to recognize the informativeness of kinematic configurations. In 1952 he wrote:

If we follow the qualities of acts such as approaching and withdrawing, it is because we respond to their *form*; we would not perceive them if we saw merely a sequence of separate, specific movements (Asch 1952, p. 151, italics original).

In support of this he referred to the experiments of Heider and Simmel (1944), who presented a cartoon film of geometrical shapes moving in and out of a 'door'. Observers interpreted these as the movements of purposive beings interacting with each other, and Asch drew the conclusion that . . .

we initially perceive movement-forms in persons in a dynamic–causal way . . . movements which form kinetic structures possess the properties of happenings or actions (Asch 1952, p. 156).

As in the Gibsons' shadow-caster experiment, information specifying these 'biological motions' must be contained only in the movements on the screen, not in the nature of the shapes themselves. Johansson (1973) carried this technique further with the use of 'point-light displays', which he generated by filming the movements of people with lights attached to parts of their bodies. Only the lights were visible on the film, which presents a compelling appearance of animate movement. Cutting *et al.* (1978) and Runeson and Frykholm (1981, 1983) have demonstrated that such information can specify properties as diverse as gender, personal identity, the weight of objects being lifted, and intention. Runeson and Frykholm have proposed a lawful relationship between these properties and the kinematics of the body, which they call the KSD principle; kinematics specifies dynamics. They explain this in terms of biomechanical necessities inherent in maintaining balance and coping with reactive impulses—bodily constraints thus combine with the requirements of any action to produce, for a perceiver, an invariant configuration which specifies its source. This configuration reflects anatomical and other properties of persons, as well as the workings of the motor-control system.

Recent experiments at Durham (Good 1985) have used point-light displays to study the invariants that underlie the perception of interactions between two people. The immediate aim is to demonstrate the existence of these invariants, not to describe their exact structure—that will be attempted later. Invariants are thus analogous to hypothetical constructs (MacCorquodale and Meehl 1948); although at present they may be unobservable, they can in principle be identified. By contrast, cognitivist models usually deal with intervening variables, or aspects of a purely conceptual model.

The point-light displays were generated from video recordings of actors simulating various encounters, including an accidental collision and help, a collision and argument, a chance meeting of old friends, a reprimand, and an unwelcome sexual advance. These sequences were selected in order to explore the information in point-light displays from a variety of both intended and accidental events, and a range of personal properties. Observers all reported perceiving intentional social actions, and many were able to give accurate accounts of the encounters displayed or selected the correct description from a list.

But in two related respects these demonstrations of invariants that underlie social perception fall short of the theoretical requirements of Gibson's programme. First, the ideal of an active, exploratory perceiver is not met. Instead, as in traditional perceptual experiments, the observer is passive, and it is not easy to introduce active participation. The equivalent to the active pick-up of information in the optic array, for instance, is presumably social participation through questioning and other means, and hence it is neither by passive watching, nor by active exploration of passive objects, that we come to know intentionality in others. Second, the self cannot be specified by the information available in these experiments. Affordances point both ways, to environment and to organism, but only when the perceiver is utilizing the affordance in some way. Likewise the social self can only be specified, in an analogous fashion, when the person is actively engaged socially, and thus in direct contact with others. As Neisser puts it, in a comment on contributions to a symposium on social knowing:

The theories and experiments described here all refer to an essentially passive onlooker who sees someone do something (or sees two people do something) and then makes a judgment about it. He . . . doesn't *do* anything—doesn't mix it up with the folks he is watching, never tests his judgment in action or in interaction. He just watches and makes judgments . . . when people are genuinely engaged with each other, nobody stops to give grades (Neisser 1980, pp. 603–4, italics original).

Thus, just as Dewey in 1896 pointed out the essential interdependence of stimulus and response, so in social psychology we must face the additional fact that the transmission and reception of information are simultaneous and not to be treated separately. This was recognized by the sociologist Erving Goffman.

Goffman saw our face-to-face communication with others as embodied, an emphasis that accords with the immediacy of perception reported by observers of point-light displays. But Goffman also stressed the mutuality of social perception:

Each individual can *see* that he is being experienced in some way, and he will guide at least some of his conduct according to the perceived identity and initial response of his audience. Further he can be seen to be seeing this, and can see that he has been seen seeing this (Goffman 1963, p. 16, italics original).

Nevertheless, point-light displays, while not fully meeting the methodological requirements of ecological theory, do provide a means of demonstrating that ecological information which specifies the properties of people and their actions, and which is conveyed by kinematics, is available to perceivers. Point-light displays also offer the possibility of exploring, through computer simulation and other means, the precise nature of the information involved. But potential limitations remain when measured against the expectations of mutualism, and they may be illustrated further by considering what is involved in a situation that has been much studied by social psychologists, that of doctor–patient relationships. We will attempt to describe this using the language of ecological psychology.

Social affordances in doctor–patient relationships

Together, doctor and patient form a system of mutual affordances. For an ordinary patient, the doctor affords an ear attuned to certain kinds of question and complaint. For the doctor the patient affords a body available to medical inspection and receptive to advice. Doctors dispense a special kind of knowledge and patients receive the knowledge in a form geared to their needs. The case is different when the patients are not merely ill but dying, where the affordances of the situation, related as they are to what can be talked about, depend on whether the fact of the patient's dying is openly acknowledged by both parties. It appears from interviews with both doctors and patients (Todd and Still 1984; Still and Todd 1986) that it is not always simply a matter of the doctor telling the patient—that can happen without being followed by open acknowledgement, and sometimes there is open acknowledgement without explicit information having passed between the two.

When affordances are conditional in such complex ways upon what has gone before, can we really continue to treat the behaviour as based upon stimulus information, and avoid appeal to role-playing and cognitive representations? Gibson believed that we can. He wrote of social affordances in general:

The perceiving of these mutual affordances is enormously complex, but it is nonetheless lawful, and it is based on the pickup of the information in touch, sound, odor, taste, and ambient light. It is just as much based on stimulus information as is the simpler perception of the support that is offered by the ground under one's feet. For other animals and other persons can only give off information about themselves insofar as they are tangible, audible, odorous, tastable, or visible (Gibson 1979, p. 135).

If this is so, what are the informational invariants that underlie the perception involved in encounters between doctors and patients? Mutuality must presumably hold. The patient's perception of the doctor as someone to whom he or she can talk openly about the illness and its implications, entails a corresponding perception of self as somebody who might, here and now, talk in such ways. In these cases there are well documented 'signals' that might serve as 'cues'. The manner, the dress, and the surroundings are characteristic, but they can never provide a complete account of the information available. As patient, one enters a situation that is part of the ongoing activity of 'going to the doctor', and an appreciation of the situation ensures a proper readiness towards the affordances that then become available.

To account for this sequential aspect of everyday experience, we may call upon what Gibson called 'higher order invariants', based on information structures that transcend particular modalities, and that may be picked up over relatively long periods of time. But there is a danger, in such an account, of losing sight of the mutuality that we have assumed to be essential to the ecological functionalism being developed here. Costall (1986) has recently drawn attention to the related danger, which Gibson himself does not always avoid, of treating the environment as a passive partner to an organism negotiating a rigid and unchanging world of affordances. Organisms act upon environments and change them, and are thereby changed themselves, on both a phylogenetic and an ontogenetic time scale. If this dialectical process operates in the case of the physical environment, then how much more so when dealing with social activity. There, the ongoing directed activities that are necessary to pick up information themselves have a more or less continuous effect on the information that is available in the ambient arrays, and it is therefore in the unfolding of activities and effects taken together that intentionality manifests itself. It is not merely greater complexity or the involvement of others that contributes to the social cognition, but this intrusion of joint activity into the information that specifies affordances.

Thus it can be misleading to say, with Gibson, that . . . 'the other person has a surface that reflects light, and the information to specify what he or she is, invites, promises, threatens, or does can be found in the light' (Gibson 1979, p. 136). This is misleading because if the information for such social affordances is in the light it is not passively waiting there. It is not, like the information that specifies surrounding surfaces and objects, there in the ambient array, available for pick-up by a suitably equipped and active organism. A smile or a squeeze of the hand may be specified by information in the optic or tactile array, but its exact meaning, and therefore what it affords, is tightly conditioned by the nature of the ongoing activity of which it forms a part. For a cognitivist, the meaning is added to the purely physical input through interpretation, with the aid of an internal representation or schema. For the ecological psychologist the nature of the explanation sought is quite different; the meaning of a smile is usually to be drawn out with reference to the actions within which it is embedded, not by interpretation of a single input. As Gibson himself wrote:

What the other animal affords the observer is not only behavior but also social interaction. As one moves so does the other, the one sequence of action being suited to the other in a kind of behavioral loop. All social interaction is of this sort — sexual, maternal, competitive, cooperative — or it may be social grooming, play, and even human conversation (Gibson 1979, p. 42).

Thus Gibson understood the problem arising from the unbroken flow of social interaction, though he sometimes seemed to overlook it, and never explained how to solve it. He gives no detailed account of activities which are not merely exploratory of available information, but which themselves provoke the transformations of informational structure which specify affordances. Such transformations must specify animate rather than inanimate movement, and allow for some form of continuous, causal correlation with the provoking activities.

In Durham an approach towards such an account has been made by using *interactive* point-light displays. In these the two 'actors' wear reflective patches, which appear as point-light sources for kinematic information. Thus each faces a camera, and views the other as a dynamic display on a video monitor. This enables us to explore the ways in which such information can support the social co-ordination of action, and it meets the requirement that the transmission and reception of information should be simultaneous. It also does justice to Asch's claim that 'we initially perceive movement-forms in persons in a dynamic–causal way'. Whether it can do the same for the complexities of the social situations we have considered and for Goffman's analysis of social action as embodied communication remains to be seen.

References

Asch, S. E. (1952). *Social psychology*. Prentice-Hall, Englewood Cliffs, NJ.
Bloor, D. (1983). *Wittgenstein: a social theory of knowledge*. Macmillan, London.
Bruce, V. and Green, P. (1985). *Visual perception: physiology, psychology and ecology*. Erlbaum, Hillsdale, NJ.
Coulter, J. (1983). *Rethinking cognitive theory*. Macmillan, London.

Costall, A. P. (1986). The 'psychologist's fallacy' in ecological realism. *Teorie and Modelli* **3**, 37–46.

Cutting, J. E., Proffitt, D. R., and Kozlowski, L. T. (1978). A biomechanical invariant for gait perception. *Journal of experimental psychology: human perception and performance* **4**, 357–72.

Dewey, J. (1896). The reflect arc concept in psychology. *Psychological review* **3**, 357–70.

Dewey, J. (1929*a*). *Experience and nature*. Allen and Unwin, London.

Dewey, J. (1929*b*). *The quest for certainty: a study of the relation of knowledge and action*. Minton, Balch and Co, New York.

Dewey, J. (1899/1973). *The philosophy of John Dewey*, (ed. J. J. McDermott). University of Chicago Press, Chicago.

Gibson, J. J. (1979). *The ecological approach to visual perception*. Houghton-Mifflin, Boston.

Gibson, J. J. (1962). Observations on active touch. *Psychological review* **69**, 477–91.

Gibson, J. J. and Gibson, E. J. (1957). Continuous perspective transformations and the perception of rigid motion. *Journal of experimental psychology* **54**, 129–38.

Goffman, E. (1963). *Behavior in public places*. Free Press. New York.

Good, J. M. M. (1985). The perception of social actions from point-light displays. Paper presented to the *Third International Conference on Event Perception and Action*, Uppsala, Sweden.

Good, J. M. M. and Still, A. W. (1986). Tolman and the tradition of direct perception. *British journal of psychology* **77**, 533–9.

Heider, F. and Simmel, M. (1944). An experimental study of apparent behavior. *American journal of psychology* **57**, 243–59.

Johansson, G. (1973). Visual perception of biological motion and a model for its analysis. *Perception and psychophysics* **14**, 201–11.

James, W. (1904/1912). *Essays in radical empiricism*. Longmans, Green and Co, New York.

Johnson-Laird, P. N. (1983). *Mental models: towards a cognitive science of language, inference, and consciousness*. Cambridge University Press.

Knowles, P. L. and Smith, D. L. (1982). The ecological perspective applied to social perception: revision of a working paper. *Journal for the theory of social behaviour* **12**, 53–78.

McArthur, L. Z. and Baron, R. M. (1983). Toward an ecological theory of social perception. *Psychological review* **90**, 215–38.

MacCorquodale, K. and Meehl, P. E. (1948). On a distinction between hypothetical constructs and hypothetical variables. *Psychological review*, **55**, 95–107.

Markova, I. (1986). The concept of the universal in the Cartesian and Hegelian frameworks. *Cognitive psychology in question* (ed. A. Costall and A. W. Still). Harvester, Brighton.

Mead, G. H. (1938). *Philosophy of the act*. Chicago University Press, Chicago.

Neisser, U. (1980). On social knowing. *Personality and social psychology bulletin* **6**, 601–5.

Reed, E. S. (1982). Descartes' corporeal ideas hypothesis and the origin of scientific psychology. *Review of metaphysics* **35**, 731–52.

Reed, E. S. (1986a). Why do things look as they do? The implications of James Gibson's *The ecological approach to visual perception*. In *Cognitive psychology in question* (ed. A. Costall and A. W. Still). Harvester, Brighton.

Reed, E. S. (1986b). Gibson's ecological approach to cognition. In *Cognitive psychology in question* (ed. A. Costall and A. W. Still). Harvester, Brighton.

Rorty, R. (1982). *Consequences of pragmatism*. Harvester, Brighton.

Runeson, S. and Frykholm, G. (1981). Visual perception of lifted weight. *Journal of experimental psychology: human perception and performance* 7, 733–40.

Runeson, S. and Frykholm, G. (1983). Kinematic specification of dynamics as an informational basis for person-and-action-perception: Expectation, gender recognition, and deceptive intention. *Journal of experimental psychology: general* 112, 585–615.

Shalin, D. N. (1986). Pragmatism and social interaction. *American sociological review* 51, 9–29.

Stich, S. (1983). From folk psychology to cognitive science. MIT Press, Cambridge, MA.

Still, A. W. (1986a). Tolman's perception. In *Cognitive psychology in question* (ed. A. Costall and A. W. Still). Harvester, Brighton.

Still, A. W. (1986b). The biology of science: an essay on the evolution of representational cognitivism. *Journal for the theory of social behaviour* 16, 251–67.

Still, A. W. and Todd, C. J. (1986). Role ambiguity in general practice: the care of patients dying at home. *Social science and medicine* 23, 519–25.

Todd, C. J. and Still, A. W. (1984). Communication between general practitioners and patients dying at home. *Social science and medicine* 18, 667–72.

15

Worlds apart: towards a materialist critique of the cognitive–social dualism

LIAM GREENSLADE

The resolution of *theoretical* contradictions is possible *only* through practical means, only through the *practical* energy of human beings (Karl Marx, cited in Bottomore and Rubel 1963, p. 87).

In opulent or commercial societies, to think or reason comes to be, like every other employment, a particular business which is carried on by a very few people who furnish the public with all the thought and reason possessed by the vast multitude that labour (Adam Smith, cited in Rothblatt 1985, p. 28).

Introduction

Since the inception of the human sciences, their history has been characterized by a number of oppositions: between the individual and the social, between the rational and the irrational, between nature and culture, between cognition and emotion. The incorporation of these oppositions as reified entities has a number of consequences for both practice and theory in the human sciences. First, they facilitate the constitution of different disciplines each taking as its focus a permutation of the opposed terms. Thus, the labour of the psychologist (whose primary concern is with the individual) becomes divided from that of the sociologist (who focuses upon the societal). In addition to this, such oppositions serve to furnish the terrain for practical activity by identifying the problems to be solved within a given focal range (e.g. the psychological) and also delineate acceptable methods of arriving at solutions.

It is in such a way, for example, that a 'gap' (in terms of both ontology and epistemology) comes to be perceived between cognition and the social world, and its bridging becomes a chronic problem deserving of inter-disciplinary research. Henriques *et al.* (1984) characterize this gap ironically, but not without accuracy, as 'a bridge too far'.

It is my contention in this paper that within the epistemological and ontological terms set by current socio-cognitive theory we are rendered incapable of thinking about this gap in any terms other than that of an indissoluble opposition, bounded by infinite regress on the one side and vicious circularity on the other. The causes for this incapacity are manifold, but they can be understood in terms of a contradictory interaction between the traditional organization, practices, and preconceptions of intellectuals in the West, the political role and function of social scientists under capitalism since the end of nineteenth century, and the wider ideological imperatives of capitalism itself as they become manifest around the notion of the person and the constitution of individual subjectivity. The first term limits the ways in which the community of social scientists confront the problem of cognitive and social and their relationship to it, the second provides the motivation for this confrontation, and the third furnishes the conditions for the chasm between individual and social itself.

Within the terrain produced by these interacting factors, theoretical and empirical research in the social sciences have been stifled and largely incapacitated by the necessity of producing politically and scientifically reductive conceptions of social being. In consequence, the common-sense generalities of capitalism have been transformed by social scientists into the point of departure for the consideration of social and psychological existence at all times, in all situations, and for all foreseeable futures. The purpose of this paper is to provide a materialist critique of this universalizing, reductive discourse. My intention is to 'theorize the theory' in such a way as to show its limitations and its functions in what Habermas (1973) has termed 'today's crisis of legitimacy'.

On materialism and other things

Before I set out on this critique I would like to explain briefly my use of the term 'material' and its various derivates in the present essay. The theory of the material world used throughout this paper derives from Marxism. In particular it derives from the premisses given by Marx and Engels (1970, pp. 47–8).

> . . . we do not set out from what men (*sic*) say, imagine, conceive, nor from men as narrated, thought of, imagined, in order to arrive at men in the flesh. . . . This method of approach is not devoid of premises. It starts out from the real premises and does not abandon them for a moment. Its premises are men, not in any fantastic isolation and rigidity, but in their actual, empirically perceptible process of development under definite conditions.

It is the process of development under definite historical conditions which concerns a Marxist materialism. Thus it is concerned with ideas only insofar as they can be placed in relation to and interpreted by reference to the actions of the human beings of whose lives they form part, not as entities in the abstraction of a logical calculus.

Materialism of this kind cannot be separated from revolutionary social practice. To paraphrase Marx, the task is not to interpret circumstances but to change them. My critique is materialist in the sense that it is not concerned with untying the abstract logical incoherences of social cognitive thought and practice, but with developing a political analysis of them which can be used to change the very circumstances from which they arise. The fate of social cognition as a mere discourse of the intellect is of less significance than the uses to which the academic labour from which it is constituted is put in a given cultural–historical epoch.

In the present essay, the materialism adopted entails the consideration of the social–cognitive relationship as a cultural product arising from the conditions mentioned earlier. Just as factory workers produce concrete objects for consumption in a given socio-historical context, so academic labourers produce conceptual objects for consumption. The particular form of the commodities under consideration (e.g. conceptualizations of the cognitive-social relation) cannot be privileged in any way. For the purposes of this essay, production of such objects cannot be separated from the conditions obtaining in the wider society and, despite the claims to ahistorical, universal truth which social scientists implicitly attach to their findings and other pronouncements (i.e. that which renders them scientific), the process of production must be subject to scrutiny and considered an essential part of the products themselves.

Like any worker, the intellectual labourer does not confront the means of production as a *tabula rasa*. He or she comes to them with a cultural and social biography, a class-historical position which exerts a determinate effect upon the way in which a particular intellectual problem is recognized and dealt with. Similarly, just as factory workers do not create anew their own raw materials or manufacturing implements, intellectuals are equipped with a variety of concepts and symbolic devices which enable them to participate in the process of academic production. There is, necessarily, a body of knowledge and practice to be learned and applied in appropriate ways under the guidance of the community. As the history of science would suggest, these 'knowledge technologies' are not immutable but are subject to constant modification, selection, and mutation (cf. Feyerabend 1975; Kuhn 1970). Finally, there is the organization and management of academic labour in the various institutions, the granting and witholding of economic and symbolic rewards to direct activity along certain paths and according to certain rhythms.

This may seem to be obvious, but when we work in the realm of ideas the extent of the social–historical determinations upon those ideas themselves is often forgotten. From a materialist perspective it is crucial to bear in mind the inseparability of the objects of production from the processes of production themselves. Such things did not emerge from nothing, but are themselves the products of historical predecessors arising under definite historical conditions. Furthermore, there is also the effect of the present historical situation to consider.

Both the process and the products of academic labour are shaped in the here and now by the administrators and economic controllers of the system of academic production itself. The framing and following of research programmes, the constitution of the teaching curriculum, and indeed the teaching and research community itself, are all the subject of constant economic and ideological incitement. Historically, we find evidence for this assertion in both the social and the physical sciences. IQ testing, atomic research, and the 'blue sky' research associated with the Strategic Defense Initiative, are all striking examples of the effects of economic and political shaping of research. It is not the insupportable assertion it once was to argue for the social determination of scientific knowledge (cf. Collins 1985; Foucault 1984). The relativization of science which results when we admit such a contention is regarded as threat to knowledge in some quarters (e.g. Gibbons and Wittrock 1985). In the present essay it is regarded as an inevitable consequence of the production of social scientific knowledge which has been effaced for political and ideological reasons. In the remainder of this paper I shall attempt to explicate this point and demonstrate its bearing on the relationship of cognitive to social.

The impossible subject: human science and the imaginary self

The pivotal reductive conception which conditions our practice in relation to the cognitive–social dualism is, in its most mundane formulation, the notion of 'self'. We think of ourselves and others as 'selves', if the clumsiness of this phrase may be forgiven. And in doing so we give substance to the myth which ties us to the very problem we seek to address. For in our commitment to the notion of our existence as 'selves' we are forced into a series of other commitments, most of which are a good deal more difficult to ground. The I-that-speaks is presupposed in a whole conceptual framework of mentalism, of individualism, of psychologism generally. Behind every utterance there stands this rock solid core 'the self', and we are led to the belief that if we can explain this, then explanations for all our conceptual problems, and the social beside, must follow.

Such a belief of course has no more or less validity than the Azande belief in sorcery, or the Christian belief in an eternal soul. They serve ultimately the same purpose; namely to preserve existing social practice and to keep power in the hands of those who already possess it. The difference between our belief in self, and Azande and Christian belief is that the first is wholly naturalized by a scientific discourse and technological apparatus which gives it a status denied to the others within our contemporary culture.

In social psychology we are currently undergoing a new phase of discovery *vis-à-vis* the 'self' (cf. Gergen 1982; Greenwald and Pratkanis 1984; Suls 1982).

Unfortunately, this new wave of 'born again' egocentrism seems determined to repeat the central errors of its historical predecessors (e.g. James 1890; Mead 1934) by redefining the concept to render it 'manageable' within the terms of contemporarily available and/or fashionable philosophical or socio-scientific discourse.

The regeneration of interest in the self, and in the issue of relations between selves, demonstrates a number of overt characteristics. One is the desire to create 'stronger' conceptualizations of wider applicability and epistemological force, something which is common to all scientific systems. Another is the desire to return theorizing to some identifiable object of investigation. It is clear that, in social psychology at least, the objects of theoretical discourse had become increasingly abstract and unworkable. A third feature is the process of 'general humanizing', which might be characterized as a return to 'common sense'.

What is missed in the course of this 'self-discovery' (if the pun may be forgiven) is that the project itself, which has been repeated at various times during the past three centuries, consists in very little more than a justificatory reification, the main goal of which is to provide a universal, non-defeasible basis for bourgeois practice. Its proponents, in turn, fulfill little more than a role as the bourgeoisie's '. . . conceptive ideologists, who make the perfecting of the illusion of the class about itself their chief source of livelihood . . .' (Marx and Engels 1970, p. 65). It is this function of human scientists under Capital which becomes the absent centre of their discoursing about the self.

In generating formulae and algorithms for the 'universal self', human scientists enter into a series of antagonisms which they then seek to reconcile conceptually: mind–body, mental–manual, self–other, individual–social. The difficulties which they encounter in the reconciliation process reinforce the ever-present tendency to treat such things as immutable and universal. As Sohn-Rethel (1978) has shown, these non-empirical abstractions can be seen as an inevitable outcome of advanced commodity production wherein dominant concepts derive their nature from the abstraction inherent in the exchange process itself. His critique of intellectual labour reiterates the Marxian notion that in order to understand ideas prevalent at any time, we must not detach them from the material context of production (Marx and Engels 1970). The idea of the self, of the constitutive subject itself, arises out of such a detachment. As a number of analyses have shown (e.g. Cherry 1967; Morris 1972; Whyte 1962) the idea of an individuated subject did not spring *ab nihilo* as a part of general human nature but was, in fact, a product of changes in historical, economic, and intellectual practices. It would seem that a significant part of the project of human science since the seventeenth century has been to repress this fact. In order to resolve the problem that we face today in 'interfacing' individual to social, it becomes necessary to revise the history of the subject in such a way as to emphasize its material basis in a commodity society.

Technological society based on commodity exchange creates and naturalizes the atomistic self and the system wherein it can be realized. It is not 'natural' but is made so in the course of economic and technological practices which by their very action render unintelligible any other form of experience. In a culture where Technology, backed up by a neutral, impartial Science and a similarly constituted system of Law, determines the organization of day-to-day existence by transforming us all into interchangeable machine parts, short-term survival depends on a firm grasp of the notion of identity which such a culture permits. As Wilden (1980, p. 91) has put it:

The atomisation of social relationships which was the necessary corollary of the atomisation of economic relationships produces that impossible and imaginary entity: the bourgeois individual.

In more historical terms we can describe the situation as follows. The development of capitalism in the West sundered the old social relations of the medieval world. The 'new consciousness' of the bourgeoisie entailed the establishment of an ideological subject which stood in opposition to the integrated hierarchy of the feudal social world. Under feudalism order was derived from the insertion of persons into a structure of unchanging social relations and social differences. It depended upon each person having a recognition of his or her place in the order of things and acting accordingly. Personhood itself was derived after ritual incorporation into the social whole which was seen as prior to and extending beyond the existence of the person (Ullman 1967).

The paradigm of bourgeois subjectivity, the Cartesian *cogito*, is an inversion of this. The Cartesian subject is self-confirming, with an ontological status given not by the social system but by the operation of individual consciousness. Such a subject is a product of the transformation from feudalism to capitalism (Wilden 1980). The individual ceases to be tied to a social system or a fixed place within it. While it is possible, as Descartes' work indicates, to produce in the abstract a relatively coherent notion of individual subjectivity, a problem arises when one turns to consider the concrete problem of how a society comprised of such individuals operates.

In the production of the new ideological subject a problem was simultaneously generated regarding the constitution of the social (cf. Hobbes 1651/1968). An ideology of universal egocentric individualism might efficiently serve to disrupt the ordered system of feudal sociocentrism, but the practical problem of extending this ideology in an uncontrolled way to the whole of society beyond the owners and controllers of the means of production could never be sustained. The ontological equality of human subjects had to be maintained at the conceptual level in order to facilitate the identification of slave with master. At the same time, however, a prior social order based on the unequal division of wealth, labour, and opportunity had to be practically sustained so that those who had wrested power in the bourgeois revolution could maintain their hold on it.

In effect the historical project of social psychology has been to find some way of reconstructing the individual–social relationship, conceptually and practically, to meet these contradictory requirements. Its failure to accomplish this has proved no obstacle to the development of social psychology as a discipline, since the problem continues to exist and solutions need to be sought. What is misunderstood is that the 'problem' of the relationship between individual and social is not one of conceptual or of technical matters, but is a political consequence of capitalism for which the solution is and can only be political.

The problem of individual and social

Central to any understanding of the division of labour within the human sciences is the dualistic opposition between individual and social: the present book bears witness to the way in which we address and otherwise engage with this issue. In my own discipline, social psychology, the past decade has seen a plethora of publications, so-called new theories and empirical procedures all attempting to deal with the problem of the collective and the individual, the psychological and the sociological, the cognitive and the social. Ethogenics, social representations, hermeneutics, and indeed the 'new paradigm' of social cognition itself all promise ways of resolving this knotty old problem.

The 'problem' of cognitive and social is neither more nor less than an expression of economic and cultural experience under capitalism. The binary conception of a cognitive (or individual) 'interior' and a social 'exterior' as separate or antithetical analytic domains is part of an ethnocentric illusion specific to the experience of intellectuals since the development of the capitalist mode of production (cf. Cherry 1967; Volosinov 1973). That we can regard this bifurcation as a universal, or even significant feature of all experience, such that its absence becomes just as much a problem as its presence (as in the case of children, traditional societies, and the insane), is symptomatic: not of its universality, but of the material dominance of capitalism as a global system, and the ethnocentrist perspective to which it gives rise (cf. Said 1985; Sartre 1967).

The ontological and epistemological divorce which, in our signifying machinery,[1] disjoins cognition from the social world stands itself in two imbricated formations of material power and effectivity: the ideological and the administrative. In both cases it becomes a point of departure for practice. Like all such machinery, the creativity of which is ultimately dependent upon metaphysics, its fate is to reveal its contradictions at a theoretical and practical level (Wilden 1980).

The failure of social psychology to establish itself as a viable scientific discourse is a case in point. The inability of social psychological practice to provide meaningful findings beyond the artificial world of the laboratory has not been the fault of social psychologists themselves nor, directly, of the methods and theories at their disposal. The problem is rather more complicated than one of either bad tools or bad workers.

All societies objectify particular codes and practices in order to signify subjectivity machinically. This is undertaken primarily as a way of explaining and/or legitimating the social relations which exist at a given period in their historical development as societies. Creation myths (cf. Bateson 1973), totemism (cf. Lévi-Strauss 1966), religion (cf. Douglas 1973), and indeed science itself (Wilden 1980), have all been used to perform such functions. These machinic systems are observed (in the religious sense) as if they fall into the domain which Moscovici (1981) has term the 'reified universe'.

In Althusserian terms (e.g. Althusser 1971) such systems constitute the always-already, the 'et cetera' conditions (Garfinkel 1967), from which practice, theoretical and empirical, departs. They render possible 'unthought' by furnishing a natural base for thought itself, a position where the latter no longer has to question itself. A characteristic feature of such systems is that, whatever their material base, their articulation involves a denial or repression of that base. This puts a distance between themselves, their proponents, and the order of things. And yet, despite this, there is a simultaneous claim that they possess an imperative force of some kind and that their authoritative effects follow from, or by virtue of, their socially abstract nature.

Such assertions are clearly mutually exclusive and contradictory. Yet it seems that it is precisely such machinery which overdetermines what it is social psychologists do, how they think about what they do, and their failure to do the things which they set out to accomplish. It appears that it is the very system of Western thought and practice in its objectification of a particular machine for signifying individual–social relations which is the greatest obstacle to the development of a *social* psychology. The material contradiction arises because the machinery which generates the necessity of a social psychology, legitimates the practices of social psychologists, and provides the administrative imperatives which determine the ends towards which those practices were and are directed, simultaneously presents it with a problem insoluble within its terms.

The project of social psychology is denied a point at which it can reach the closure demanded of it (i.e. a once-and-for-all solution to the problem of individual and social relations in the material world) because its point of departure is the abstract individual, the given of what Therborn (1980) has termed the 'class ego-ideology' of the bourgeoisie. The centrality of this abstract concept to the development of social psychology is matched only by the extent to which it renders the concrete domain of the social largely opaque and scientifically barely accountable. As a result, the operation of the social psychological signifying machine becomes an exercise in contradictions which, by analogy to capitalism itself,

. . . are constantly overcome, only to be again constantly re-established. Still more so. The universality towards which it is perpetually driving finds limitations in its own nature, which at a certain stage of its development will make it appear as itself the greatest barrier to this tendency (Marx, cited in McClelland 1971, p. 112).

The problem of critical social psychology

A critical socio-psychological science has, inevitably, to deal with the problem presented to it by the individual–social relation. Unfortunately, it would seem that present and previous approaches to social psychology from within the academic establishment, including those which might not necessarily be regarded as such (e.g. ethnomethodology, psychoanalysis, etc.) have foundered because the wrong fundamental perspective was adopted at the outset. In short, social psychologists have failed in practice to recognize the individual–social relationship for what it is: a function of political practices and social organization, which does not permit the adoption of an uncontradictory position outside of this organized practice itself.

This problem stems from the central contradiction of social relations within capitalism itself. Ideologically, the system of capitalist social relations depends upon the enforcement of particular notions of subjectivity. The inversion of social relations which capitalism engendered historically involved a substitution of the egocentric for the sociocentric orientation of human being to human being. As Marx has put it (1973 p. 83)

In this society of free competition, the individual appears detached from the natural bonds etc. which in earlier historical periods make him the accessory of a definite and limited human conglomerate.

However, while the system of production constantly seeks to legitimate the concept of the subject as an isolated, self-grounded monad, ontologically prior to the social, at the level of actual social practice, this insistence disintegrates.

That is, it becomes clear to many subjects, implicitly or explicitly, that the theory of subjectivity which informs their lives under capitalism is in practice unworkable, unless of course they are white, middle class, male owners of the means of production. In effect what occurs amongst women, workers, blacks, and other subjects of domination and exploitation is that their experience of their oppression is constantly elided by the ideological formation of social practice. In the presuppositions of language, of economics (the 'free market'), of politics, there is a constant incitement for such individuals to identify their particular needs with the needs of capitalism and ignore the conditions which contribute to their oppression.

The marginalization of such human beings and the practical delegitimization of their subjective position which takes place under capitalism generates a recognition of its own which is signified in a multiplicity of ways (cf. Fanon 1970; Foucault 1984; Turner 1984; Volosinov 1973). Attempts to define, signify, or materially obtain a position different from those legitimated within the dominant ideological discourse are subject to resistance and recuperation (i.e. transformed or incorporated into a capitalist rationality) in such ways as to render them harmless to the hegemony of capitalism over subjectivity.

As people struggle with their oppression under capitalism, either overtly or implicitly, they come to realize that struggle rooted in the consciousness of the individual is of limited utility; it is only in the context of a social grouping of some sort that meaningful resistance can be effected. Collective action on an organized basis by any oppressed group is the thing most feared within the capitalist social order. When it occurs and cannot be constrained sufficiently to pose no threat to that order, it is quashed by whatever means necessary. Where collective resistance is effective and can be controlled sufficiently to avoid a direct threat to the hegemony of capitalism over social relations, concessions may be made and individual 'leaders' such as Lane's (1974) 'top-hatted trade unionists' of the nineteenth century created in order to be bought off. Alternatively, oppressed groups may be provided with collective models through which their experience of oppression may be re-articulated as one of 'aspiration'. In this mode we find, for example, the ubiquitous *Cosmopolitan* woman; rich, beautiful, and competitive in both the bed and the boardroom.

Whichever strategy is adopted, however, the material contradictions of life under capitalism still exert their effect. Access to capital, economic and symbolic, is still unevenly distributed, the mental is still privileged over the manual, labour is still subject to division, and unequal reward, patriarchy, and racism still structure our social relationships. Such things can only be effaced at a very superficial level. It becomes clear, one way or another, to the factory worker that he or she will never own the factory, to the woman that motherhood and domestic labour will never be valued as highly as a 'career', and to the member of the social or ethnic minority that their cultural heritage and life-style will always be subject to one or another form of apartheid.

At the level of the individual, the experience of these contradictions manifests itself in a multiplicity of ways, and coping with them becomes a significant feature of day-to-day existence. The use of drugs to alter consciousness, mildly or extremely, (e.g. tobacco, alcohol, valium, heroin, etc.), the projection of contradictions onto less advantaged individuals or groups (e.g. racism, sexism), the practical oppression and exploitation of those groups (e.g. pornography, fascism, child abuse), the rejection or displacement of hegemonic values (e.g. various 'youth' cultures, extreme religious sects) all become viable, short-term strategies for individuals, signifying the effects of contradictions in the base and superstructure of capitalism.

The 'problem' of individual and social, and consequently of the relationship between the latter and the domain of the cognitive, arises because the material differences which exist between people in capitalist culture have to be masked over in ideological practice. Part of this masking entails the naturalization of an ideological model of the human being such that it becomes seen 'not as a historic result but as history's point of departure' (Marx 1973, p. 83). The historical development of the individual, bourgeois, subject form, articulated as a de-historicized, self-sustaining entity is constantly effaced in order for it to function as the hegemonic lynchpin of social identity. The history of the 'self' is necessarily restricted to the personal biography which is constantly re-interpreted to naturalize any given state of affairs within the terms of the ideological model presupposed. As Rotenberg (1978) has pointed out, to accomplish this there is a constant search for confirmatory evidence in the subject's biographical past. Any serious internal contradictions to such a narrative are subject to elision (as Hessen's 1931 study of Newton demonstrates). The trivial ones are rendered the subject of curiosity or amazement (e.g. Hitler's love of his dog).

Each one of us is required to internalize this practice in the consideration of our own 'self' and produce restricted, non-contradictory narratives which deny our location in the wider socio-historical process, as the subjects of history. Pathology arises when we fail to internalize and repress the contradictions of life under capitalism and our culture has provided us with various signifying machines to facilitate self-naturalization. The psychoanalytic machine is perhaps the most striking exemplar of the process I have in mind here. As Volosinov (1976) intimates, the practice of Freudianism serves primarily to re-interpret the socially pathological ('unofficial') consciousness of the patient (e.g. the hysteric) into a form for internalization which is intelligible to and does not threaten the 'official' consciousness of the hegemonic order.

When the history which is denied in this process of naturalization begins to assert itself, when the hegemony of capitalism is threatened (culturally or economically), then the signifying machinery of civil society works overtime to restore threatened order. When those marginalized subjects produced as result of the hegemony of white, patriarchal, capitalism start to act in concert on the knowledge that their positionality does not coincide with that presupposed in the legitimating narratives of capitalism, a crisis is generated and the legitimacy of those narratives is undermined. Under such conditions it becomes necessary to repair, replace, or otherwise modify the 'subsystems' of legitimation in those areas where resistance is encountered directly, or often, merely anticipated. Signifying machinery is put into play which, in Habermas's (1973) terms, 'structure attention' in such a way as to direct it towards or away from certain themes which confirm or render problematic the legitimating narratives of capitalism. Social cognitive research is no more or less than a component in this machinery.

The focus of its work is rarely if ever the social, but the individual, which is necessarily its point of departure. Its task is that of minimizing any alterations in the structure of the former by working on the recuperation of the latter. Its modes of signification are many and varied, but they share in common a reductionism to the level of individual. The social being, the product of specific socio-historical determinations thus becomes processed and *re-presented* as the legal person, the psychiatric subject, the subject of an egocentric morality and ethical practice, the subject of scientific management, the subject of social casework, of narrative biography (whose form is that of nineteenth century realism), or at base, the biological organism. The list of these subjectivities is as long as the list of machinic subsystems where power is applied to shape or create for the purposes of maintaining hegemony (cf. Guattari 1984). In each of these conditions, the militant other becomes separated off from others, from the social body as a whole: a clear and distinct problem, unique and isolated.

It is from the consideration of this distinctness that the disciplines of psychological science arise, but their task is as contradictory as the individual around which they are focused. For example, within the purview of the psychological sciences all forms of socialized resistance to capitalism, all signifiers of difference, be they race, class, gender, or more extremely, delinquency, madness, alcoholism, theft, perversion, have necessarily to be reduced to two points of departure: The autobiography and/or the body. Conversely, all the virtues which come under scrutiny are similarly accounted for (cf. Rotenberg 1978). Psychology produces accounts which privilege the internal because to do anything else would be to undermine the purpose of psychology as an ideological pursuit, as an authorized machine of signification (cf. Bourdieu 1975). The machinery of individuation which the psychological disciplines operate become, historically, the basis of their claims to be scientific and the socially validated authority which accompanies that characteristic.

Moscovici's (1972) seminal paper *Society and theory in social psychology* concluded with a call for social psychology to abandon its scientific fetishism in order to become what he described as 'dangerous'. For Moscovici, the constitution of 'dangerous science' resided in the willingness to overturn the conceptions which are current in a given age in order to 'create new aspects of society' (p. 65).

While I do not disagree with Moscovici's sentiments, the formula he presented by which this project of 'becoming dangerous' might be fulfilled depends on an inadequate and partial analysis of the true state of affairs. It is clear in this paper and in much of his work subsequent to it that Moscovici adheres firmly to a theory which sites the consciousness of the individual as the primary locus of the force for change. It is as if all social psychologists had to do was change their minds about what constituted good scientific practice in the context of the discipline and Moscovici's dangerous science would follow.

While well-meaning, a critical project for social psychology which depends upon such foundations simply misses the point. Consciousness is not typically changed by an act of will on the part of individuals. The effectiveness of a rational appeal to a rational subject is inevitably circumscribed by the more potent effects of the material conditions and social relations within which subjects (rational or otherwise) live their lives. The moralizing Manicheism which affects so much of what passes for critical practice in social psychology—the work of writers like Moscovici, Shotter, Harré, *et al.* comes to mind here—is precisely *an effect* of material practices and social relations, and not the panacea for them that they are intended to be.

The problem is that such theorizing implicitly transcendentalizes individual consciousness and its role in the production of social change in a way entirely analogous to the universalizing discourse of non-radical, conventional social psychology. Both conceptual systems commit the error which Volosinov (1973) identified. That is, they depend upon the deliberate or accidental generalization of individualistic self-experience typical of the bourgeoisie as the basic and universal form of human subjectivity. Thus, for example, when Ostrom (1984, p. 12) seeks to humanize social cognitive research by declaring that 'people are not pet rocks', he conveniently ignores the fact that in certain practical and ideological contexts, they might as well be. It is not difficult to think of situations, including some of Ostrom's own experimental work, where the status of pet rock would be an improvement upon that granted by the given micro-structure of social relations!

What liberals, radicals, and conservatives within social psychology, and the human sciences as a whole, have to come to terms with is the fact that it is not what theoretical perspective one has on the individual–social relationship which makes a difference. That dualism is always–already imposed politically, administratively, and ideologically. It cannot, by its very formulation, provide the basis for a human science that would be viable in the same sense as, for example, physics or chemistry. We can change what we say, we can change what we say about what we do, we can even change what we do, or seem to do, but until we come to terms with the political, historical, and economic framework wherein that saying and doing takes place, very little can or will alter materially. Such factors do not merely form a background to the constitution of their subject matter; they form the material out of which the subject matter arises. *Without the political economy and its history, there could be no such thing as social psychology.*

Anti-individualism and the development of radical human science

Bourgeois individualism, and I refer here to a political practice rather than a mere conceptual system, is impossible both theoretically and practically. The subject form it creates is imaginary, because it seeks to deny in its practices that which Marx has termed human 'species being'. That is, it attempts to turn history on its head by an insistence on priority of the individual over the collective. In order to operate 'effectively' capitalism must on the one hand rigorously oppose the individual to the social and, on the other, attentuate this opposition in order to draw into the sphere of its own hegemony those for whom the experienced social reality of capitalism belies the opposition of which it makes so much.

Human science in general, and social psychology in particular, internalizes the antagonisms which result and attempts to resolve them in terms set by its own logical concepts. What is neglected is, of course, that the concepts themselves, as part of academic common sense, are merely signifiers of the same contradictions. Human scientists seek to speak about their society in a language which has literally turned itself away from that society (Sohn-Rethel 1978): a language in which the imaginaries of immutability and universality have replaced the realities of the culturally specific and historically delimited. At times of systemic crisis, such as the present, the retreat from history and from a material relationship to society becomes an even greater necessity if the 'socially necessary labour' of the human scientist is to be performed. Unfortunately for human scientists, the very areas from which they would wish to retreat at times of systemic crisis are precisely those with which capitalism demands they engage.

Under present conditions the signifying machinery of human science demands that its operatives become more efficient technologists of the ideological and/or theoreticians of the imaginary. The development of a more efficient conception of the individual–social relationship is part and parcel of this. As the law of the market-place returns us ever closer to the conditions of Hobbesian chaos, there is a corresponding increase in social fragmentation and divisiveness. Ways must be found to recuperate those dispossessed by market forces or oppressed by sexism or imperialism, to induce them to see their condition as natural or inevitable, and to undermine their resistance, preferably before it begins to find its own voice. They must be induced to co-operate, taught to cope, educated to change their minds rather than their situation, or as a last resort, but ever present sanction, bombed, beaten, or starved into submission. The task of human science is to furnish some of the ways and means by which problems of the social may be turned into problems of the individual, where both terms are defined by reference to developments in the mode of social production itself.

However, the socio-economic conditions which produce the present situation do not restrict their effects solely to those culturally external to the capitalist class and those whose task it is to police them. The present crisis is generating a transformation internal to capitalism in the West. Old alliances based on cultural and economic interest are undergoing revision as the site of production is transferred increasingly to the Third World. In the West knowledge itself becomes more overtly subject to the dictates of commodity production as it becomes increasingly the dominant site of productivity remaining in the West (cf. Gibbons and Wittrock 1985; Lyotard 1984). It becomes increasingly difficult for scientists of all kinds to see their own traditional, cultural, and historical interests as quite so tightly knit with capitalism as was formerly the case. As Salomon (1985 p. 95) has put it

The image of the learned scholar, the *savant* involved in research for its own sake or for his (*sic*) own pleasure is an image of our culture, not a reality in our societies. . . . Science has become a technique among others and scientists fulfil functions that are today as far from those of the Greek philosophers as an abacus is from a microcomputer.

As the logic of the production line comes to dominate the academy a variety of responses, varying in their novelty, become possible. The first is, of course, to deny the course of our historical development as producers of knowledge and accept the present state of affairs as we find them. Our short-term interest invites us to follow this course, in the hope of something better around the corner, as a way of continuing in work of a kind we are used to. There are those of us who opt for this course, either because it corresponds with our own class or cultural interests or because we can see no way of effectively resisting it. The inevitable result is further fragmentation and demoralization as we compete amongst ourselves for stringently controlled and increasingly scarce resources. The possibility of becoming 'micro-capitalists', each of us competing overtly against the others in the exchange process of knowledge commodities, with the inevitable consequences, cannot be ignored.

It is, however, without undue optimism, possible to conceive that such circumstances could, in the human sciences at least, engender conditions where it is possible to reject once and for all the ideological and epistemological premisses upon which the issue of the relationship between individual and social is based.

I have argued that the problem of the individual–social relation derives from the fact that there are inherent contradictions in the way this problem is formulated, the political motivation for its treatment as a problem, and the epistemological and technological equipment with which human scientists set out to resolve it. Because of these factors the machinery of human science is incapable of materially and effectively confronting the individual–social relation and stripping it of its mysterious nature. The numerous, competing formulations and re-formulations of the problem which the present century has witnessed amount to little more than attempts to bring about radical alteration in the structure of this relationship and common-sense understanding of it by tinkering with the 'means of production'. The struggle for human scientists has been one focused upon the improvement of the machine rather than changing the basis upon which it produces.

As any (manual) worker knows, one does not bring about a meaningful improvement in the relations of production by making the lathe turn faster or the line run more smoothly. Improvements in the means of production invariably worsen the state of affairs for those who are forced to operate it (cf. Marx 1976, p. 790). While workers outside the academy are constantly incited to forget this by the operation of the machinery itself and a whole array of 'total ideological' phenomena besides, professional intellectuals, because of their class-historical position, have until now had little or no cause to learn its lesson. It cannot be too strongly stated: one does not bring about meaningful change by improving the means of production, *one does so by changing one's relationship to the means of production.*

Human scientists are in the process of learning that under capitalism their material position is no different from that of any other group of workers. They are little more than appendages of a commodity machine, dependent for their survival on the sale of their labour and the vagaries of the market. From the recognition of this fact and the imposition of its consequences arises the possibility of demystifying the nature and purpose of labour in the human sciences. From the process of demystification and the struggle which it entails comes the possibility of a genuine and radical change in material practices.

The first victim of this struggle is the 'problem' of the individual–social relationship. By recognizing one's position first as part of a working community engaged in struggle with the owners of the means of production, it is possible to extend this recognition to other workers, despite the seeming differences in their material position. Under capitalism intellectuals are incited to see themselves (and others) as part of '. . . a society of individuals where each person shuts himself (*sic*) up in his own subjectivity, and whose only wealth is individual thought' (Fanon 1967, p. 36). Their reflections on the relationships between individuals and the social world simply mirror this incitement.

By engaging in a practical struggle which cannot, if it is to succeed, take place at the level of the individual '*cogito*', but must occur at the level of the group, the intellectual automatically turns on its head the received wisdom of bourgeois common sense. And with this inversion the possibility for reconceptualizing experience arises. Fanon's (1967) writings on the colonial struggle in Algeria recount the effects of such struggle on intellectual consciousness:

Individualism is the first to disappear. . . . Now the native [intellectual, L.G.] who has the opportunity to return to the people during the struggle for freedom will discover the falseness of this theory. The very forms of organisation of the struggle will suggest to him (*sic*) a different vocabulary. Brother, sister, friend — these are words outlawed by the colonialist bourgeoisie, because for them my brother is my purse, my friend is part of my scheme for getting on. . . . Henceforward, the interests of one will be the interests of all, for in concrete fact *everyone* will be discovered by troops, *everyone* will be massacred — or *everyone* will be saved (pp. 36–7, italics original).

I do not intend to suggest that in Fanon's account there resides the miraculous panacea to our ills; that all we have to do is 'change our minds' (or even our vocabulary), and from that all else will follow. The Algerian people's struggle described by Fanon extended over many years and involved much bloodshed. Furthermore, it involved a culture where a structure of pre-capitalist community still existed to form a basis for resistance strategies and provided an alternative mode of social relation. Nevertheless, the central point he makes, that struggle as a group exerts a determinate effect on the way one theorizes and experiences individual consciousness, is still applicable.

In my opinion, however, human science can make a serious and significant contribution to such a struggle by using its accumulated knowledge and received wisdoms against itself. In the development of a new 'radical culture' we can no longer take our point of departure from the empty concepts and vacuous platitudes of bourgeois individualism. The point at which we start this contribution is with ourselves, not as 'consciousnesses to be raised', but as a community of workers, like any other, for whom the only effective strategy, for both survival as a group and for defending the values of a critical scholarship, is to link our struggle with a wider community of resistance. We can only do that by giving up some of the privileges we claim for ourselves and our labour.

If we as a community can begin to understand the effects of the individual–social relationship 'from the other side', that is, from the point of view of those whose interests and conditions are not so intimately tied to the ideology and practices of capitalism, then we can also begin to deal with the practical (as opposed to conceptual) problems this relationship presents in a truly emancipatory fashion. To do this, however, we cannot proceed from our own common-sense understanding, because the point to which it leads us is always already determined, primarily by the economic and social history of our own culture and our own function within it. Nor, however, can we proceed from the authoritative vision of science to which we have traditionally aspired, since science, and with it philosophy, it itself imbricated with the common sense from which we must necessarily escape.

Acknowledgements

Acknowledgements for their kind help in the production of this paper go to the following people (in alphabetical order): John Bowers, Alan Fair, and Jacqui Nicholl, not forgetting, of course, the editors of the present volume for their critical and patient assistance.

Note

My use of the term 'signifying machine' is derived from the theoretical work of Felix Guattari (1984). In Guattari's work the notion of machine is both metaphor and reality. That is, the model of the technical machine, with the organized patterns and rhythms of productivity it implies, is extended to apply to all forms of productivity: semiotic, social, theoretical, and so on. Guattari distinguishes machines and the 'machinic', as open systems, from the closed system of mechanics. A significant characteristic of machines is that they can never be considered in isolation; they always operate as part of an interacting aggregate, each one forming a subsystem of the others. For example, the factory machine, he observes, operates interdependently with a training machine, a marketing machine, a social machine, an R & D machine, and so on. In this context, therefore, signifying machines are systems of varying organization the function of which is to produce signs. They correspond approximately to Volosinov's (1973) 'fields of ideological creativity'.

References

Althusser, L. (1971). *Lenin and philosophy*. NLB, London.

Bateson, G. (1973). *Steps to an ecology of mind*. Paladin, London.

Bottomore, T. and Rubel, M. (1963). *Karl Marx: Selected writings in sociology and philosophy*. Penguin, Harmondsworth.

Bourdieu, P. (1975). The specificity of the scientific field and the social conditions of the progress of reason, *Social science information* **14**, 19–47.

Cherry, C. (1967). There is nothing I have is essential to me. In *To honour Roman Jakobson, vol. 1* (ed. T. Sebeok), pp. 462–74. Mouton, The Hague.

Collins, H. M. (1985). *Changing order: replication and induction in scientific practice*. Sage, London.

Douglas, M. (1973). *Natural symbols*. Penguin, Harmondsworth.

Fanon, F. (1967). *The wretched of the Earth*. Penguin, Harmondsworth.

Fanon, F. (1970). *A dying colonialism*. Penguin, Harmondsworth.

Feyerabend, P. (1975). *Against method*. Verso, London.

Foucault, M. (1984). *The Foucault reader* (ed. P. Rabinow). Penguin, Harmondsworth.

Garfinkel, H. (1967). *Studies in ethnomethodology*. Prentice-Hall, Englewood Cliffs, NJ.

Gergen, K. J. (1982). From self to science: what is there to know? In *Psychological perspectives on the self* (ed. J. Suls). Erlbaum, Hillsdale, NJ.

Gibbons, M. and Wittrock, B. (eds.) (1985). *Science as a commodity*. Longman, Harlow.

Greenwald, A. G. and Pratkanis, A. R. (1984). The self. In *The handbook of social cognition, vol. 3* (eds. R. Wyer and T. Srull). Erlbaum, Hillsdale, NJ.

Guattari, F. (1984). *Molecular revolution*. Penguin, Harmondsworth.

Habermas, J. (1973). Was heisst heute Krise? *Merkur* **4/5**, 644–67.

Henriques, J., Hollway, W., Urwin, C., Venn, C., and Walkerdine, V. (1984). *Changing the subject: Psychology social regulation and subjectivity*. Methuen, London.

Hessen, B. (1931). The social and economic roots of Newton's *Principia*. In *Science at the crossroads* (eds. N. Bukharin *et al.*) CASS, London.

Hobbes, T. (1651/1968). *Leviathan*. Penguin, Harmondsworth.

James, W. (1890). *The principles of psychology*. Holt, New York.

Kuhn, T. (1970). *The structure of scientific revolutions*. University of Chicago Press, Chicago.

Lane, T. (1974). *The union makes us strong*. Arrow Books, London.

Lévi-Strauss, C. (1966). *The savage mind*. Weidenfield and Nicholson, London.

Lyotard, J.-F., (1984). *The postmodern condition: a report on knowledge*. Manchester University Press, Manchester.

Marx, K. (1973). *The Grundrisse*. Penguin, Harmondsworth.

Marx, K. (1976). *Capital, vol. 1*. Penguin, Harmondsworth.

Marx, K. and Engels, F. (1970). *The German ideology* (ed. C. Arthur). Lawrence & Wishart, London.

McClelland, D. (1971). *Marx's Grundrisse*. Paladin, London.

Mead, G. H. (1934). *Mind self and society* (ed. C. W. Morris). University of Chicago Press, Chicago.

Morris, C. (1972). *The discovery of the individual 1050-1200*. SPCK, London.

Moscovici, S. (1972). Society and theory in social psychology. In *The context of social psychology: a critical assessment* (eds. J. Israel and H. Tajfel). Academic Press, London.

Moscovici, S. (1981). On social representations, In *Social cognition* (ed. J. Forgas). Academic Press, London.

Ostrom, T. (1984). The sovereignty of social cognition. In *The handbook of social cognition, vol. 3* (eds. R. Wyer and T. Srull). Erlbaum, Hillsdale.

Rotenberg, M. (1978). *Damnation and deviance*. The Free Press, New York.

Rothblatt, S. (1985). The notion of an open scientific community in historical perspective. In *Science as a commodity* (eds. M. Gibbons and B. Wittrock) Longman, Harlow.

Said, E. W. (1985). *Orientalism*. Penguin, Harmondsworth.

Salomon, J.-J. (1985). Science as a commodity—policy changes, issues and threats. In *Science as a commodity* (eds. M. Gibbons and B. Wittrock). Longman, Harlow.

Sartre, J.-P. (1967). Preface. In Fanon, F., *The wretched of the earth*. Penguin, Harmondsworth.

Sohn-Rethel, A. (1978). *Intellectual and manual labour*. Macmillan, London.

Suls, J. (1982). *Psychological perspectives on the self*. Erlbaum, Hillsdale, NJ.

Therborn, G. (1980). *The ideology of power and the power of ideology*. Verso, London.

Turner, B. (1984). *The body and society*. Basil Blackwell, Oxford.

Ullman, W. (1967). *The individual and society in the middle ages*. Methuen, London.

Volosinov, V. N. (1973). *Marxism and the philosophy of language*. Seminar Press, New York.

Volosinov, V. N. (1976). *Freudianism: a marxist critique*. Seminar Press, New York.

Wilden, A. (1980). *System and structure: essays in communication and exchange* (2nd edition). Tavistock, London.

Whyte, L. L. (1962). *The unconscious before Freud*. Tavistock, London.

Author index

Subject index